D0680461

WITHDRAWN

How You Play the Game

"From Hungry Hill to the top of the mountain. What a great story from a guy who has seen it all."

—Jerry Reinsdorf, Chairman,
Chicago White Sox and Chicago Bulls

"When Jerry Colangelo speaks, the rest of us listen. He's a family man, community leader, patriot, and sports businessman of the first order. Americans from all walks of life will enjoy this book."

—Dan Quayle, 44th Vice President of the United States

"If only Jerry's crystal clear vision, personal integrity, and energized leadership could be bottled and sold. . . . He's simply the best in the west. His book, *How You Play the Game,* sparkles like a diamond.

—Harvey Mackay, author of
Swim with the Sharks Without Being Eaten Alive

How You Play The Game

Lessons for Life From the Billion-Dollar Business of Sports

Jerry Colangelo
with Len Sherman

CALVIN T. RYAN LIBRARY
U. OF NEBRASKA AT KEARNEY

AMACOM
American Management Association
New York • Atlanta • Boston • Chicago • Kansas City • San Francisco • Washington, D.C.
Brussels • Mexico City • Tokyo • Toronto

This book is available at a special
discount when ordered in bulk quantities.
For information, contact Special Sales Department,
AMACOM, an imprint of AMA Publications,
a division of American Management Association,
1601 Broadway, New York, NY 10019.

This publication is designed to provide accurate and authoritative information in regard to the subject matter covered. It is sold with the understanding that the publisher is not engaged in rendering legal, accounting, or other professional service. If legal advice or other expert assistance is required, the services of a competent professional person should be sought.

Library of Congress Cataloging-in-Publication Data

Colangelo, Jerry.
    How you play the game : lessons for life from the billion-
dollar business of sports / Jerry Colangelo with Len Sherman.
      p.   cm.
    Includes index.
    ISBN 0-8144-0488-X
    1. Colangelo, Jerry. 2. Sports team owners—United
States—Biography. 3. Phoenix Suns (Basketball team)
4. Arizona Diamondbacks (Baseball team) 5. Professional
sports—Economic aspects—United States. I. Sherman, Len,
1956– . II. Title.
GV697.C63A3 1999
338.7′61796′092—dc21
[B]   98-56068
                                          CIP

© 1999 Jerry Colangelo.
All rights reserved.
Printed in the United States of America.

This publication may not be reproduced,
stored in a retrieval system,
or transmitted in whole or in part,
in any form or by any means, electronic,
mechanical, photocopying, recording, or otherwise,
without the prior written permission of AMACOM,
an imprint of AMA Publications,
a division of American Management Association,
1601 Broadway, New York, NY 10019.

Printing number

10 9 8 7 6 5 4 3 2

For my wife, Joan,
And my children,
And my grandchildren,
For a lifetime of love and support

Contents

CONTENTS

Foreword

I FIRST HAD the pleasure of meeting Jerry Colangelo over thirty years ago when he, at the age of twenty-eight, became the youngest general manager in professional sports and I was a much younger (twenty-seven-year-old) lawyer working for the NBA. Over the years, Jerry has demonstrated success at every level of sports ownership, arena and stadium design and construction, and community involvement, but it was obvious back then that Jerry Colangelo was destined for a fulfilling, inspiring, and remarkable life in sports and in business.

At Jerry's core is a passion for basketball that is pure playground. It rose out of his years scrapping on the cement courts of Chicago Heights, playing starring roles in high school and college, battling it out in a tough semi-pro league, and finally coaching the Phoenix Suns for two seasons. He has always loved basketball with an intensity that is natural, joyous, and complete. He loves the game and he loves the players, both as athletes and as people.

Jerry has also had a remarkable appreciation for the business side of sports. Just as he studied and understood what happened on the court, he was a student of the deal and knows how to build winning teams and successful leagues. His great success with the Phoenix Suns, the fact that he has been named NBA Executive of the Year an unprecedented four times, and his successful launch of the Arizona Diamondbacks are all testaments to his vision, his skill, and his know-how inside the boardroom. America West Arena, home of the Suns, and Bank One Ballpark, home of the Diamondbacks, demonstrate Jerry's ability to forge the private-public partnerships that are required for arenas and stadiums and the renewals that they bring to communities.

But most important, Jerry has always lived his life and conducted his business without ever compromising his strong sense of ethics and his deep commitment to doing what's right. He is a true believer, not just in the purity of the game, but in the fundamental values that give meaning to our lives. His devotion to family and friends, his respect for colleagues and loyalty to employees, and his commitment to the community all represent Jerry's fierce desire to live a life that is balanced, enlightened, and good.

You can learn a lot from Jerry Colangelo, perhaps in more ways than you are anticipating as you open this book. I have. He is a teacher, a leader, and a valued friend.

Enjoy!

DAVID STERN

Foreword

WHEN JERRY COLANGELO first contacted me about the possibility of a Major League Baseball expansion franchise for the Phoenix area in 1993, I was receptive to his ideas. I had spent most spring trainings in Phoenix with the Milwaukee Brewers and had many opportunities to get to know him. I was well aware of his reputation as a dynamic and successful sports entrepreneur, his knowledge and love of sports, and his ability to traverse the sometimes difficult civic and business roadblocks that confront owners of sports franchises. Most important, I knew that Jerry's first love was baseball. He was a terrific high school pitcher from the south side of Chicago—having pitched ahead of former major leaguer Jim Bouton one year—and might have made it to the big leagues had he not blown out his pitching arm.

Jerry pursued a major league franchise with all the passion and vigor that he exhibited in turning the Phoenix Suns into one of the preeminent franchises of the National Basketball Association. He performed all his due diligence with great care and embarked on the construction of a state-of-the-art baseball facility for the baseball fans of Arizona. His planning was extraordinary and impressive, and he was awarded the franchise—the Arizona Diamondbacks—on March 9, 1995, and Bank One Ballpark was built in time for his club's first pitch in 1998.

In just over a year, Jerry has established the Diamondbacks as one of the game's most successful expansion franchises and himself as one of the leaders of our industry, through his keen business insight and his ability to develop and nurture personal relationships. One of the reasons for his success is that he has participated in just about every level of the sports industry—as an athlete, as a marketing director, as a coach, general manager, and franchise operator and owner. The transition from athlete to owner is a fascinating story of hard work, dedication, and loyalty, which Jerry has achieved with grace, sensitivity, and intelligence. I am proud to have him as a colleague and a friend.

Read this book. It's a sports story on one level, but a story of life and how to achieve your dreams on another, more important level.

ALLAN H. (BUD) SELIG

Acknowledgments

RARELY DOES THE opportunity arise to thank all the people who have played a significant role in your life in such a public forum, and I, for one, shall not let this opportunity pass by.

All the stories and ideas inside these pages are the result of a lifetime of experience and relationships, personal and professional. No one walks that journey alone, and neither have I. A few people, outside my family, have been with me year after year, decade after decade. They are woven into the fabric of my life in a profound way.

First among all the people in my life is Ruthie Dryjanski, whose commitment and dedication are unparalleled.

I would like to acknowledge and thank Frankie and the whole gang back in the old neighborhood, who've been with me through the years, from the beginning, and also all the people who have backed me, from the media and the business community, in both Chicago and Chicago Heights, since my boyhood days.

My journey with the Suns has been a tremendous ride, and I've been blessed by great people who've made exceptional contributions. Most notable in this group are Harvey Shank, Bob Machen, Tom Ambrose, Ray Artigue, Ted Podleski, John Sakata, Chris Bianco, and Joe Proski. I also want to recognize all the coaches and players, and everyone else who has helped build and sustain the franchise.

The Diamondbacks have just begun what promises to be an equally amazing journey, and the people who have had the greatest impact on the franchise's genesis include Buck Showalter, Rich Dozer, Joe Garagiola Jr., Scott Brubaker, Tom Harris, and Roland Hemond, as well as all the coaches and players, and the entire baseball staff.

I also would like to thank my attorneys, Jay Ruffner, Mike Kennedy, and Mike Gallagher.

I'd also like to mention my long-time partners David Eaton, Mel Schultz, Eddie Lynch, and John Teets, along with Bill Shover and Chip Weil.

Now to the matter at hand: the publication of this book. I'd like to express my appreciation to the people at AMACOM who were so enthused, from the start, about the prospects for this work. In particular, I would like to thank publisher Hank Kennedy, editor Ellen Kadin, and copy editor Karen Boyd.

I would be grossly remiss if I did not express my deepest appreciation to all the fans, in Phoenix, in Chicago, and throughout the country, who have supported our organization, our teams, and me, and have made every venture and championship run worth all the effort.

Finally, the very first page of this work is surely one of the most important: the dedication to my family. It is perhaps beyond my ability to fully express in words what each of them means to me, in every way, and so I shall say no more, trusting that they know that they are always in my heart.

How
You Play
the Game

Prologue

THIS BOOK IS about what I believe. Of course, what I (or anyone else) believe is the culmination of many things: family and faith and experience, education and intuition, all mixed together to provide a share of knowledge and—hopefully—a touch of wisdom.

I have been interviewed on many occasions and have spoken about some of these ideas, values, and experiences. Despite all those interviews, this forum, this book, is my opportunity to speak fully and completely, for the first and only time, without interruption or editing.

I have spent more than thirty years in the sports industry, and I have learned many lessons. A few I learned easily, and others I learned the hard way, through trial and error, and sometimes error and error. Still, through it all, I have worked and persevered and gone on to build a business and an organization that employs thousands, and brings a measure of joy to thousands upon thousands more.

My career, both as an entrepreneur and as a corporate executive—not to mention athlete, scout, general manager and coach—has taken me throughout the country and around the globe. I have visited places unimaginably distant, and not merely in physical terms, from my boyhood home on Hungry Hill in Chicago Heights, Illinois. My work has led me to the business brink and back through endless rounds of jousting and contending with fellow owners and governments, sports agents, and transnational corporations. I have passed through the infinite layers of horse-trading and deal-making, compromise and intrigue, that command industry, sports and otherwise. I have become intimately familiar with the rules and risks that dominate the world of power and influence.

I have also had an awful lot of fun. And I have succeeded at attaining most though certainly not all of my goals, frequently far beyond what I ever dreamed conceivable.

When I consider the trajectory of my life, from the old neighborhood of my youth to the glossy arenas and glistening fields of professional sports that now constitute my home ground, I recognize that my career mirrors the explosive growth of professional sports in this country. And that mirror reflects not only the evolution, or revolution, in sports, but also the extraordinary changes in American culture and society. Some of these changes, both in sports and society, are for the better, and some are not. Nothing exists in a vacuum, and that definitely applies to the business of sports.

I began with the expansion Chicago Bulls, an uncertain proposition in a city where two professional basketball teams had already failed, then moved to Phoenix to take on another untried expansion club, the Suns, which also reached amazing heights and suffered ignoble calamities. Now I am immersed in Major League Baseball and our latest franchise, the brand-new Arizona Diamondbacks. Along the way, I helped build two state-of-the-art venues for the Suns and the Diamondbacks and created unique public-private partnerships to facilitate the costs of America West Arena and Bank One Ballpark, to the accompaniment of widespread sound and fury. I have participated in the transformation of professional sports from an often hit-and-miss proposition, with unpredictable profits and prospects, to its emergence as a major component of the global entertainment industry, with leading performers as famous as presidents and as privileged as movie stars.

And while the Bulls, the Suns, and the Diamondbacks are the best known and most successful of my plans and projects, I have a handful of other successes, and a couple of failures, to my name. We brought the Phoenix Coyotes to town, where they have flourished. The Arizona Rattlers of the Arena Football League have acquired a loyal following, and the Phoenix Mercury of the WNBA is quickly building its own fan base. On the other side of the ledger are the late, widely unlamented Phoenix Smash of World Team Tennis and the Arizona Sandsharks of the Continental Independent Soccer League. And I would be remiss if I neglected my start in organized sports, before the pro ranks beckoned, in my high school and college teams.

Through this reel through my athletic endeavors, both on the court or field, and behind the scenes, too, I intend to explain where I began and where I am now, and what I have known about not only sports but business and other matters as well.

For my life has not been and is not only about work. Joan and I married while in college, and we have four children and eight grandchildren to show for it. And without her, without them, and without everything we have done and gone through together, I would not be the man I am.

We have many topics to discuss, replete with many places and people; memories and stories; the past, present, and, most consequently, the future, mixing together, as we explore the reasoning and risks and responsibilities that have always determined and directed my decisions.

This book is about what I believe and what I have learned, and what I hold to be true and important. I hope it rings true and perhaps even a bit important to you, too, for I have something of a larger purpose here, larger than merely recounting the hows and whys of my personal journey for re-counting's sake. I'm going to tell you what that purpose is right now, giving away a little bit of the ending.

As you will soon see, I started pretty much at the bottom and have worked my way to a position where I have been able to fulfill many of my ambitions, achieve many of my goals. I did not use the secrets of the Knights Templars to accomplish this, or a trust fund, or magic. I used whatever abilities God granted me, and I worked hard and then harder. Expressed another way, my story is a story of passion. Passion for my family, my work, my beliefs. That passion has carried me through life. And the point to all this, the underlying, essential, crucial point, is that if I can do it, then so can you. So can anyone who truly wants to, and truly believes in what he is doing.

If you haven't already realized the remarkable scope of possibilities that are out there, I hope I can help you recognize them. If you have realized the possibilities, then I hope I can help you find a better way to reach them. If you have reached most of your goals, then I hope I can help you see that even more awaits.

CHAPTER ONE

Back to the Beginning

HOME.

For more than thirty years, Phoenix has been my home. It is where I settled my young family so long ago and labored to build a business, a reputation, and a life.

But there was a time for me before that, a life before Phoenix, and it began in Chicago Heights, a working-class suburb south of Chicago. And today I have returned to Chicago Heights, to my first home. Today I have come full circle.

This is not to suggest that I haven't returned in three decades. Not at all. Not by a long shot. I still have family here. I still have friends here.

I still have my roots here.

Nonetheless, today—these past few days, in fact—are special, for reasons that are both personal and professional. For starters, I did not travel to Illinois alone, but accompanied the Arizona Diamondbacks, Major League Baseball's newest team, scheduled to play a three-game stand against the Chicago Cubs in Wrigley Field. The Cubs were the first team I loved, the team I loved and followed and supported during my early years—until March 9, 1995, when a group of investors I assembled and led was granted a MLB franchise that would soon become the Diamondbacks, a franchise I would head as the managing general partner.

And Wrigley Field. . . . Wrigley is a special gem of a ballpark, as beloved as the Cubbies themselves, and the stadium where I attended my first professional sports event. How old was I then? Seven years old? Eight? The place seemed immense, unbelievably gigantic. This was pretelevision, so the closest I could get was listening to the games over the radio. Seeing the players live, face-to-face, to actually be there, was incredible.

Back then, of course, I was happy—thrilled, even—to sit in the bleachers. Now, my seat is directly behind the visitors' dugout—the Diamondbacks' dugout. And I'm surrounded by dozens of old friends from the old neighborhood, whom I invited for this occasion.

Wrigley epitomizes what is best about baseball, with its foul lines set close to the stands, the ivy growing up the wall, the fans yelling and cheering from every corner. Wrigley is an integral piece of Chicago, part of the fabric of the community, as vital to Chicago as the subway or parks. Approaching Wrigley Field on the elevated train, affectionately known as the El, the cars jammed with those going to the game, riding through the neighborhoods and past the apartment buildings and houses, so many of which have rickety wooden porches and staircases grafted onto the backs, facing the tracks, Wrigley slowly comes into view, big, solid, commanding. The energy on the streets surrounding the ballpark pulsing and electric; the sounds of the gathering inside Wrigley echoing in waves of exhilarated anticipation; the smells of the ballpark— hot dogs and peanuts and pizza and beer—mixing together, brewing a heady, unmistakable elixir; the roofs overlooking the ballpark filled with fans getting a free view of the game; traffic halting as people rush around buying hats and miniature bats and tickets; so much motion, so much excitement, so much laughter. . . .

This is Chicago. This is baseball. This is terrific.

I recall another Cubs game in June 1993, almost exactly five years ago. I was in town because the Phoenix Suns were battling the Chicago Bulls in the NBA Finals. The team had an off night, and I came to Wrigley Field to take in a game. It was a night game, the first one I had ever seen at Wrigley, and the stadium was filled and the place was jumping. I sat there and imagined how terrific it would be to have Major League Baseball in Phoenix.

Two weeks later, I had a visit from a couple of fellow Arizonans—a politician and a lawyer—intent on achieving exactly that dream, bringing a major league expansion franchise to Arizona. They wanted my assistance; actually they wanted me to take the lead. I had to think long and hard and do some diligent investigating before determining if I was willing to assume that imposing commitment. A couple of months later, I made the decision to put together an investment group and raise the money and try to get that franchise for Arizona.

Now, half a decade later, I'm back at Wrigley, back with the Arizona Diamondbacks, back to take on the Cubs. The Diamondbacks won the first game, 5–4, before a sellout crowd. To return home with our own team and win . . . amazing. The memories flood back. I remember being about nine years old, sitting in the upper deck at Wrigley, and Roy Campanella of the Dodgers, future Hall of Famer, smacked a foul ball right at me. I reached out my hand and the ball landed in my palm.

Which was more amazing? A nine-year-old's foul ball or a grown-up man's team winning one from the Cubs?

Why choose?

It has been a whirlwind trip, punctuated by events, flavored by family and friends, resonating with those memories. A couple of nights ago, the National Italian American Foundation held a dinner in my honor. Mayor Richard Daley was in attendance and declared Thursday, July 2, 1998, Jerry Colangelo Day throughout Chicago.

The Diamondbacks moved on to Houston this afternoon. After taking that first game from the Cubs, we lost the next two. We'll work to do better next time, and better yet the time after that. Count on it.

I've stayed in town because I've been invited to serve as the grand marshal for Chicago Heights's 1998 Independence Day parade, this year held on July 3. And so this morning we drove south to the Heights, a small caravan in tow, the cars filled with three of my four kids and seven of eight grandchildren. Having my family along with me to enjoy these events and this week renders it all that much more special.

We stopped at Louise and Frank Narcisi's house. I've known Frank since I was a kid. We played together and then, for a short while worked together, before I joined Dick Klein, and together we created the Bulls. Frank stayed in Chicago Heights, recently retiring as the superintendent of maintenance of Bloom Township High School, our old high school. I make sure that he and Louise travel to Phoenix each year for an extended visit.

Frank greeted us as we parked in his driveway. He and Louise had breakfast waiting, highlighted by a huge box of long johns, donuts stretched like long, thick cigars, topped by vanilla icing. Long johns are a tradition between us, reaching back to our youth, when we used to eat two each in the early morning to start the day.

The parade was much like those experienced across small-town America. The route wound down Chicago Road, which was lined with older people seated in their lawn chairs, families spread out on blankets, children chasing each other in circles.

A brief review of classic cars kicked off the parade, followed by a police motorcycle, a fire engine, both with sirens blaring, and a Marine Corps color guard. Politicians running for office—governor, lieutenant governor, attorney general, so on—were interspersed throughout the ranks. Ronald McDonald waved to the kids from his perch on top of a giant shoe. A seven-man Mexican band played, courtesy of a local

Mexican restaurant. Teenage cheerleaders from the Chicago Heights Park District leapt about the street. Senior citizen square dancers from the Chicago Heights Happy Swingers swung their partners to the urging of a caller. The Order of Sons of Italy of America, Lodge 1430, was represented, as were the members of the Catholic High School marching band, Polish-American dancers, the Majestic Star Casino, the Lions Club, and the Jesse White Tumbling Team.

That was Chicago Heights. And right in the midst of all this working-class diversity was a float with a staircase on either side, forming a pyramid, covered with white paper and streamers, and adorned with the words "Phoenix Suns" and "Arizona Diamondbacks." That was the Colangelo family float, and we climbed aboard, Joan and myself, and all the kids and grandkids, and were driven along the parade route, waving to the townspeople we had known all these years. That's the way it is with Fourth of July parades in small-town America—even when they're held on July 3.

Afterwards, we all went to the Crossroads Festival of Chicago Heights, the local carnival with games and rides and food. When I was in high school, I used to attend the local fairs and act as the designated shooter for my buddies. They would give me their quarters; I would find the basketball toss concession, score, and win dolls or other prizes for them. For my efforts, I was informally banned from more than one such attraction.

On the stage, I was introduced to the crowd by Mayor Angelo Ciambrone. "Chicago Heights has a long history," the mayor said, and he talked about a community that was diversified, schools that nurtured, families that cared.

"And one native son has always felt Chicago Heights is his native city," he said, presenting me with a plaque commemorating the occasion. "Jerry, you make us proud."

Burt Moore, my high school basketball coach, was next up, and he presented me with my old jersey, number 23. "I don't know who had it first," he said, "you or Michael Jordan."

He recalled how I went out for the team as a freshman, causing him to ask his assistant coach, "How in the devil are we going to put some meat on this guy?"

It was my turn at the microphone, and I handed Joey Longo the trophy representing the first Jerry Colangelo Award, lauding the eighth grader and basketball star for leading his team in several categories and "exemplifying an attitude of hard work, dedication, and commitment."

It had been a busy day, and a busy week, but the climax of the trip still awaited. The family, Frank and Louise, and Mayor Ciambrone drove over to 22d Street, on Hungry Hill. I don't know for certain why Hungry Hill was so named, though I suspect it was because the people *were* hungry— hungry for work, hungry for success, hungry for security— and probably just plain hungry, too.

I was raised on Hungry Hill, on 22d Street: 156 22d Street, to be exact. And now we are there again because my hometown is putting up a marker in front of my old home.

With minimal fanfare, a cardboard cover is removed to reveal the marker, prepared by the Chicago Heights Historical Association:

Boyhood Home of Jerry Colangelo
Dedicated July 3, 1998
City of Chicago Heights
Mayor Angelo A. Ciambrone

It is a wonderful moment. The couple who live in the narrow house now—reshingled and its green exterior repainted white with blue trim—graciously invite the family inside to see where I grew up. And as they walk up the few steps, the grandchildren eagerly mounting the stairs ahead of the adults, my mind whirls back half a century ago, to when I was maybe seven years old and my grandfather would bang on the pipes to wake me up for my paper route.

Giovanni and Rosina Colangelo immigrated from a

mountain village east of Naples around the turn of the century. They made their way to Chicago Heights, a working-class town south of Chicago, dependent upon its steel mills and foundries. A lunch-bucket community with large concentrations of Italian and Polish immigrants. Every corner had a saloon, and the successful entrepreneur owned a small grocery store.

I learned about roots before roots were popular. Chicago Heights was a close community. Homes were kept unlocked and open, and a closeness existed between families and between neighbors that must seem inconceivable to many younger people today.

Sometime during the 1920s, my grandfather, who worked as a laborer for the city, county, and state, built our house with his own hands, using the lumber from two railroad boxcars for his primary construction material. It was a small, two-story affair, with a kitchen, living room, and bedroom downstairs, and two rooms upstairs. He and grandma had five children: Angelo, Hugo, Christina, Levio, and Dorothy. Levio, who went by Larry, was my father.

My grandmother was not only a great cook but also the neighborhood medic, dispensing Old World remedies to all in need.

When I was born, my grandparents lived downstairs, along with an aunt and uncle. My father and mother slept upstairs. My mother's name was Sue, and she came from Joliet, Illinois. As was common at the time, she left school after the fourth grade. Although she was of Russian-Czech heritage, she adapted to the Colangelo family Italian mores and manners.

I also slept upstairs and shared a room with my younger sister. When grandfather judged that she and I were getting too old to sleep in the same room, he took his tools and built another upstairs bedroom. This was my room, but it was so small that, as I grew to six foot four, my feet literally stuck out the door, back into my sister's room.

The family, frequently along with other relatives as well, would congregate downstairs for our meals. Everyone in the neighborhood had a tiny garden, where vegetables were meticulously grown. It was a simple existence; few people finished school and continued on to college but rather went to labor in the local factories and foundries. People worked hard, and they often played hard, too, keeping the taverns open until late, drinking and arguing and laughing, and playing bocci ball. The 3-Star Ristorante (which was more of a saloon than a restaurant back then) was just two doors away, and its outdoor bocci court was inevitably busy. Most nights I drifted off to sleep to the sounds of bocci balls clicking against one another.

Mine was a typical Italian upbringing; we shared everything with one another, knew everybody's business, our sense of family extended far beyond our four walls, and we felt safe and secure and loved.

Then there was grandfather. As I've mentioned, he would grab a spoon and bang on an exposed water pipe between five and five-thirty in the morning to wake me so I could deliver newspapers. Beginning around the age of nine, I delivered five newspapers: two in the morning, two in the afternoon, and the *Chicago Heights Star* a couple of days a week. Grandpa would give me a cup of coffee to get me going, and, when it was cold enough—and nothing beats a really cold Chicago dawn—toss in a drop or two of whiskey. I remember two dogs from the neighborhood—Spot and Tippy—who used to wait for me outside my door, and accompany me on my route. Funny what you remember after so many years.

When I got a little older, I also caddied at Idlewild Country Club, in nearby Flossmoor. Hitchhiking back and forth to the club, I earned three dollars for carrying a bag for eighteen holes, double if I could manage two bags. I knew the meaning and the value of hard work early on, for that was one of the lessons the family and the neighborhood taught, with unmistakable clarity.

Nonetheless, I can't claim that work dominated my youth. Nor, truth be told, did school. Sports were my passion, my preoccupation, my purpose, and my point.

I'd leave the house with a salt shaker stuck into my pocket, and snatch a tomato off somebody's vine for lunch, not letting anything slow me down on my way to the next game. We mainly played baseball and basketball, and we played wherever we could find a park, schoolyard, field, or alley.

Our equipment was makeshift at best. The baseball bat we used was held in one piece with literally dozens of nails, and the ball was more tape than ball.

I was a dedicated athlete and achieved a modest amount of recognition in the neighborhood. By the time I was a teenager, I had already learned about the work ethic and responsibility; soon, my athletic successes would make me feel that I had a further responsibility in representing my family and my town. This feeling would only grow with time, and I still carry it with me, in everything I do, in representing not just Chicago Heights now, but also Phoenix and Arizona.

I was a diehard Cubs fan, and many a night I fell asleep listening to the game on the radio. I dreamed about one day pitching at Wrigley Field for the home team. There were only eight teams in the National League and eight in the American, and many of us young fans could name every player on not only our hometown teams but many other teams, too.

I encountered one stumbling block on my own path to glory. In seventh grade, I was cut during tryouts for the junior high basketball squad. A southpaw, I couldn't shoot a layup with my right hand with any consistency. The cut constituted a severe setback to this playground athlete, and I worked for a year until I had the layups down pat. I returned to try out for the team in eighth grade and was the last person kept. By the end of the year, I was in the starting lineup.

In high school, I pitched for the baseball team and played guard for the basketball team.

Anyone who follows high school basketball—or saw the

movie "Hoosiers"—knows just how competitive and important the sport is in secondary schools throughout Illinois and Indiana. When I was in my teens, the best basketball in the country was being played in those neighboring states. My goal—my one, overriding, absolute goal—was winning the state championship for Bloom Township.

In my junior year, our team was 22–6. I was confident this was it, this was our time, even though our starting team was kind of young, with three juniors, one sophomore and one freshman. However, we ran into Oak Park in the first round of the championship tournament, a matchup that should have occurred a lot further down the road. We fought down the wire, but we ended up losing. I still see the score in my mind's eye: 62–57.

It was a tough loss, but there was always next year, and next year we were ranked in the top five among all high schools. We notched a few victories, as expected, and then dropped a shocker in our fourth game to Lockport. We proceeded to reel off twenty-four straight, and finished the season 27–1.

With a record like that, the postseason looked promising. Even so, we faced another tough challenge in the very first round, another testament to a lack of seeding. Elgin had an undefeated team we could have faced in the finals, if things had broken a certain way. Instead, it was Elgin versus Bloom in the opening round.

The contest was fiercely played. I later confirmed what we assumed from the beginning: Elgin's scouting and strategy had focused on stopping me, the team's point guard and leading scorer. Coach Moore assumed as much, and devised a counterplan: let the others do the shooting and scoring.

The plan worked. We led through three quarters and most of the fourth—until the last twelve seconds. Elgin scored, we didn't, and we lost 53–52.

This was a shattering defeat for the team and almost

overwhelming for me. I had based my high school career, my high school life, on winning the state tournament, and I had come up short. I had failed. And I didn't know what to do. I simply hadn't considered the possibility of defeat.

I took my parents' car and drove around till three o'clock in the morning. Then I realized the reality of the situation. The sky hadn't fallen. A lightning bolt hadn't stuck me dead. Life went on. So would I. Winning was good—winning was great—but there was always another day, another game, another opportunity.

I drove home, got some sleep, and went to school the next day.

In the meantime, my baseball career was progressing in fine fashion. I was the number-one pitcher on our team, and that was no mean accomplishment. In fact, Jim Bouton, who would go on to perform distinguished service with the New York Yankees, moved to Chicago Heights when he was a junior. Back in New Jersey, he had been a first-string star in baseball, basketball, and football. In Illinois, at Bloom Township, he was in for a shock: he was cut from the basketball team, demoted to our fourth-string quarterback on the football squad, and had to pitch in the second spot behind me on the baseball club. (That was, until the middle of our senior year, when Bouton would come on strong and start to emerge as a pitcher with real prospects.)

And I haven't even mentioned the track team yet, which had won three state titles in a row. The track coach tried to recruit me, saying that if I quit baseball he would turn me into a state hurdling champ. I thanked him but declined. I liked baseball too much.

In addition to the high school team, I played for the American Legion club, coached by "Stork" Garzaloni and Earl Detella. American Legion ball was tough, high-caliber ball. The summer before college, I pitched in five games in one week—nine innings on Sunday, and four each on Wednesday,

Friday, Saturday and Sunday. That week just about killed my arm, as far as my big league prospects were concerned, although I didn't know it at the time.

My championship dreams were thwarted once again in the American Legion national tournament, held in Cincinnati, Ohio. We lost in the semifinals against the club from Bentley Post of Cincinnati.

We lost to Terre Haute in the consolation game. It was the last inning, and I was the last batter up. The opposing pitcher hit me in the hand. The blow, and my frustration at the defeat, caused me to lose control and punch home plate as hard as I could. I succeeded in breaking almost every bone in my hand, and was rewarded with a cast that reached from my thumb to my elbow.

And that was how I arrived at college to commence my freshman year.

I made the Illinois All-State high school basketball team my senior year, in 1957, and the All Illinois-Indiana team. The honors garnered me sixty-six scholarship offers from colleges around the country. I also received six offers from major league franchises, after showing my stuff at various baseball tryouts around the country.

Baseball was great, but I knew my future lay elsewhere. In any event, I wanted to further my education. Sports had already opened up my world, taken me out of my neighborhood, and shown me a bit of the country. Competing for my high school, or for whatever team I was playing on, had also made me feel that I was more than just one kid with a fiery fastball and a wicked outside shot, that I represented my town, that I was responsible, even in a small way, for other people's hopes and aspirations.

I had given a lot to sports, and sports had returned the favor. Now it was going to give me a higher education. I would be the first Colangelo to attend college.

I narrowed my choices down to four universities, for four different reasons; Illinois was close to home, Michigan had a tremendous program, Notre Dame was steeped in tradition, Catholic and athletic, and Kansas had one extraordinary asset—Wilt Chamberlain.

I had missed out on my chance to win a state championship in high school. I was determined to do even better and win the national championship in college, the NCAA national championship.

Over seven feet tall and massively strong, Wilt Chamberlain was the best college player of his day. He was surrounded by a fine supporting cast. (In fact, that cast promised to only get better. Bill Bridges, who would enjoy a long and illustrous NBA career, was entering Kansas in my freshman class.)

Kansas was in prime position to take the NCAA title.

I was sold. I wanted that title.

So I showed up on the Kansas campus in the fall of 1957, temporarily disabled with my arm in that cast, but raring to go, ready to work and play and win.

A few months after I arrived, and before the season started, Wilt confided in several of his teammates, myself included, that he was quitting school to join the Harlem Globetrotters.

I was devastated. I had left home and gone far, far away, leaving behind everyone and everything I knew, to enroll at Kansas and get that championship. Now those dreams were definitely dashed. Without Wilt, we didn't have a chance.

I decided to return home. I had departed Chicago Heights to much fanfare and expected triumphs just around the corner, and now I was back, a lot sooner than expected, with neither fanfare nor triumphs, with my tail between my legs. Illinois still wanted me, but the NCAA rules stated that I would have to skip a year of basketball eligibility if I transferred. This was going to cost me dearly. After finishing the first semester at Kansas, I skipped the second semester at Illinois, intending to enroll a freshman in the fall, with fifteen credits in my educational bank.

I took a job with the Chicago Heights sewer department

and occasionally rode a garbage truck. When I wasn't hauling trash, I played basketball anywhere I could, and especially in a very rugged and good Amateur Athletic Union (AAU) league.

Winter passed, then the spring, then summer, and it was time to go back to school. In addition to my scholarship, I got a couple of jobs to help make ends meet: I waited tables at the Moose Club, and distributed ice skates at the University of Illinois armory rink.

I was elected captain of the freshman team and was asked to practice with the varsity, usually taking the role of whoever was the best player we were going to face in the next game, so the team could prepare its plan of attack.

I had a good first year and set a specific goal for my sophomore year: to break into the starting lineup, which was wholly composed of juniors and seniors.

Our first tournament during my second season was the Los Angeles Classic, held in the brand-new L. A. Sports Arena over Christmas 1959. The cast of competing squads was impressive. The incomparable Jerry West ran the floor for West Virginia. All-American Daryl Imhoff played center for Cal, a terrific team that was coached by Pete Newell, a college coaching legend.

We were 7–0 going into the tournament but lost the first game to Cal. That put us in the consolation bracket, and we proceeded to beat Stanford, and then Northwestern.

In the course of the loss to Cal, I had gotten into the game and played pretty well. Well enough, in fact, to break into the starting lineup for the next game. In short order, I had achieved my first goal.

The team traveled on to Columbus to face Ohio State, and future NBA all-stars Jerry Lucas and John Havlicek, along with Larry Siegfried, Mel Novell, Joe Roberts, and Bobby Knight.

We were riding high. I was riding high. And now it was Ohio State's turn to fall before us.

I knocked in my first three shots, and we were quickly

ahead 6–0. Then the whirlwind struck, and Ohio State started racking up the points. As we were in the midst of being blown away, I was taken out of the game. I never made it back into the starting lineup that year.

I was elected captain of the team the next year, but our coach, Harry Combes, called me into his office and said no underclassman had ever acted as captain, and that was a tradition he intended to maintain. So I had to wait until the following season, when my teammates once again chose me captain.

After the season, I was selected to the All–Big Ten team. While that was a terrific honor, I remained frustrated in my quest for a championship.

I also pitched for a couple of years at Illinois. Through the kind of wear-and-tear I experienced in my American Legion ball days, along with inadequate conditioning and rehabilitation (back then, a pitcher with a swollen elbow or shoulder might sit under a hot shower for few minutes before getting dressed and going home, which was exactly the wrong thing to do, only helping increase the inflammation) my arm wasn't what it used to be.

Finally, after getting shelled in Memphis, in Houston, in Minnesota, all around the country, in fact, I resolved, with my coach's assent, to hang up the glove.

School ended, and I was not selected by any of the NBA teams in the draft. Of course, with just eight teams, and only twelve players on a team, there were not many spots open for rookies—approximately ten players made it per year.

The NBA might not have wanted me, but someone did, and that someone turned out to be the most important person in my life. Joan and I were married during our junior year.

I graduated from Illinois with a degree in physical education. I was qualified to teach, but my interest increasingly lay in business. I had taken a lot of business courses and found myself drawn to the entrepreneurial world. In some ways, it reminded me of sports: the individual challenge, the all-out pressure, the winning and losing.

I returned with my wife to Chicago Heights and went into the tuxedo-renting business with an old friend. We would scour the newspaper for engagement announcements and solicit prospective clients.

Later, we added dry cleaning to our enterprise. For three years, I worked very long hours and took home one hundred dollars a week, plowing our profits back into the business. In addition, Joan and I had bought a little house, our first house, and were struggling to make ends meet. Joan had already given birth to three of our kids.

At the end of the three years, things didn't work out as I had hoped and anticipated. It was time to move on. I was disappointed in the faltering business, and disillusioned because of the relationship. And yet in the midst of this misfortune, I discovered something about myself. Prior to this experience, I regarded myself as pretty capable of taking care of myself. I considered myself self-reliant. Whatever life threw at me, I thought I could handle it. Now, all of a sudden, the walls had come tumbling down, and I found myself at the kitchen table, surrounded by a wife and three small children, nothing in the bank, nothing to show for three years of hard work. I didn't know where I was going to be the next day, because I had nowhere to go, no place to turn.

To put it simply, it was a very humbling experience.

At the same time, I wasn't about to panic. I looked around and said to myself, This is what has happened, this is what I'm doing, this is who I am, everything will be fine. I wasn't thinking, How am I going to send them to college? I didn't think that far down the line. I was more interested in finding a way to deal with the here and now.

One aspect of my life that kept me calm and optimistic was my strong personal faith. I came to believe and understand that there is a lot more to life than just self-reliance. I came to believe and understand that if you have a true faith and a true belief, that if you looked for the direction that I believe you have to look for, the direction that comes with a belief that I have in my God, Jesus Christ, you can go on in the face of any crisis or problem with confidence and hope.

I was brought to this faith by my wife, who has brought me so many of the best things in my life. Joan had been attending a small Baptist church for some time before I started going with her. The minister, who had come from an Italian Catholic family, had left that faith and become a Baptist minister. He made a big impression on me, partially because of his ideas and his faith, and particularly because of the similarities of our backgrounds.

The transformation he effected in my life, the realization he led me to, the faith he ignited in my mind and soul, made me a better person, a better husband, a better father. I was so busy doing my thing, trying to build my business, that I didn't have a good picture of where I really needed to be in my life.

In any event, an extraordinary occurrence took place on that distressing night. I was sitting at the kitchen table, with nothing to do and nowhere to go, when I took my wallet out of my pocket and, rather absentmindedly, started cleaning it out, throwing away the scraps of paper and other debris one accumulates. I found a business card stuck in my wallet, crumpled and worn. It had been there about two years. My father-in-law had handed it to me one day, saying he thought this was a guy I should meet.

Busy with my business and growing family, I promptly forget all about the business card. Now, my present position left me with more than enough time to act on my father-in-law's suggestion. Why not? I certainly had nothing to lose. I was twenty-six years old, and my only income was the fifty bucks I got per game for playing in a semiprofessional basketball league at night.

The next morning I phoned Dick Klein. He invited me down to his office for a cup of coffee and a chat. I agreed, not thinking much about it.

Little did I know at the time, Dick would change my life forever, and together, we would change the course of professional sports in America.

Of course, all that was in the future. Now, over thirty years later, we are back in Chicago Heights, back where I began, back with a sizable portion of my family, back where I will always be home, back before the first home I knew.

Chicago Heights has honored me in many ways. The junior high school gym in which I played so long ago has been renamed the Jerry Colangelo Gymnasium. The street on which I grew up now has a sign that announces that 22d Street is Jerry Colangelo Way.

And now my grandparents' home, and my parents' home, and my home, will always have this plaque before it. If this is not the greatest honor of all, it is surely the most personal honor.

My son, Bryan, couldn't be here with his family because he is the general manager of the Suns and the draft is tomorrow. My three daughters and their husbands have brought all their children—and the kids are scrambling up the few stairs and are entering the house. They see the small, narrow front room, which is open to the small kitchen. An even smaller room is off the front room. A staircase behind the kitchen, which was once outdoors but is now enclosed, leads to the second story. The doors are locked, but I know there are three small rooms, three bedrooms. They peer through a glass pane in the door into the room that grandfather added on to serve as my bedroom.

Joan, with some help from our daughters, who hold some memories of Sunday dinners and other visits when they were very young, explains to the grandchildren how this home was once the center of the Colangelo family universe, how it throbbed with hope and dreams, and the daily joys, problems, and realities of life.

The grandchildren are too young to understand this house, this history, the long road from the railroad boxcars that became a home on Hungry Hill to the sunlit world of Phoenix where they live today.

I understand this house, and I understand the history—my history. I know what it took, and what it still takes to stay in the game, to stay on top of the game. That's what I'm here to tell you.

My story is an especially American story, with especially American successes and failures, and especially American lessons.

You have heard something of my beginning. Let's get to the business at hand.

On to the Bulls.

CHAPTER TWO

The Birth of the Bulls

THE CHICAGO BULLS won their sixth world championship (in 8 years) in 1998, an astonishing achievement in any professional sport. They are fabulously profitable, consistently sell out their arena, and successfully market their logo and products around the world. The Bulls, embodied by Jerry Reinsdorf, who is as skilled an owner as any in pro sports, and Phil Jackson, an absolutely terrific coach, and a tremendous line-up, which begins but does not end with the phenomenal Michael Jordan, created a standard of excellence and professionalism that is admired throughout sports. In fact, this standard is so unassailable, so unwavering, that it must seem to many (particularly those in the younger set) that the Chicago Bulls have somehow always been there, like the Great Wall of China or cotton socks.

In reality, the Bulls are a relatively recent invention—and all that tradition was built and all those logo-driven products had to be devised from scratch—beginning not much more than thirty years ago.

It began with that dog-eared business card I plucked from my wallet. I called Dick Klein, who remembered me from my basketball days at Illinois, and invited me to his office to chat. I headed downtown the next morning, without any expectations, without any preconceived notions, just going because it was something to do. If not definitively forward progress, it would be better than standing still, at least. Instead of a quick chat, we spent the entire day talking.

Dick Klein owned an incentive merchandising company, which assisted other companies in putting together gift packages and other programs to give to clients, distributors, and suppliers. Dick, who basically ran a one-man shop, was swamped with work, and needed help. By the end of the day, he offered me a job at double what I had been earning in the tuxedo business, along with potentially sizable commissions. I readily accepted.

I had no need to consider and evaluate before deciding. The job sounded promising, I certainly needed a promising job, and I took it. Even as the stage on which I've operated has gotten larger, with big stakes for everyone involved, I've always behaved in that manner: If the opportunity sounded right, if I knew in my bones it was the right move, then I acted.

This is not to discount the value of diligent research. Before I decided to plunge into Major League Baseball, I spent months examining the baseball business from every angle. That commitment demanded no less.

However, as valuable as research is, facts and statistics and flow charts and projections by themselves cannot provide every answer, cannot warranty every contingency, cannot ensure every outcome. Nor can they tell you how much you will enjoy the work or ultimately be fulfilled by the result.

It's a fine line between being reasonably cautious and being unnecessarily fearful. There are no guarantees in business, just as there are no guarantees in life. Education and experience will teach you how far you can trust your intuition. The trick is to learn to rely on your best instincts, decide, and act without looking back.

I decided to take two weeks off before starting, which was one of the best decisions I ever made. Between the business and basketball, I had been working days and nights, and finally had the chance to get reacquainted with my wife and children. It was a cherished two weeks, and I learned how precious such times are. I resolved to never again get so caught up in my business, no matter how exciting or important, that I allowed it to steal too much time from my family. It is a vow I have kept, and now I have been fortunate in that all my children and grandchildren live in Phoenix today.

My vacation passed, and my first day on the job entailed accompanying my new boss on a business trip in order to learn the ropes. We were driving somewhere along Route 41 in Indiana when Dick told me of his long-held, heartfelt wish to start an NBA franchise in Chicago, and his frustrated efforts to accomplish this goal. Dick was singing my song. I was a basketball guy all the way and offered to do anything I could to help.

Dick Klein was an excellent athlete who hailed from Fort Madison, Iowa. Two or three inches over six feet, Klein starred in both basketball and baseball at Northwestern. He was as good a promoter as I would ever encounter. Not only was he a large, imposing man, he had one of the best smiles you'd ever see.

His concept was to help other companies sell their products, motivate their personnel, or create more traffic in their stores. One example from my own work in the business: I put together a "dealer-loader" program for Helene Curtis Industries, the cosmetics giant. This was regarded as dealer-loader because the idea was to motivate the company's many dealers to take on additional product, urging them on to extra effort in order to win prizes such as trips and silverware.

Other incentive programs were consumer-oriented. For instance, we devised a program for a large grocery chain in Chicago to offer silver trays as a gift to customers who spent a certain amount of money in its stores. Today, of course, every credit card, supermarket, and magazine has some sort of incentive program for customers and workers, but that wasn't the case in the Sixties, and Klein was a pioneer in his field.

I plunged into the incentive business, racking up sales

and commissions. At the same time, I was becoming immersed in the basketball side of the enterprise, Dick Klein's glorious basketball quest. I attended meetings with bankers and other potential investors. I might have known a lot about basketball, but the business side of sports was a playing field I had never before encountered.

However, while this might have been new to me, professional basketball was not an entirely new concept for Chicago. Two—not one, but two pro teams, the Chicago Stags and Chicago Packers, who also changed their name in mid-stream to the Zephyrs—had already failed in the Windy City. This sad history didn't exactly inspire instant enthusiasm on the part of the money men, private or corporate. Indeed, it was a considerable obstacle we had to overcome.

In our initial basketball/banker meetings, my role was to sit and listen and learn. I would watch with intense interest as Dick laid out his game plan to make pro basketball a Chicago reality, proffer his proposals to the bankers and other money types. Particularly in the beginning, Dick's scheme and ideas were primarily met with negative responses—basketball wasn't a viable commodity, at least not in Chicago; basketball wasn't a business the bankers understood; basketball wasn't always a game the bankers cared about; on and on.

Dick didn't give up. We went from door to door, person to person, pushing the plan, pursuing the dream, talking, explaining, responding, building contacts and relationships. Eventually, we made a convert or two, then more, and then more.

I learned a lesson in perseverance, though in truth individual drive was an emotion with which I was already familiar. More important to me, I learned a great deal about the mechanics of putting a deal together, and structuring a limited partnership. What an extraordinary opportunity—to be invited into the inner workings of a totally involving venture, and granted a front-row seat to observe and absorb the scene, the players, the emotions, the facts, the exchanges, the negotiating, as your boss carried the water and did the heavy lifting.

We made more progress. Step by step, piece by piece, we found believers and uncovered investors.

We raised the money. Seven hundred fifty thousand dollars. In the bank. The price of a franchise in the National Basketball Association, circa 1966.

That should be where the first part of the story ends. Unfortunately, before Klein flew off to New York to hand over the money and sign the papers, we learned that the owners of the National Basketball Association—Dick's new fellow owners—had decided to raise the price by $500,000 to a cool $1.25 million.

Why did they suddenly demand more money?

Because they could.

Was this fair? Was this right? Was this ethical?

Welcome to the big leagues, in any sport, anytime, anywhere.

As the NBA figured, Dick still wanted his team, and he sought out Elmer Rich, one of the investors. Rich, whose family owned Simonize Wax, stepped up with the extra half-million in interim financing, and we closed the deal. Dick ended up with twenty percent of the franchise, which was a respectable piece of the total.

Dick went to New York and I stayed in Chicago, preparing a news release to announce this momentous event. Dick's secretary, Ruthie Dryjanski (who would later, to my immeasurable advantage and eternal gratitude, move with me to Phoenix), and I waited and waited. Finally he called to say we're in, the deal's done, full steam ahead.

I was ready to go. I had ideas and schemes on how to promote the team off the court, and how to build the team on the court, swirling through my mind.

Not too long after we got the franchise, I leased a flatbed truck and rented a bull—a live bull, mind you—to place on that flatbed. We took that truck and bull and drove down Michigan Avenue at lunch time, passing out our pamphlets, declaring the arrival of the Chicago Bulls on the scene, looking to sell tickets.

That was our first marketing pitch.

Of course, nobody in Chicago cared. The town had a bunch of pro teams. Basketball was a minor sport compared to baseball or football or hockey, and the Cubs and the Sox and the Bears and the Blackhawks were established icons. In addition, the local media had seen it all before with basketball, and the results had been discouraging.

Basketball was definitely relegated to the second tier of pro sports. Just nine franchises constituted the league. Our first year, the Bulls' payroll for the entire team, all twelve players, was $180,000. Compare that to the NBA today where the average player salary is $2.6 million. Compare that to the hundred-million-dollar contracts being demanded, and sometimes received, by individual athletes.

Regardless, when Dick phoned to say we were in, I sent out my press release—via telegram, in those days: "An important announcement of both local and national interest will be made tomorrow at the Water Tower Inn at 9 A.M. Signed, the Chicago Bulls."

A word about the name. Dick Klein basically picked the name—the Bulls. "The Bulls" fit like a glove: direct, tough, reminiscent of Chicago's past as a prime stockyard and shipping point. He asked me what I thought and I said, Yes. That's it. The Chicago Bulls it would be.

Our next task was finding a place to play. The choices were only two, one old and far from state-of-the-art. The Chicago Stadium the more modern stadium, owned by the Wirtz family, was being used by the Blackhawks of the National Hockey League. While this did not necessarily preclude a basketball team from playing in the stadium, the Bulls were not invited to share the facility.

Then there was the International Amphitheater. The Amphitheater had served in a previous life as the stockyards, where the cattle were led to the slaughter. Anyone who has read about them in Upton Sinclair's *The Jungle,* let alone visited a slaughterhouse, knows that it is not just another place of business, with offices and furniture that can be neatly stacked away in an afternoon, obliterating all signs of the occupants. A slaughterhouse is a messy, bloody, gory place, whose legacy lingers long after the cows are gone on to their greater reward.

So the place certainly had a reputation, and the smell to back it up. That smell. . . . It just permeated the entire building, although the stockyards had been out of business for years.

And that was where we going to call home.

The Bulls. Dick had this belief that the newspapers and other media preferred short names—the Cubs, the Bears, the Sox (for the White Sox), the Hawks (for the Blackhawks)— and the press was key to the success of any professional sports venture. Of course, I later broke Dick's rule with "the Diamondbacks," but you can be sure that the media immediately shortened the name, usually to "D'backs," to fit their requirements.

"The Bulls" was perfect. We went to Jack Mathis, who owned a small advertising firm in town, and he devised this mean-looking bull for a logo. We thought that fit quite nicely, too. More than thirty years later, the Bulls still have the same name, and the Bulls still have the same logo, which obviously speaks to the value of those initial choices.

Our first big press conference was scheduled for the next morning at nine. I left the office and loaded our press releases in my car. It was starting to snow and I had to get to Grand Rapids; even with all that was going on, I was still playing for fifty bucks a game in my semi-pro league, the North American Basketball League.

I drove around Lake Michigan, the snow getting worse.

I'd just been traded by the Chicago team to Grand Rapids, which was kind of amusing, considering that I was helping bring an NBA team to Chicago.

One of my new teammates was Manny Jackson, who is now the owner of the Harlem Globetrotters. Years later, I had something to do with Manny moving the Globetrotters' headquarters to Phoenix.

In any event, we played the Chicago team. We beat my old team, too. In fact, I sunk the game winner in overtime, which was a nice way to go out. You see, this was the end of my pro career; now that the Bulls were getting started, I was not only inundated with new responsibilities, but I also immediately hit the road in my role as scout.

After the game, I got dressed and realized I couldn't find my car keys. I later learned that Manny had accidentally absconded not only with my keys, but also with my wallet— and had left for Detroit! By the time I figured out what had happened, everybody else was gone. I was alone and stranded in an authentic Midwest blizzard.

This was not good. Aside from the sheer unpleasantness of getting stuck, truly stuck, in the middle of a snowstorm, I had to find my way back to Chicago for my press conference. So, with no other choice, I broke into my own car without really knowing what I was doing and somehow found a spare ignition key in my glove compartment. To this day, I don't know how or why it was there, but to this day, I'm grateful it was.

I drove home, arriving just in time to change and report to the Water Tower Inn and pass out the releases.

Sleep would come another day. Now it was time for the Bulls.

My responsibilities were many and varied, as befitted a startup operation. I was the director of marketing and chief (and only) scout, which covered a myriad of realms and responsibilities. Today, the marketing for a pro basketball franchise is handled by twenty to twenty-five employees, and a scouting department consists of four or five people.

Every single day of that first year was very, very exciting. We were new to the business, we were building something, we were learning as we went along. It was a tremendous experience for me. Little did I know, in 1966, at the age of twenty-six, that my work with the Bulls was preparing me for even bigger things. Similarly, little did I know that this mom-and-pop league was going to explode into a multibillion dollar industry.

I didn't think about such things. I was a Chicago guy involved with a major league sport. That was enough for me. I couldn't have been happier. This was who I was, this was what I did. That was all I had to know.

I learned on the job. More precisely: I learned *everything* on the job, from fleeting, promotional gimmicks to overriding, relentless, pounding priorities.

One of those lessons I learned early on—one of the most important lessons I ever learned—occurred on one of my first scouting trips. In those days, though this might be hard to believe, most clubs didn't scout college players. Instead, they relied on a couple of magazines to spread the word about prospects. Having been a player, I appreciated the importance of getting out there and seeing not only who could jump and shoot, but also who was motivated and aggressive and a leader—who could not only play but also who *wanted* to play.

I landed in Kansas City for the National Association of Intercollegiate Athletics (NAIA) tournament, which was the competition of choice for the smaller colleges. I'd already been traveling for two or three weeks. Scouting can be quite a grind, moving from city to city, tournament to tournament, game to game. At a tournament like the NAIA, you watched eight games in a day, starting at ten in the morning and finishing at eleven at night.

The competition was held in downtown Kansas City, and

the tournament headquarters' was next door, in the Muelbach Hotel, where everyone associated with the tournament stayed. Around the corner from the hotel was the Italian Gardens, where the small scouting contingent from the NBA would gather each night to eat and drink. The group totaled just five: Red Holzman from the New York Knicks, Pepper Wilson from Cincinnati, Buddy Jeannette of the Baltimore Bullets, Marty Blake of the St. Louis Hawks, and me. These were the days when general managers sometimes doubled as scouts, as was the case with Wilson, Jeannette, and Blake. In addition to the eating and drinking, we'd talk basketball. Actually, I'd sit and listen while the others, who had been around the league for years, talked.

While the talk might have been casual, dinner conversation, the basketball wisdom imparted to anyone paying close attention was invaluable. Two of this quartet, Red and Buddy, were future Hall of Fame inductees, and all four were skilled, sure pros.

After three nights of this, Red Holzman, who was soon thereafter named the coach of the Knicks and eventually led his team to two NBA championships, turned to me.

"Kid," he said, in that blunt style that would become famous in New York. "You know what?"

"What?" I said.

"You're going to do pretty well in this game."

"Why's that, Red?"

"Because you don't know anything," he said. "Because you keep your mouth shut."

While not exactly your standard compliment, I did appreciate Red's words. I also took them to heart, always trying to listen before I spoke, always trying to learn before I decided. It's a lesson I've attempted to pass on to other people as they came into our organization or into the league. My manner has been perhaps a bit more genteel, but the message is the same: You may have an opinion, or many opinions, but when you have the opportunity to be around Jerry West, for example, or another of the really accomplished, knowledgeable professionals that are on the staff of every club, be a good listener.

I never had a true mentor, in the sense of an employer, teacher, or coach who guided me through my career, but I have relied upon many people who have had substantial influences on my life. Apart from the short note of encouragement already mentioned, Red Holzman offered valuable advice to me for years.

(Actually, on one occasion, I returned the favor. Red and I had started to travel together quite a bit on our scouting trips, arranging to hit the same colleges and tournaments. We were finishing up at a pre-Christmas tournament in Huntington, West Virginia, and Red and I were rushing back to the airport to fly home for the holiday, Red to New York and me to Chicago. Back in New York, things weren't going so well for the Knicks, and Dick McGuire's coaching days with the club seemed numbered. Red and I were scheduled to meet up in Portland for another tournament the day after Christmas, and I said I didn't think Red was going to be there.

"I think you're going to be sitting on the bench," I said, meaning he was going to be the next coach of the Knicks.

"What are you talking about?" Red said gruffly. "No way. No. Never happen."

We argued about it for a minute, and then parted ways.

Christmas came and went, and I left the following morning for Portland. I waited for Red at the hotel, but he never showed up. Turning on the television in my room, I learned that Red had indeed ascended to the coach's job in New York. I sent him a telegram, effectively saying, I told you so.)

Eddie Gottlieb was another influential person in my life. Eddie had the owned the Philadelphia Spas, which played in a league that preceded the formation of the National Basketball Association. In those early days, it was a common occurrence that a dance would be held in the gym, bringing in a crowd, followed by the Spas running onto the court to take on their opponent. Eddie went on to be one of the founders of the NBA. He used to make the schedule for the whole NBA, requiring just one pencil and one eraser. That was it. Whenever I went back east, I availed myself of the opportunity to sit and speak with him.

Pete Newell was one of the great college coaches of all time. Enshrined in the Hall of Fame, he coached Cal to the NCAA title, and coached the 1960 Olympic Team that included Jerry West and Oscar Robertson. Pete's eighty years old and still does some scouting. The mindful student can learn so much from such a great teacher, as Pete talks about the game, about its past, its rich traditions and history. The rules of the game, the tactics on the floor, the strategy developed in practice: they all began somewhere and evolved and matured. Understanding the layers of reasons, mistakes, and changes that make up the present structure of the game—or the company or industry, in any business or endeavor—can be of benefit only to someone seeking to maximize his abilities and opportunities. That is what a sense of history can give you. That is what tradition truly means. That is what Red Holzman, Eddie Gottlieb, or Pete Newell helped me grasp.

I've spent a lot of time and swapped a lot of theories and proposals and plans with some great players who went into management once their playing days were through, great players like Jerry West, Wayne Embry, Rod Thorn, Lenny Wilkens, and Billy Cunningham. They became my colleagues and my friends; sometimes we worked in concert, and sometimes we worked in opposition. That was the nature of the business. But always we remained colleagues and friends.

In short, it's all about appreciation for the game, respect for the game, and that's something that deepens over a long period of time. That kind of appreciation and respect is often a victim of this fast-paced, hypercompetitive world, in basketball and out. There's scant time for that—it's make your decision and move on, boom, boom, boom.

Tradition, history, respect. We have it in the NBA, and

so do Major League Baseball, the NFL, international tennis and golf, and all professional sports, much more so than in most other industries. Still, with so much money coursing through sports, we have to remember that money alone will not sustain us, that we have to work hard to maintain the link that binds us to our past, that link between the past and the present that makes sports special.

When I entered the sports business, it was basically a very simple, straightforward enterprise. It has become a very complex business, which is a direct and inevitable result of the size and growth of the industry. Where franchises were selling for two million dollars in the mid-sixties and late sixties, today those same franchises are selling for hundreds of millions of dollars.

The business has changed, but it remains the same old game. The same terrific game. And we have to treasure it in order to nourish and protect it.

Another sign of the changes in the sports business over the past three decades can be found in shoes. We have all heard about the fantastic millions the shoe companies have spent on athletes, stamping their names on basketball shoes, using their faces in ads, having them perform in commercials. Well, it wasn't always that way.

I was busy reviewing our needs for that first season, and recognized that basketball shoes were going to be a high priority for the Bulls, and potentially an expensive one (relatively speaking for a franchise with ticket prices ranging from two to five dollars), over the course of a season. I gave Converse a phone call because everybody wore their sneakers in the Sixties. Chuck Taylor's canvas shoes were the gold standard. They came in black or white, low-top or high—and that was it. Though I don't exactly remember the exact price, Chuck Taylor's probably cost about fifteen to twenty bucks; not a lot today, when basketball shoes can set you back one hundred fifty dollars, but a lot of money in 1966.

Anyway, I called a fellow named Gib Ford at Converse (Gib eventually went on to become CEO of the company.) Because I was always looking to save money or increase revenue and this was one more opportunity, I had a deal in mind and explained the details to Gib. Converse would supply the Bulls with shoes, and the team would provide Converse with some tickets and advertising and a few other incentives and perks. Converse accepted the offer, and the Bulls were able to save a small bundle on shoes.

That, I believe, was the first shoe deal in professional sports.

In January 1966, I put together our first game program. Jack Mathis, a good friend of mine to this day, whose firm had designed the Bulls logo, helped me put the program together. Jack had always loved basketball. He sponsored his own AAU basketball team, named JAMACO, which stood for the Jack A. Mathis Advertising Company. I played for JAMACO, and we had an excellent team.

After printing our game program and other expenses, we netted $15,000 in ads and game sales. That might not sound like much in the today's billion-dollar basketball business, but I was really happy with it because it meant we had made a profit.

Again, let me run through the small numbers, and smaller margins, with which we were working. Tickets were priced at two, three, four, or five dollars; our share (equally split among the teams) of the NBA's national television revenue was $100,000; and our dozen players cost the franchise a grand total of $180,000.

With that in mind, you can understand that a $15,000 profit was nothing to sneeze at.

On the other hand, not every idea worked out so well. We had scheduled a promotional night, a basketball give-away night, for one of our games. This was a pretty new idea in

1966, but not completely new; the Everlast Company, the famed boxing supply company, staged what was perhaps the first promotional give-away game at Yankee Stadium on August 4, 1927. Everlast arranged for a "Boys' Day," whereby a handful of lucky boys under the age of fifteen would win athletic equipment if the other half of their game tickets were selected by Babe Ruth, Lou Gehrig, or other Yankee stars before the start of the day's contest.

So while I can't take credit for give-away games, the Bulls were still early innovators in the NBA, and handing out basketballs was definitely not a routine event.

Anyway, as people entered the arena, we distributed the balls to the kids. Between the twin attractions of hosting the Knicks and giving away basketballs, we had a crowd of some ten thousand, which was a very good turnout. Thoroughly pleased with the result, I suddenly had a brainstorm during the first half and headed to the booth to make an announcement: All the kids who wanted to could bring their brand new balls down to the court at half-time and shoot. And, just as expected, many kids did troop down to the floor and toss up their balls. However, not expected, especially not by me, was how many kids would lose their basketballs between leaving their seats and returning to them. That resulted in a stream of irate parents demanding replacement balls at the end of the game.

We distributed more basketballs, and I learned a lesson. Give away the stuff that could easily get lost not as people entered the arena but as they were leaving.

I've never dwelled on mistakes, and I never ranked mistakes in order from bad to the worst. I recognized long ago that making mistakes is part of the process. And once you've made them, the only thing you can do is learn from them and go forward. In my case, my business acumen has always been centered around professional sports. I learned in the trenches, I learned on the job. My methodology was trial and error.

One lesson I learned had to do with the basic ethics of the

business. Early on in my Bulls' career, I was having a phone conversation with Marty Blake, the general manager of the St. Louis Hawks. We were chatting about players, as general managers are wont to do, and I mentioned a player we were bringing in for a tryout. Porter Merriweather was his name. I had played with him in my semi-pro league and thought he had a legitimate shot at the NBA.

In those days, the rules regarding such matters were loose. There were all kinds of lists of players floating around, denoting players who were available for one reason or another, or unattached to any NBA team, and protocol permitted you to simply take a guy's name off the list and put him on your own list.

Anyway, we concluded our conversation, and I went back to my business. Eventually, though without any sense of urgency—I knew that no one else was interested in him—I got around to dealing with Porter Merriweather and moving his name to our list.

Lo and behold, I suddenly discovered that Merriweather was no longer available. Marty Blake had snatched Porter Merriweather for his Hawks. I was out of luck and had no recourse for any complaint I might have wanted to register.

That was the way business was conducted. It was simply a lesson I had to learn. I didn't hold it against Marty. Actually, we have always had a great relationship over the years and still do. And we still laugh about the Merriweather deal.

By the way, two things: Porter didn't work out for Hawks. And I never made that mistake again.

Here's another one from the trial-and-error—emphasis on the error—department, though I'm pleased to say that this one wasn't mine.

One not atypical Chicago morn in 1967, the skies opened and it snowed. And snowed and snowed, until twenty-four inches of snow covered the city, in classic Chicago blizzard style.

The city was shut down. A doubleheader at Chicago Stadium was canceled. Lew Alcindor, later known as Kareem Abdul-Jabbar, was playing for UCLA, but that game was also scratched. Cars were buried, walking was slow and difficult, and trains were the only way to get around.

In the midst of all this, the Los Angeles Lakers were coming to town, the great Lakers, with Jerry West and Elgin Baylor, to play the Bulls.

Now I thought we should cancel the game. I took the train into Chicago from Chicago Heights and implored Dick Klein to reschedule for another day.

"No one's going to show up," I said. "There's not going to be anyone there."

The parking lot was unplowed, as were most of the streets. Not only would the fans have trouble getting to the Amphitheater, the Lakers were having difficulty reaching the arena.

"Let's catch it another time," I said.

Dick was convinced that the show must go on. Besides, he had a feeling it was going to be our night. "If we can beat the Lakers," he said, "I want to take the win."

The Lakers were clearly unhappy about trudging through this very un-California weather. Dick dispatched me to their locker room to extend a sort of a peace offering.

"Tell them we'll buy them dinner after the game at the Stockyard Inn," he said.

So I went to their locker room and gave Fred Schaus, their coach, the glad tidings about dinner. And even though the Stockyard Inn was and remains a very good restaurant, the news didn't brighten up the coach's distinctly unhappy mood.

In fact, the Lakers were collectively so unhappy that they went out and beat us by forty points. And maybe a thousand people showed up to witness the rout. And then the Lakers, still unhappy, walked over to the Stockyard Inn and ate a fine meal on the Bulls.

In the end, not a happy night for anyone.

Another learning experience.

Not everything I learned had to do with marketing. On the less glamorous side of the business, I had to learn how to read a balance sheet, and understand how accountants and bankers fit into the picture.

Balance sheets didn't always fall within the sophisticated scope of accountants. Take ticketing, for instance. Of course, today everything is computerized, with backup systems and built-in redundancies and safeguards, a process instant and flawless—usually—but thirty years ago was another story.

Back in 1966, you had hard tickets, that was all, and a ticket manager who literally would keep track of sales by "listening to the unsold tickets," the "dead wood." These tickets were kept wrapped in bundles, and the ticket manager would put up a stack, riffle through it, and unfailingly know how many tickets were in his hand. And that was it, that was the accounting; after that riffle, you had dead wood or you had cash.

I learned something about that process with the Bulls that first year. We hired a guy, Eddie Edelstein, a renowned old Chicago Cub ticket seller, to function as our ticket manager. In those days, we had all the tickets for the whole season printed and then locked them in a vault. After every game, he would remove the unsold tickets from the vault and figure out how many he had left over. This would be referred to as the "reconciliation," and the reconciliation told the all-important tale of profit and loss.

It was a fascinating process—almost a performance. I would watch Eddie as he grabbed the tickets, which were all stacked up, and hold them to his ear and rip his finger through those tickets—whoosh!—and mark down fifteen or fifty or whatever the number was. I was amazed how sure and certain he was, game after game. Oh, a quick check now and then would show he might have been off a few dollars off here or there, but it was absolutely transfixing.

Of course, then when we got to the last game of the season and added up the totals for the year, I saw how short he actually was—thousands of dollars short, throwing our accounting into disarray for some time.

That was pretty much the end of Eddie. And I made sure I kept my eye firmly fixed on those tickets from that day on.

I had been a local athlete and had gained a certain amount of credibility with the press because of my own sports career. I had always enjoyed positive relationships with many members of the media, on and off the court.

Now, with the Bulls, from the outset, I came equipped with an appreciation of the importance of the media and maintaining good relations with them. It just made sense. The press, through the sportswriters and columnists who staffed the four major newspapers in town, was an aggressively powerful presence.

This was a different era, when the papers ruled the media roost. Chicago had a quartet of important newspapers, brimming with skilled, knowledgeable, assertive writers, as accomplished a lineup as could be found in the country. The *Chicago Tribune* was represented by the great sports columnist Dave Condon. The *Chicago Sun-Times* held its own with Bill Gleason and Jerry Holzman.

Those were just the morning papers. In the afternoon, the *Chicago Daily News* and the *Chicago American* flooded the streets with their own editions. The *American* had Jimmy Enright, and Dick Dozer also wrote for the *Tribune*. Dick's son, Rich, would become a prominent player in our endeavors in Phoenix.

With such a continual flow of information inundating the city, it was clear that what the papers thought of the Bulls would determine what Chicago thought of the Bulls.

We couldn't make the reporters and columnists write what we wanted, nor did we try anything of the sort. We could, however, be as accommodating and as friendly to the press as was acceptable and reasonable.

And that friendship was real. Just one example: In the

course of those first couple of seasons in Chicago, Tom Fitz-patrick, who later won a Pulitzer Prize for his news reporting, was covering the Bulls. And in the course of those seasons, Fitzpatrick and I became rather close. In fact, on a fairly frequent basis, after a Bulls game, I would wait for him to finish his story and file it, and then give him a ride home. Nothing particularly dramatic about that, nothing extraordinary, just a couple of guys riding home after work—but something that probably wouldn't happen in today's often charged and contentious relationship between management and the media.

Our paths would cross again when Fitzpatrick moved to Arizona and went to work for a couple of newspapers in Phoenix.

Another old-timer we hired was Ben Bentley. He headed our public relations, and he was an authentic character straight out of a Damon Runyon book. He accommodated the needs and interests of the press in his own special way on behalf of the Bulls, as the franchise's point man in dealing with the media.

Ben was from the old school. He was popular all over town, knew everybody, and was one of Chicago's truly colorful characters. A legend in his own time, you could say. Ben believed in servicing the media and knew what appealed to all his press pals. Thus, twice a day, once in the morning and once in the afternoon, he would leave our office at 221 North La Salle and walk across the street to the newspaper offices, bearing a bottle of booze or a fistful of cigars, and stop in and spend some time. One-on-one attention—that was Ben's way.

Ben and I shared an office, and I never tired of watching him operate. He had three phones on his desk. One was for the Bulls, for basketball business. The second was for his boxing interests, for Ben was a boxing promoter and a ring announcer. He knew all the old boxers and managers and trainers, and they'd constantly be calling, asking for a job or a match or the latest inside scoop. The third phone was for his side deals, which might mean dropping the name of a new restaurant into a newspaper's society column in return for free meals at the joint. Ben had so many of these side deals going that I doubt he ever bought himself a meal or paid for a suit or paid for much of anything, for that matter.

I would sit there, watching him, amazed at his ability to juggle the three jangling phones at once. He would be talking with one guy, discounting a story about an injury to one of the Bulls, and then the second line would ring and it would be a middleweight champ asking for an update on his upcoming fight, and all the while he would be jawing on the third phone with some new bar owner in town about how to properly promote his spot.

Ben was a performance artist before there was performance art.

Of course, as we grew we needed more help, more brains, more eyes, more hands. Even before then, from the very outset of the Bulls, prior to our playing a single game, I was already getting resumes from people looking for jobs. I was amazed at the caliber of the people who were applying, people whose training and experience rendered them more prepared than I was to do my job—or my jobs, I should say. Of course, we couldn't hire everyone who applied, no matter how qualified. We had neither the positions nor the money. Sorting through all those resumes, it made me wonder about the hiring process, about how people—in almost any company, in almost any field—get a chance.

Our organization stayed small because we had to. But those resumes kept coming.

Today, that process has only gotten more complicated and more difficult. With such high stakes, such intense pressures to succeed, and all the costs that make the game, any pro game, so expensive, there is little time or tolerance for someone learning on the job the way I was able to try and test and experiment and learn. This is an unfortunate situation, given my own experience with the Bulls.

Clearly, many people wish to be involved in the sports business, as is true with all aspects of the entertainment industry. There exists a reservoir of candidates from which to choose, some outstanding candidates—people with not only the type of enthusiasm and commitment you seek, but also with proven track records. I received some terrific resumes back in 1966, but they are dwarfed by the scores of sensational resumes I see today.

At the same time, let me stress that however hard it is to get into the sports industry, it is more possible now than ever before because there are so many more teams and leagues and sports.

I got a lucky break when I met Dick Klein and he included me in his basketball dream. And I was ready to act on it, because I knew how to work hard and I knew what I was capable of accomplishing. The point is not to wait and hope for that break, but to do everything possible to make it likely that you will be in position to recognize a chance and will be prepared to take advantage of it when it comes along.

And that break—that encounter or conversation or offer or opportunity—will come, sooner or later, in one form or another. Perhaps not as dramatically or as perfectly as you might wish, perhaps not even in the field or place or business that you prefer. But those encounters or conversations do occur, those offers and opportunities do arise, on a remarkably consistent basis. Maybe it's just the chance to ride a garbage truck and collect trash for the city, but if that chance comes when you need it, it will take you to the next place, the next job, the next chance.

Study, work, learn, be ready. That's all you can do. That should be enough.

I haven't tried to provide a catalogue of every deal we made and every decision we took and every game we played that first year. My intention has been to serve up some examples that would represent what it took that extraordinary first year to ensure that the franchise would have the financial foundation to eventually prosper, as well as providing the fans the embryo of a team and a tradition worthy of supporting.

The bottom-line reality that first year was that survival meant success. It was make or break, and that's a hard way to learn, but make it we did, and learn I did.

The Chicago Bulls grossed $425,000 in 1966. After paying off all our expenses, there was a small net profit, too small to even remember with any specificity. But that profit grew a little larger the next year, and larger the year after that, and now the Bulls are a beloved Chicago institution, a national obsession, and a global catchword for excitement and excellence.

All because Dick Klein had a dream and dared to make it happen.

By the way . . . the Bulls won thirty-three games that first year and lost forty-eight. We also made the playoffs and lost three straight to the St. Louis Hawks, led by their great guards, Lenny Wilkins and Richie Guerin.

The Bulls would eventually do a lot better.

CHAPTER THREE

From Chicago to Phoenix

THAT FIRST YEAR with the Chicago Bulls was more exciting than I can possibly relate. Everything was new and untested and possible. Some of it worked, and some of it didn't. But enough of it worked so that we made a profit, started building a fan base, and survived to enjoy another season fighting on the boards.

While the first year was incredible, the second year wasn't bad either. Now we had a season and off-season under our belts, a base upon which to build. We were still learning as we went along—that was for sure—but we knew a thing or two ourselves.

Perhaps the most important change from the first year was our move from the Amphitheater to Chicago Stadium. The Amphitheater was antiquated years before we moved in, and it was never intended for basketball. Chicago Stadium, the home of the Black Hawks, the preeminent, established venue in the city, gave us an instant boost of credibility. The Wirtz family, which owned the arena and wasn't willing to have us in the place the first year, decided it was in its best interests to bring the Bulls inside. And they were right on that score because we had been pretty successful our first season:

we had made some fans, generated some media attention, sold some tickets. Some tickets, mind you—we averaged around 4,000 tickets per game our first year.

Still, it was a start. My biggest challenge that second year was moving the team into its new venue, and getting acquainted with the building. The Amphitheater had been deserted except for the Bulls; Chicago Stadium, on the other hand, was a busy, ongoing venue, with lots of activities always on tap. The Bulls had to fit into the stadium's schedule, work around other events, while making the most of our marketing opportunities.

Even with this boost in our fortunes, we had to watch every penny going out and capture every penny coming in. Remember the shoe deal with Converse? While exceedingly modest in comparison to today's shoe mega-deals, it filled a need for our young club. That was how it worked—I was always looking for ways to create revenue or save money, because we had to. As much as I was thrilled with being in basketball, I never forgot that it was a business, and we had to operate like any other business. That meant making a profit and always remaining aware of how and where we were spending our money.

Money cuts more than one way. As with any business, profits were necessary, first, in order to reward investors and shareholders, and second, to pay expenses, and invest in new equipment and improvements. In pro basketball, improvements referred, first and foremost, to better players. The more money we earned, the more adept athletes we could draft and trade for and hire. The more adept athletes we hired, the more games the team would win, the more fans would buy tickets to come see the winning team, the more money we would collect, the more accomplished athletes we could hire, so on and so on.

Unfortunately, the young Bulls didn't have an excess of funds on hand. This state of affairs came into sharp focus during one draft. Walt Frazier was an underclassman who had decided to turn pro, and we certainly wanted him. However, in discussions with his representation, I soon realized that the Bulls, with our limited resources, didn't have a hope of meeting Frazier's financial expectations. Most reluctantly, we would have to pass on this great player.

As unhappy as I was with the outcome, I knew somebody who would have a different reaction. I called Red Holzman to let him know he was going to get his shot at Frazier.

Red was suitably thrilled. The Knicks drafted Frazier, and signed him to a contract. Walt Frazier went on to become one of the great guards in the NBA, not just as a player but as one of the classy, stylish individuals who helped take the Knicks to new popularity and then to the championship. Frazier spent almost his entire career in New York and retired as one of the most beloved players ever to don a Knicks uniform.

In summary, Red had reason to be thankful for the Bulls' thin purse for many years.

One thing that kind of surprised me when I entered the league was the lackluster quality of practicing and training. This was due to the methods most of the coaches employed. Many of them were former players without any formal coaching background. Practices were essentially a series of scrimmages, during which coaches would sit and drink coffee and smoke cigarettes and watch.

Dick Klein and I agreed that this was not good enough for the Bulls. His original concept was to hire one or two college coaches to assist our head coach, and then we thought about hiring a college coach to run the team. College coaches were in the teaching business; they taught fundamentals and skills. They understood the need to motivate and the need to instill discipline.

We interviewed Ray Meyer of DePaul University for the

head job. Meyer was definitely one of the top college coaches in the country, winning at one of the top basketball colleges. Meyer had tentatively accepted the job, and then changed his mind.

We had already offered the assistants' positions to two men, who had followed what was then more typical paths to coaching in the National Basketball Association: As a player, Al Bianchi had led Bowling Green University to a berth in the National Invitational Tournament before playing in the NBA for the Philadelphia 76ers and for the Syracuse Nationals. The Bulls were his first coaching job. Johnny "Red" Kerr had also come to us straight off the court, recently retiring from the Baltimore Bullets. Long before his pro career, he had been a great high school star at Tilden Tech in Chicago and then attained All-American status at Illinois.

With Meyer dropping out, we moved Kerr up to head coach. During that first year, the more I saw of the NBA, the more I became an early and vocal proponent of bringing college coaches into the pro ranks. During the Bulls' second season, I was scouting out in deep in the wilds of Idaho, watching Weber State play Idaho State. Dick Motta was Weber's coach.

After the game, I was sitting in the coffee shop of the town's sole hotel when Motta walked in. I introduced myself, and Dick sat down and we started to talk. We talked until four in the morning.

When I returned to Chicago, I told Klein I had found a new candidate for assistant coach of the Bulls: Dick Motta.

"Dick Motta?" Klein replied. "Who's Dick Motta?"

I explained he was the successful coach of Weber State.

"Weber State?" Klein said. "Where's Weber State?"

Before too long, Bianchi would depart for the head coaching job in Seattle, Kerr would leave with me for Phoenix, and Motta would wind up in charge of the Bulls. And Dick Motta, in the course of a long and distinguished career, would win 918 games, making him the third most victorious coach in league history.

My appreciation for college coaches did not diminish when I moved to Phoenix. We hired Cotton Fitzsimmons out of Kansas State in 1970, where he had just been named Big Eight Coach of the Year after taking his Wildcats to the Big Eight Championship and to the regional semifinals of the NCAA Tournament. In 1973, John MacLeod became the Suns' coach after six years at the University of Oklahoma, where he took the Sooners to the National Invitational Tournament twice. MacLeod would coach the Suns for thirteen years, finishing with 579 regular season victories and 37 playoff victories.

These three men represented a lifetime of experience and success in the NBA, and were joined by other coaches from colleges, large and small. Bill Fitch, Hubie Brown, Jack Ramsay, to name just a few. The list quickly grew long and their results were impressive.

Today the NBA coaching ranks are mixed between college coaches and former players. In the latter category, Phil Jackson, Pat Riley, Lenny Wilkins, Don Nelson, Paul Westphal, Doug Collins, Danny Ainge, and Larry Bird, among others, have performed admirably and achieved success. It seems plausible to contend that we have achieved a sort of balance, taking the best from wherever we find them.

In the course of those first years, I learned one more invaluable lesson in addition to the ones I've already enumerated. I learned the importance of building relationships within the industry with players, coaches, general managers, and, finally, agents.

Ah, the agents. Early on in my career, it became apparent to me that sports agents would only become more influential as the industry grew and revenues increased, and so did the salaries of its players. It needs no explanation to unequivocally proclaim that the players are the game's prime asset, both on the court and off, as athletes, marketers, and good-will ambassadors.

It was thus inevitable that as the National Basketball Association grew more powerful and more public, and the players grew more powerful and more public, sports agents representing their interests would increasingly take center stage.

The relationship between the agent and the team was necessarily fraught with difficulty from the start. Nonetheless, a basis of trust, then and now, must be developed and maintained between the team and the agent, for that relationship was destined to be one of the key levers that made the league go round.

From the beginning, I dealt honestly with agents, proving by my actions that my word was my bond. As time went on, and both my role and the agent's role became more visible and more important, this long-standing effort would pay dividends.

In the meanwhile, I was traveling and scouting, trading and dealing, cutting costs and generating profits for the franchise. Through all these different aspects of my work, which brought me into contact with people across the NBA, top to bottom, my name started to become familiar to the powers-that-be.

The NBA expanded during the Bulls' second year, adding franchises in Seattle and San Diego. I received a call from one of the new Seattle owners, offering me the number two position with the club. I was flattered but not interested. I was happy with the Bulls, and incredibly busy.

The next year, the league added its thirteenth and fourteenth teams, in Milwaukee and Phoenix. I was quite familiar with Milwaukee, situated in neighboring Wisconsin, but Phoenix, Arizona, was another story. Phoenix—my first thought was, Why would anyone put a basketball team in the middle of the desert?

Milwaukee asked me to be its general manager, even before the ownership group was awarded the franchise. I was enthused about the club's prospects, especially because Al McGuire, the very successful coach of Marquette University, had been prospectively tapped to assume the same position with Milwaukee. I had a relationship with Al and knew him as a terrific coach and a terrific guy.

Though Milwaukee was interested in Al, Al wasn't sure he was interested in the pro game. In the end, he decided to stay where he was.

So all the talk and speculation led to naught. But that was all right with me; I was more than happy where I was and was hardly aching to depart.

Suddenly, however, things got a little more serious. I was in Denver on a scouting trip, watching a seven-foot stiff stumble around the court when I got a call from Richard Bloch, an Arizona investment banker who lived in Beverly Hills. He was heading a group that owned the Phoenix franchise. Just a couple of days after his group had been awarded the club by the NBA, I was recommended to him by the Seattle owner who had wanted me for his franchise. Bloch had done some checking and said he was prepared to offer me the Phoenix GM job.

I was always willing to talk. I had told Dick Klein each time someone had approached me with the possibility of a new position. Klein was most vehement in his desire for me to stay in Chicago. He said he didn't intend to stay in his position as president and general manager for too much longer and assured me I would take over. That was great news, but I didn't want to wait indefinitely—not if I had a choice.

Dick offered to increase my salary, but I told him I was already adequately compensated. While money was always important, it wasn't the only issue; I wanted to do more. I believed it was necessary for me to explore my options and opportunities.

Dick understood, and told me to go ahead. He continued to make it clear that he didn't want me to leave Chicago.

I flew to Beverly Hills and met Dick Bloch. He had

moved to Los Angeles from Tucson to drum up business for a construction/development business in which he was a partner. Bloch wanted to talk about an administrative job in the front office. I was favorably impressed with him as an individual. He was a young man who had obviously been very successful.

Nonetheless, the first thing I discovered was that the owners had already selected a coach, and the coach's wife was slated to keep the club's books. I told Bloch flat-out that wouldn't work, and it particularly wouldn't work for me. I wasn't interested and headed home to Chicago.

By the time I landed at O'Hare, the deal had changed. The coach had been haggling over too many aspects of his contract, arguing over each nickel and dime, and it had become too much for the owners. By the time I got back to Chicago, the coach and his wife were out, and messages were waiting for me at my home and my office from Bloch. He wanted me to fly to Phoenix and have further discussions with his partners.

Bloch said he couldn't be there himself, but he asked me to fly to Phoenix, take a cab to the Black Canyon Freeway, and go to Eller Outdoor Sign Company. Karl Eller was another partner in this venture.

I agreed to go, but I was still extremely skeptical about this whole Phoenix deal. To my surprise, Dick Bloch met me at the airport. He had deemed it important enough to be there when I arrived, and I was duly impressed. We took a cab together to the meeting.

My trip to Arizona quickly erased my skepticism. In truth, it was literally that trip, from Chicago to Phoenix, that had a tremendous impact on my state of mind. Actually, it wasn't getting on the plane that did it; it was stepping off.

I had left Chicago in winter. It was twenty degrees below zero that morning. When I landed in Phoenix three hours later, the sun was shining and it was seventy degrees.

Score one for the desert.

I met Karl Eller and Donald Pitt, who was a prominent

Tucson attorney, and he and Bloch were partners in the construction/development company. The three were to constitute the principal ownership group. The investors were smart businessmen, but they weren't basketball men, and they didn't pretend to be. I would be the general manager, and I would be in charge.

I was well aware that general managers around the league were earning between $10,000 and $12,000 per year. I asked for a three-year contract starting at $20,000 for the first year, and rising to $25,000 by the third.

No guts, no glory.

The owners countered with a two-year deal at $22,500 per year.

I responded that I wasn't sure and had to return to Chicago and ponder the offer. Before departing for the airport, I wondered whether I could use the phone.

I called home. Joanie answered. I told her to pack the bags and the three kids. We were moving to Phoenix.

I was twenty-seven years old, and had eight hundred dollars in the bank. In truth, it wasn't as easy to leave Chicago as it might have sounded. The Bulls were improving on the court, and so was the franchise's financial state. Personally, my future with the club held the promise of greater excitement and reward. If I stayed around long enough, Klein had promised that I would end up in the top position with the franchise. Finally, I was a Chicago boy, born and bred, and everything and everyone I knew was there.

Nevertheless, Phoenix presented an opportunity to run the whole show my way. I couldn't pass up the chance and the challenge.

I remember telling Bill Gleason from the *Chicago Sun-Times* that I was leaving. Gleason was a very strong Chicago partisan from the south side of town, and he was shocked by my decision.

"Jerry," he said, "you can't do it. You can't go out there to Arizona. You're a Chicago guy."

"Bill," I said, "I have to. It's my time."

Nonetheless, despite my departure, the Chicago media has remained friendly towards me personally, and more often than not has written favorably about me professionally. Over the years, I've tried to maintain a solid relationship with many members of the Chicago press. Of course, many of those people with whom I started are now gone. Time takes its toll. Regardless, Chicago is still Chicago, and, as far as my old friends and colleagues are concerned, I'm still one of them, a point of view that is fine with me.

Dick Klein was sorry to see me go, but he wished me well in most generous and heartfelt terms. There was never any animosity involved, no hard feelings. He understood why I was leaving. We remained close, and continue to be close to this day.

(An opportunity for me to pay Dick back in small measure for his having given me a career arose just a few years later. When the owners of the San Diego franchise decided to move to Houston, they asked me to consult and help them get started. During the course of my stay in Houston, I recommended Klein to the owners to serve as their GM. At that point, he was having trouble with his partners back in Chicago. Klein had been removed as president and general manager, though he retained his financial interest in the franchise. Dick was offered the Houston job, but he had a conflict because of his shares in the Bulls. He chose not to sell those shares and stayed in Chicago. Though this didn't work out for Dick, I later hired him as a part-time scout for the Suns, a position he holds to this day from his home in South Carolina.)

Karl Eller had to drop out of the ownership group. He was busy forming Combined Communications, which included his outdoor sign business, a Phoenix radio station, and a television station, which today is the NBC affiliate in town. Eventually Combined Communications merged with media giant Gannett Company, Inc. With that sort of high-stakes venture going, this was not the best time for Eller to get involved in a start-up basketball team.

Donald Diamond, another friend and partner of Bloch and Pitt in Tucson, took his spot as one of the three principals. Through Bloch's California connections, Rosenfeld, Sussman, and Meyer, a Beverly Hills law firm, got into the game. They had a bunch of Hollywood types as clients, and soon Andy Williams, Henry Mancini, Tony Curtis, Bobbie Gentry, and Ed Ames were investors in the team.

It was time to get started. The owners advanced me ten thousand dollars to get the club going. We turned a storage room in the state fairgrounds into an office, pushing a few boxes around to make space for desks. I had become quite close to Ruthie in the past couple of years, and she wanted to join me in Arizona to tackle this new venture. I tried to talk her out of it, and not only because her roots were in Chicago and her family lived on the south side of the city. I felt it was one thing to take a chance on this risky venture with my life, it was quite another to bring along another person for what could prove a colossal disaster.

Fortunately for me, Ruthie insisted on coming. I landed in Phoenix on March 1, 1968, and she joined me exactly one month later, on April 1. Ruthie is still with me and the organization to this day.

By the time I reached Phoenix, I already had a pile of resumes waiting for me. One of those resumes was from Joe Proski, whom I had hired not that long before to be the trainer of the Bulls. Prior to his entry into the basketball arena, Proski had worked for years as a trainer in professional baseball, most recently with the Cubs. Baseball had brought him to Arizona for spring training. He had liked it so much, he wanted to return on a permanent basis.

Joe was one of the original Suns' employees and is still with the franchise to this day.

Ruthie, Joe, Ted Podleski, our first marketing pro and later the general manager of the San Diego Clippers, Bob Machen, our first ticketing manager and now the president and general manager of our Sports and Entertainment Services, and myself constituted the entire Phoenix Suns organization. Our task was simple in conception, though not nearly so simple in execution: to find enough players to stock a team and then find enough fans to fill the 12,471 seats of the Veterans Memorial Coliseum.

The Vet was only two years old, but it was small and not designed for basketball. Rather, it was intended to host all manner of shows, from circuses to concerts—most everything but sports. Thus, the arena contained no locker rooms; instead, there were dressing rooms, suitable for entertainers. The concourses were inadequate, the bathrooms too few, and there was not a scoreboard in view.

Still, it was our home, and we had to make the most of it.

A contest was held to choose the name. Twenty-eight thousand people in the valley submitted entries. "Suns" won out.

I hired my old friend, Johnny "Red" Kerr, to leave Chicago and coach the Suns. Johnny had coached the Bulls the previous two seasons and was the NBA's Coach of the Year in 1967. With Kerr in place, we began to build a team with confidence. We selected Gary Gregor, a six-foot-seven forward from South Carolina, with our first pick in the draft; we would trade him a year later to Atlanta for the redoubtable Paul Silas. We selected Dick Van Arsdale, a six-foot-five swingman who had spent three seasons with the Knicks, with our first pick in the expansion draft. We also got guard Gail Goodrich from the Lakers in that same expansion draft. Van Arsdale would spend the next nine years with the Suns, earning All-Star honors three times. Goodrich would play two seasons with the Suns before being traded back to the Lakers, where he would finish his Hall of Fame career.

The team played its first NBA game before 7,112 fans in Veterans Memorial on October 18, 1968. The Suns won 116–107. Limited partner Andy Williams performed after the game with the Phoenix Symphony. The symphony was conducted by another one of our investors, Henry Mancini.

The Suns averaged 4,340 fans per game that first year. We sold precisely 735 season tickets. That probably doesn't sound like much, and in truth it wasn't. Many a night, the Coliseum was a lonely place to be. Still, it was a start.

With the team taking shape, we concentrated on filling those empty seats. For years now, every game in Phoenix, as well as in other cities, too, has been a guaranteed sell-out. That was not the way it was in the beginning—not by a long shot. The NBA was a secondary league, and the citizens of Phoenix had not exactly stormed city hall demanding their own professional basketball team. We had arrived in town unheralded and unknown, the investors taking it upon themselves to bring the franchise to the Valley of the Sun. The task of the entire Suns organization was to go out and convince the public that the team would be worth watching, worth leaving the comfort of home, worth driving downtown, worth spending good money on game tickets—in the end, worth watching and supporting.

From the start, my attitude in approaching this assignment, which I repeated to myself and to my employees, was plain and uncomplicated: "This city doesn't owe us anything. We have to earn its support."

This idea became more than my attitude, it became my mantra. *This city doesn't owe us anything. The people of Phoenix do not owe us anything. We have to earn their support.*

For my own part, I set about earning that support by knocking on every door in town, introducing the team to the valley. In particular, I concentrated on the business community, trying to sell every company, firm, and industry in Phoenix on the virtues of doing business courtside. I used all my salesman's skills to move those tickets.

There was another component in our attempts to establish the Phoenix Suns in the valley, and that involved how we conducted ourselves as an organization. When the nature of your business necessarily keeps you in the public eye—as is the case with sports—I think you have an extra responsibility to properly respond to that public scrutiny, and represent what is best about your business. That means, first and foremost, that you have to conduct yourself with dignity and treat others with respect when dealing with your clients and your audience.

The truth is, the more public you are, the more opportunity you will have to fail, and fail in the most public and sometimes most embarrassing manner. You're dealing with the media, you're dealing with corporations, you're dealing with big business and high finance. In that potentially volatile mix, it is inevitable that you will make mistakes: a trade doesn't work out, a player doesn't live up to expectations, the arena needs more seats, the parking lot is too small, and so on. That is inescapable and entirely human. The point is not to compound those ordinary mistakes with lapses in personal judgment and in personal and professional values. Stick to your basic beliefs, your fundamental values, to see you through and help you maintain an even, ethical foundation.

There's an adage that states, You work, you work hard, you work harder. Add on to that, You work to stay on the cutting edge of your business, and you never give up, and you keep plugging away. All together, you have a framework for a business philosophy, which, though neither revolutionary nor even especially insightful, is sound, reliable, and honest.

Of course, in spite of my philosophy, in spite of my efforts, the arena was often an empty cave that first campaign. On the bright side, this might not have been the worst thing, considering that the Suns won sixteen games and lost sixty-six.

On the court, the second year didn't start off as much of an improvement over the first. The major difference was that our relatively few fans (as well as yours truly) expected more, expected better, and it just wasn't happening. Those expectations were not unreasonable, given the changes we had made in the team. We had drafted Neal Walk, a six-foot-ten, 220-pound center from Florida in the first round and thought he could be quite an impact player. While Walk was a fine choice, he was unquestionably the consolation prize on this day. You see, we had just lost a coin flip to Milwaukee for the right to select first, with the result that the Bucks had gotten Lew Alcindor, the most sought-after player of his day. Alcindor, who would change his name to Kareem Abdul-Jabbar, would lead Milwaukee to the NBA title a mere two years later.

We traded for Paul Silas, an outstanding veteran power forward, and knew he would instantly help us. Finally, and most significantly, we obtained Connie Hawkins from the ABA.

Connie Hawkins, revered far and wide as "The Hawk," was the first of the amazingly acrobatic athletes to grace the court, to spin and dunk and fly with controlled abandon. Before Kobe Bryant, Michael Jordan, and Julius Erving, there was Connie. He gained fame as a teenager as the greatest schoolyard player in New York City, a playground legend. The Hawk had stumbled on his way to fulfilling his basketball greatness when he was accused of associating with gamblers while at the University of Iowa. He was banned from the NBA and wound up in the upstart American Basketball Association, where he immediately emerged as a leading star. The real losers in this were the fans, relatively few of whom got to see the Hawk when he was in his twenties and probably in his athletic prime, while he wandered the ABA wilderness for seven years.

Finally, some attorneys who were friendly with Hawkins

decided that this punishment was unfair, and they put together a case demanding that the NBA lift its ban. The NBA agreed to allow Hawkins into the league and provided a financial settlement as well.

It was time for another coin flip. In a contest restricted to the teams with the worst records in the league, we beat Seattle in the flip, giving us the right to sign him.

The Hawk would play in Phoenix for five seasons and would be selected as an All-Star in each of those years. In 1992, he was selected for induction into the NBA Hall of Fame.

With that kind of boost in our lineup, we expected to win a lot more games. However, thirty-eight games into the season, our record was a discouraging 15–23.

When something isn't going the way it should, you always have to look to the top for explanations, for reasons, and I realized that Johnny Kerr wasn't the right man to be coaching this team. He was an excellent coach, but every coach has to be put in the right situation, and this simply wasn't Kerr's right situation. Call it what you will—chemistry, timing, whatever—but the people have to fit, the situation has to work. And this wasn't working.

I had no choice, midway through the second season, but to dismiss Kerr. Regardless of our relationship, regardless of our friendship, the franchise—which encompassed the investors' money, the jobs of my employees, the security of my family—was my responsibility. Remember, it was by no means a sure bet that the Phoenix Suns would survive and prosper. Basketball franchises around the country had failed before and would fail again. I had to do everything within my ability to protect and promote the club.

I fired Johnny and took over the coaching duties myself for the rest of the season, but it was not an easy action to take, and I hoped that Johnny understood. Interviewed years later by a reporter, Johnny Kerr graciously explained that he had grown up in circumstances similar to mine, and thus had always appreciated why I felt compelled to act as I had, in the best interests of the franchise, personal considerations aside.

At the same time, I wasn't about to throw my good friend overboard. I asked Johnny to move over to the broadcasting side and cover the Suns for our radio and television shows. That's how highly I thought of his basketball savvy and his insight into the game. As far as I was concerned, Johnny could have stayed with the club in Phoenix forever.

Kerr, however, thought it was time for him to leave. He joined the ABA, reuniting with Al Bianchi in a front-office post with the Virginia Squires. Eventually, he accepted a broadcasting position with the Bulls, a position similar to the one I had offered him, and has enjoyed a terrific career.

I decided to take over the coaching job, instead of hiring someone else, for a couple of reasons. I had been a player long before I became a general manager. I knew basketball, and I still retained my fire, a real passion, for the action. I became a coach because I felt I could do the job.

On another level, on a more personal level, I took over because I was the guy writing the checks. We were heading in the wrong direction, and it had to stop. To be blunt, as the man who hired and fired, I had great leverage with the players. Additionally, as part of the franchise from the start, the players already knew me and understood that I cared as much as they did, I had as much at stake as they did. I felt I could quickly reach them and connect with them, surely more quickly than a coach—even the perfect coach—brought in from the outside in the midst of a tough season.

The team did pretty well under my coaching reign. The Suns posted a twenty-four and twenty record during my tenure and actually made the playoffs, where we faced a Los Angeles Lakers squad that included Jerry West, Wilt Chamberlain, and Elgin Baylor. We lost the first game, and then won the following three. Then, in the fifth game, Jimmy Fox, our starting center, sprained his ankle. The Lakers took that game, and the next, too.

The big contest was Game Six, played in Phoenix. We had the chance to close out the series, and the Lakers were fighting to tie it up. We lost an exciting contest, 104–93.

We traveled to Los Angeles for the rubber game. On their home turf, the Lakers blew us away and clinched the series.

The Hawk led the Suns with twenty-five points and fifteen rebounds in that last game. Through the seven games of the playoffs, he had averaged 25.4 points per game, and 13.9 rebounds. Through the season, Connie had averaged 40.9 minutes per game, 24.6 points, 10.4 rebounds, and 4.8 assists.

When I took over the club, one of my priorities was increasing the Hawk's role in the team's offense. In my opinion, he had not been sufficiently integrated into the offense, he had not been acknowledged as the dominant factor in the offense.

I made no bones about putting the onus on Connie's shoulders. He was going to be our main man, our prime weapon. We were going to rise or fall on his abilities and his leadership. And Connie came through big time, he came through and was the chief reason we were able to turn around our season.

An example of the Hawk's greatness: Our last regular season game was in San Diego. The Rockets (who would later relocate to Houston) were long out of the race. This contest, however, counted for us; a win would position us one rung higher in the division, which would mean a better position in the playoffs and more money for the players.

In other words, San Diego had nothing to lose, and we had something to gain. That translated into the Rockets coming onto the floor loose and ready, and the Suns more than a bit tight.

By half-time, we were down by twenty-three points. I was a young coach, I was emotional, and I was prepared to do whatever I had to do to motivate my players. What I decided to do on that night—what I wanted to do—was tell my team, in no uncertain terms, that I was extremely displeased with their effort. In a phrase, I let loose with a tirade.

I put the pressure on the Hawk. The game was in his hands. He had to show us the way. And he did exactly that. He played superbly, and the rest of the team followed suit. The Rockets tried to hang tough, but with twenty-four seconds remaining in the game, we had fought our way back only one point down.

It was our ball. Time out. We set up a play, designed to clear a little room for Connie to get the ball and get it by his man, who happened to be Elvin Hayes, an All-Star in his own right. What occurred after that constituted one of the most astonishing sequences I have ever witnessed on a basketball court.

Hawk got the ball on the in-bounds pass and went up for the shot. Hayes also jumped, and he blocked the shot.

Connie snatched the block with one hand, and instantly flew back up again. But Hayes was right with him, and, amazingly, blocked the shot again.

But Connie was just as quick, and once more caught the ball. This time, instead of going right back up, he put the ball on the floor, leaned back, and gave a beautiful fake. Hayes went for the fake and leaped. A moment later, Connie flew into the air, closed in on the basket, and smashed it down and through the hoop, with barely more than a second left.

I jumped twenty feet into the air. Well, maybe not quite.

The Hawk scored around forty-four points and grabbed some twenty rebounds. He was spent, finished, done. He had given everything he had to give. It was nothing less than a great performance, topped by an incredible finale.

(An interesting footnote: The Rockets were coached by the guy who came close to being the first coach of the Suns, until his negotiating got to be too much for Bloch and the other owners, and until I objected to his wife handling the books. Earlier in the season, the Suns and the Rockets had found themselves in a similar position, just a second to go, our team ahead, and San Diego holding the ball. The coach had called in a play for Hayes. It hadn't worked then, but I had a hunch he was going to try it again.

I called over Lamar Green, a six-foot-eight rookie, who happened to be one of the greatest leapers I have ever seen. I told Lamar to stand in front of Elvin Hayes, between Hayes and the ball, and jump as high as he could, straight up in the air, as soon as the ball was thrown in-bounds. Don't wait, don't look around, just assume the ball was coming your way and blast off.

Well, Lamar did my instructions one better, leaping a second before the play started. Sure enough, the same play unfolded, and the ball was aimed at Hayes. Lamar was in place, and he vaulted so high that the ball hit him in the knees, and the game ended.)

Another Hawk story: Cotton Fitzsimmons, who would emerge as one of the key figures and influential leaders in the history of the Suns franchise, assumed the coaching mantle the following year. In Detroit during that season, an opponent clobbered Connie in the midst of a play, inadvertently smashing his nose. In fact, you could see quite clearly from the sidelines that it was broken.

Unfortunately, in those less sophisticated days, we didn't have medical personnel standing by in case of accidents. In addition, Hawkins was famous for his singularly low pain threshold, which frequently kept him from venturing too far into traffic where an accident of this type was more likely to take place.

Given that the coaches were constantly urging the reluctant Connie to mix it up a bit—after all, basketball is a tough, physical sport, and this was a facet of the game where the Hawk needed some improving—there was something amusing about the fact that when he finally (and perhaps unintentionally) ended up among the flying elbows, he had taken one to the face. It was also clear that this was an injury that shouldn't be ignored. I ended up driving him to the hospital during the game.

When we arrived at the hospital, we were escorted to a remote corner of the building, a corner that was dark and apparently deserted.

Eventually, a doctor, or someone I assumed was a doctor, showed up. He took two long, large instruments and stuck them up Hawk's nostrils, which completely captured Connie's wide-eyed attention. The doctor turned to me and asked, "Do you think that looks straight?"

I found it interesting that the doctor would ask my opinion, so I gave it serious consideration. "No," I said, "just a little bit the other way."

The doctor pushed and pulled this way and that, until he got it straight. And the whole time the Hawk was dying. He more or less held it together, despite his natural inclination to suffer not in silence, but he was dying.

Now that I'm telling the story, it occurs to me that maybe I found this more amusing than Connie did.

More from the Hawk files: No doubt, the Hawk could be difficult, in a number of different ways. We were in Los Angeles, playing the Lakers, and I was the coach. Out on the floor, Hawkins was obviously going through the motions. I didn't like it. He wasn't getting back on defense, he wasn't hustling, he wasn't moving. I pulled him out and told him to sit down.

A little while later, I turned towards him and told him to get back in the game. He said no. I answered that he should leave the court, he should get out. In front of a big crowd, he walked out.

After the game, the reporters crowded around and wanted to hear what I had to say, though it was obvious to everyone what had happened. Regardless, I protected my player and told the media Connie had left the court because he wasn't feeling well.

That wasn't the end of it though. When I got inside the locker room, I pulled Connie aside. My message was simple: Don't embarrass me and I won't embarrass you.

The problem didn't arise again.

Connie was traded to Los Angeles. It was a good deal all around. When the Hawk retired a few years later, we threw a retirement party for him. To wish him well in his dotage, we gave him several presents, including a rocking chair and an automobile. In typical Hawk fashion, he took the rocker home and forgot the car.

Some time after, Connie flew across the Atlantic to play in a European basketball league. A few months later, I got a postcard stating he had run out of money. He asked me to send him some so he could get home. By that time, we had found his car, parked, unattended, and unloved.

The solution to Hawk's problem was evident: we sold the car and sent Connie the money.

The Hawk wasn't always easy, on the court or off. But no matter what he did, no matter how mad or frustrated you were with him, he would turn and give you that smile and that wink, and he would melt your heart. He was born with a charisma that couldn't be denied. There was only one Hawk. He was different, and he was magic. As *Arizona Republic* sports editor and columnist Joe Gilmartin wrote, "Connie Hawkins is a work of art. Some nights poetry in motion, other nights still life."

Connie Hawkins deserves a lot of credit for helping establish the Phoenix Suns in the public's mind. Despite the difficulties that had plagued him for years, he emerged as a star of the first rank in the NBA. He also raised the Suns' profile along with his own.

Through his extraordinary abilities, the Hawk changed the very nature of the game. Kareem Abdul-Jabbar has said that when he saw Hawkins perform, it was the first time he had seen basketball played above the rim.

There was something else about Connie Hawkins. When

I think of the difference between former and current athletes, young men today seem to regard playing in the NBA as a right rather than a privilege. Hawk loved the game so much, even when its leaders turned their backs on him, that he stayed loyal to it through his outcast years, and entered the NBA grateful for the chance to show what he could do.

After Connie's playing days were over, he encountered some tough personal times. After many years, we brought him back to Phoenix and placed him up in our community relations department, where he still works, representing the Suns, inspiring kids and adults alike. The Hawk may not fly so high anymore, but the charisma is still there, and so is that irresistible smile and that laughing wink.

That 1969–70 playoff series, and the valiant effort put forth by the Suns, went a long way to solidifying our place in Phoenix. Over the next seventeen years, the team played well enough to record a .522 winning percentage. Apart from a brief return to coaching in the course of the 1972–73 season (during which I scored a 35–40 record, bringing my total coaching account to 59–60), I had given up pacing the sidelines and concentrated on building our business, in creating new fans, and integrating the team firmly into the community. We accomplished this with a combination of marketing, winning, and getting involved in good works.

There's an old expression that goes something like this: There aren't any new ideas, just old ideas recycled new again. Regardless of the impressive vintage of the expression, I'm not convinced that's actually the case. When you throw yourself into something, when you're passionate about it, you're going to get better and better at it. You're going to learn what has already worked and what hasn't. Then you can employ that knowledge as a base, as a jumping-off point, and experiment and innovate and take your business another step forward.

I was passionate about the Bulls, and I was surely passionate about the Suns. As Red HoIzman noted, I kept my mouth shut, listened, and learned. I respected the game, and my elders in the game, and absorbed everything I saw and heard—and then I went out and tried to do things as well and maybe even a little better. Certainly I tried things that hadn't been tried before, like my shoe deal, and a few bigger deals as well, deals that eventually served as models for other sports organizations to emulate.

Seventeen years passed in this fashion, the Suns performed well on the court, and the franchise performed even more successfully off the court. Beginning with the 1975–76 season, we made it into the playoffs every year except for one through the 1984–85 season. In 1975–76, we reached the NBA Finals for the first time, going up against the Boston Celtics, led by John Havlicek and Dave Cowens. We lost the first two games in Boston and returned home to tie the series. Knotted at two apiece, the fifth game was clearly crucial. Game Five is considered by many to be the greatest basketball game ever played. The contest, held in Boston, went into triple overtime. Unfortunately, when the game ended, the score was Boston 128, Phoenix 126. The Celtics took the next game, 87–80, and the series was over. We had come so close, but the ultimate prize had eluded us. Still, it seemed only a matter of time—maybe next season—when we would gain the championship.

It had been a great season, a thrilling, marvelous season, and the franchise had been profitable while giving the fans the ride of their basketball lives. I was happy, but still . . . I wanted that title.

The frustration would continue. The following year saw the return of the core of this strong team, plus the addition of Tom Van Arsdale, playing beside his brother Dick, who also happened to be his identical twin, for the first time in their pro careers. Unfortunately, injuries decimated the line-up, knocking out the entire starting front line. We finished the year 34–48, fifth in the Pacific Division.

Though we would rebound the following year and go on from there, winning games, division titles, and conferences titles, while the franchise earned a profit, we never walked away in the last game of any season the winner and champ.

For me personally, this cast a shadow over all the accomplishments. I didn't brood like Hamlet or scheme like Othello. I worked hard and thoroughly enjoyed our many successes. But that ring, that champion ring, was still out there, distant but undeniably within reach. And I wanted it. I wanted it very much indeed.

This was already a familiar story in my life. From high school to college to the Bulls and now to the Suns, my dream of winning a championship had been thwarted. The Suns had come close, but I had been close before, and I can't say I was satisfied with the experience.

Suddenly, out of nowhere, another situation arose that thrust my championship frustrations firmly to the side and placed in jeopardy everything everyone in our organization had worked so long and hard to build.

The past seventeen years of work and effort and considerable success suddenly counted for very little when a scandal rocked the Suns. In 1986, at the end of the basketball season, three current Suns players and two former players were arrested on drug charges.

The case never went to trial and the charges never amounted to anything criminal, but an ambitious county attorney, assisted by an ill-advised local police chief, did their best to generate as much hysteria among the public—while generating a corresponding amount of publicity for themselves—as possible.

The ambition didn't take them far as the case fell apart, but the hysteria took hold. The outlandish drug conspiracy claims by the political opportunists caused much of the media and the public to turn against the franchise. Instead of the Phoenix Suns, the team was referred to as "Phoenix House," after the drug rehabilitation center. Though not even my harshest critics even hinted that I was involved in any of this, or condoned any illicit behavior, the virulence and persistence of the attacks on the franchise were such that I was soon swept up in the media uproar and became an object of ridicule. One spillover from this incessant drumbeat of blame: For the first time in my sports career, I was booed at games.

I did not find any of this either fair or rational. It was if all those years of trying to build something, something that the people of Phoenix and Arizona could be proud of, trying and largely succeeding, had meant nothing. The chance had evidently come to tear it all down and the franchise was too tempting a target to ignore. I was also a target, not only professionally but also personally, and it was soon open season on the Suns and Jerry Colangelo. Instead of attempting to join together to understand whatever problems we faced and solving them, the delight that so many seemed to take in adding fuel to this fire, in deriding and destroying what had been built, was nothing other than incomprehensible to me.

Just one example: I had met the Phoenix police chief when he was walking a beat back in 1968, when I first arrived in town. We had developed a personal relationship. We were friends, and I had no cause to believe that we were anything other than friends through the years. Hence, the notion that he could turn around and lead this ludicrous investigation, that he could try to gain political capital by attacking my organization, by attacking me, was something I would never have regarded as remotely conceivable. I was shocked, disappointed, and deeply hurt. This was both a betrayal of the public's trust and a betrayal of our years of friendship.

I never spoke to him again after this time. I had nothing to say to him. He is no longer the Phoenix police chief, and no longer lives in Phoenix.

Equally distressing was the NBA's reaction, which leaned in some high-ranking quarters towards removing the franchise from Phoenix and awarding it to another city. Columbus, Ohio, was spoken of as a leading contender for the Suns' new home base.

Making matters worse, there were influential people in Phoenix who didn't care whether basketball stayed or not, and did nothing to advance our cause with the league or the public.

A terrible witch-hunt had been conducted and not a single conviction had materialized. Nonetheless, the damage had been done, and it was severe.

The ownership was most unhappy with this turn of events. The owners mainly lived in Tuscon and Los Angeles, and sports were a second business at best for them. They didn't appreciate this unflattering spotlight shining on their investment, and decided they wanted out, out of Phoenix, out of basketball.

Even though I was only an employee, I had put my life into the franchise. Of course, I had long hoped that the day might come when the status quo might change. I didn't know when or how, but it never hurts to be prepared. Thus, when I first signed on with the Suns back in 1968, I asked the owners for the right to buy the team if they ever wanted to sell. I asked, even though I didn't have two nickels in my pocket, and they demonstrated absolutely no thought of some selling out, when I conceived this provision.

Nevertheless, the owners assented to my request, though we never formalized this agreement in writing.

Now the team was either going to be sold or moved. It was time to remind my bosses of our agreement. I exercised my verbal promise, and the owners concurred. I could have the team if—and this was a very large if—I could raise the money.

The original price for the franchise had been $2 million. The owners wanted $44.5 million.

Not a bad profit in less than two decades, especially a profit on an investment that had returned its original cost many times over.

I had spent the past seventeen years doing everything I could to make the community feel that the Suns were its team. I had done everything I could to attract local business to the arena, and include the franchise in the community's charities. I had done everything I could to make the Suns an integral part of the community.

My commitment to Phoenix was unshakable. During the past few years, I had had my opportunities to leave. Irv Levin, the owner of the San Diego Clippers (later the Los Angeles Clippers), offered me a twenty-five percent ownership stake in the team if I would move to California and run the franchise.

Perhaps an even more intriguing offer came from Sonny Werblin, the legendary New York sports owner and impresario. He invited me to his home, which was a suite in the Waldorf-Astoria Hotel, and said he wanted me to run Madison Square Garden, plus the Knicks and the Rangers. He offered me a five-year deal, at approximately $500,000 per year, as well an apartment and a limousine. It was an incredible opportunity, to manage two of the most exciting franchises in American sports, overseeing the operation of one of the most glamorous venues in the country, in the most important city in the world.

And the money wasn't bad either.

In fact, the money was many times more than what I was earning. Nor did I have any percentage of the team, as would have been the case with the Clippers.

Still, I turned down both offers with hardly a second thought. My virtually immediate responses were not brought about because I had any indication that I would ever have the chance to buy the Suns, or because I foresaw receiving a raise even close to that proposed by the Knicks.

I turned down these offers because I had raised my children in Arizona, was still raising the younger ones, because I loved living in Arizona; because I was committed to my franchise, my fellow employees, and to the work we were doing. I believe that God has a plan for everyone, and I felt in my head and in my heart—in my very soul—that this was where He intended me to stay, where He intended me to fulfill whatever my destiny held in store.

I suppose you could say that though my decision revolved around business, it was much, much more than a business decision. Thus, we have the duality of life: Taking a risk and taking stock. My career has been a series of opportunities that I have welcomed and accepted as they arose—jumping into basketball in Chicago, moving to Phoenix, starting new teams in new sports, building new venues—and I believe that each of us must always be ready to take a risk, the right risk, and go where the opportunities lead.

However, at the same time, each of us must know when to pause and consider that a job, profession, or place is the right one for us, and for our family, and then forgo the other offers and options and make a stand and put down roots and stay, at least for awhile.

No amount of money could shake me from my view that Arizona was where I was meant to be. Now I was going to find out if my instincts and my faith had been correctly placed. Now was the moment of decision. Now I was going to find out if my efforts through the years were not only appreciated, but would bear fruit, at a time when the franchise needed it most.

I went to the business community and laid out the deal: Invest in the Suns and help keep them in Phoenix.

A key player in my wooing the money for the partnership was John Teets. Teets was the head of the Dial Corporation, which was headquartered in the valley. We had become friends over time, and, as a basketball fan, he had taken a great interest in the franchise. Previous to the scandal, John had encouraged me to try to put a package together to buy the team and to include a reasonable equity position for myself. A couple of times in the past decade, I had considered attempting something, but the ownership had never been interested.

Now the situation had changed, and I recognized that great adversity could also bring great opportunity. I went to see John, and laid out for him what I thought was necessary to seal the deal. I said it required $20 million in cash to purchase the team—the rest I felt I could borrow from the banks. To accomplish this, I needed a major company to step up and invest in the franchise, and become my partner. I not only needed the money, but I also needed the credibility that a major company would give to the partnership, encouraging others to also sign up and invest.

John told me to write something up and he'd present it to his board, which was meeting in just a few days back east. I returned to my office and dictated a memo to Ruthie, proposing that Dial put up $6 million for a 25 percent interest in the franchise. I sent the proposal over to Teets that same afternoon.

Four or five days later, John called from his board meeting, The board had said yes. Dial was in. We had its $6 million.

Apart from the cash infusion, Dial's involvement accorded me serious credibility when I approached other institutions. I got commitments from Circle K, America West Airlines, Eldorado Investments, a subsidiary of Pinnacle West, and others. In addition to these corporate players, more money was pledged by individuals.

We were getting close to the deadline. Though we had cobbled together an impressive list of investors in a short period, we were far from home free. All the commitments hadn't been turned into signed contracts yet, and we weren't collecting any checks without those contracts in hand.

I was sitting in my lawyer's office, in his conference room. Jay Ruffner, one of the leading attorneys in Phoenix, was with the firm of Lewis and Roca, and had been recommended to me by John Teets.

I was seated at the head of the long conference table, before a large group gathered to settle this. Things weren't going well. At the last minute, Circle K and America West Airlines pulled out. Each corporation counted for millions of dollars that I now saw slipping away forever, taking my dream with them.

As their representatives got up and filed out of the room, I crumpled up the papers before me, and, staring straight ahead at the departing people threw them the ball almost the length of the room to the side toward a waste basket. Somehow, the ball dropped right inside the basket. It would have been a shot to stand back and admire, if I hadn't been so upset.

Everybody left the room. I swiveled my chair around and stared out the window. The office was high up in a skyscraper overlooking the city. I looked out that window for a solid hour. Finally, Jay came into the room, walked over, and said, "It was a hell of a try. You almost got it done."

"You know, Jay," I replied, with more confidence than I felt, "it's not over yet."

I got home around midnight. Joanie was already in bed. She woke and asked how the meeting had gone.

"Not very well," I said.

I lay in bed, thinking, weighing, wondering. By the early morning, I believed I had the answer. I called Donald Pitt and told him that if he wanted the deal to work—and he certainly had sufficient incentive, considering the enormous profits he and his partners stood to earn—he had to enter the deal as a limited partner. Plus he had to carry some of the debt. The total came to $3 million.

Pitt understood. It only made sense for the good of his interests to ensure that the sale was completed. He agreed to my proposal.

I called Jay and said that we were back in the game. The banks loaned me the $2 million I needed to finish off the financing. This was a personal loan, advanced to me, not to the partnership. This was a key distinction, a form of personal support.

When all was said and done, I was able to put the $44.5 million package together in six weeks. I raised $20 million and the banks lent us the rest. The franchise had no collateral to offer the banks (or the investors) because we owned nothing of any real value. Expressed in other words, the Suns did not own an arena (an obviously prized asset), or anything else of palpable worth, other than a handful of player contracts and a logo and a bunch of basketballs and uniforms—the franchise, in essence, was the collateral—and my ideas and strategies for turning those players and the Suns logo and the rest of it into a tangible, valuable, continuing commodity. Still, faced with this atypical prospectus, the banks gave the partnership funds and then they gave me more funds because, in the final analysis, they believed in my ability and my vision. I had earned their trust and faith because of my work, because of the sweat I had put into the franchise and the community.

Put bluntly: Sweat equity was my collateral.

I took a tiny portion of the deal for myself, a single percentage point of the total. That percentage that would rise only as the investors and the banks got their money back and started earning profits.

We closed the deal on Friday. Forty-eight hours later, the stock market collapsed in one of the most dramatic and disastrous days in the history of Wall Street, which came to be known as "Black Monday."

One option we considered, and a perfectly common and reasonable one, was to ask the owners for a one-week extension to give us a little breathing room to finish raising the money. If we had gotten the extension, and Black Monday had hit while we were still out there, looking for money, we would have lost everything as panic set in throughout the business community, and individuals and companies recoiled in shock and hid their pennies.

Timing is everything.

In any event, after all these years, I finally had my own team, a team I could run as I wanted, a franchise I could market as I chose.

The truth was, I had had pretty much a free hand with the Suns all along. Still, this was different. This was my deal and my show. This was what I had been waiting for. This was my chance.

It is interesting to note that this episode, this transition, was different from almost all others in my life in a very important way. I had not planned to assist Dick Klein as he pursued his dream of starting a new Chicago basketball franchise. I had not planned on moving to Phoenix to start another basketball franchise. I had seized these opportunities and made the most of them.

This was another story. I had laid the groundwork from the start, by asking for that verbal agreement from my employers, though without any specific blueprint in mind. Franchises changed hands in sports; they were bought and sold in basketball without any special notice, just as they were bought and sold in all the other major sports. Hence, it did not require any remarkable foresight to understand that the time might arise when the owners of the Suns might feel the need or desire to cash in and get out of professional basketball.

Simultaneously, as part of our normal efforts, our unceasing work to integrate the Suns into the web of the Phoenix business community now paid great dividends. Without this specific end in mind, we had labored long and hard to establish the Suns and our organization as responsible civic citizens, as citizens that the business community would want to support.

And now the business community responded in exactly that manner. Not everyone and every business, mind you, but a majority, and in the sort of strength and numbers that the Suns and the organization had the chance to take the franchise to a new and unprecedented level of success and achievement.

I must admit that I was disappointed by the rejoinder I received from sports and business types in and out of the league in the wake of this transaction. After finally raising the money and closing the deal, I heard, directly and indirectly, from people around the country who thought I was crazy. Forty-four and a half million dollars—no one had ever paid that much for a basketball team. No one had ever paid anything close to that much.

I didn't care. My attitude was, I wanted the opportunity to own the team, and here it is. Finally, here it is. And now I'll figure out a way to make it work.

Apart from my own native optimism, I recognized that we had several key factors working in our behalf. First, pro basketball was booming. Led by superstars Larry Bird, Magic Johnson, and Michael Jordan, corporations from the television networks to shoe companies endorsed the intrinsic excitement of the game and the savvy marketing skills of the NBA, and leaped on the basketball bandwagon. Second, Phoenix was booming. Despite an economic downturn, primarily caused by a collapse in the real estate market and the national savings and loan scandal, it was clear that people were leaving the cold northeast and midwest for the sunshine of the southwest and would keep coming to Arizona. More people meant more potential ticket buyers (as well as T-shirt, cap, and banner buyers) and a larger TV audience, with greater advertising revenue, on and on.

So the bottom line was this: I surely had faith in my own ability, but I also had faith in the game of basketball, the skills of the NBA, and the city of Phoenix and the state of Arizona. Working in concert, I didn't see how we could miss.

In today's world, it is necessary to comprehend that no sizable business venture stands alone, that the modern entrepreneur or corporate leader must take into consideration the relationship between his company and his community. In fact, for many ventures, factoring in only the local community is not sufficient; rather, the whole world must be reckoned with before any significant decisions are enacted.

The value of a product alone is no longer the sole consideration. What is its environmental impact? Is it socially responsible? Is it politically feasible, as it crosses international boundaries? How will the media react? Who will object, and who will support you?

Similarly, I knew that while the Suns could stand alone on the court and triumph, they could not do so in the larger and more consequential arena off the court. We had to be more than the Phoenix Suns in name—we had to embody the best of the city and the valley.

So let's briefly set the stage, as it was in 1986: the Suns had about twenty-five employees (not including the team), we played in old, inadequate Veterans Coliseum, and we minimally participated in the arena's revenues. In other words, we paid rent, and in exchange received some ticket revenue, and local TV and radio revenue. That was it.

I brought Cotton back to Phoenix, after coaching stints around the league, as our first director of player personnel. It was crucial to have another basketball man at my side to help at this time of crisis, as we sought to rebuild the franchise and its credibility. Cotton jumped in with his enthusiasm and his expertise. We made the single largest trade in the history of the franchise, dealing Larry Nance and Mike Sanders, along with the Detroit Pistons' first round pick in 1988, to Cleveland in exchange for the Cavaliers' first and second-round draft choices in 1988, and three players. Another trade sent Jay Humphries to Milwaukee for Craig Hodges.

Nance was our best player, a six-ten forward, our only real asset. To express it in business terms, dealing him away was risky. However, the first-round draft pick we got in return turned out to be Dan Majerle, and the traded players were Kevin Johnson, Mark West, and Ty Corbin. Marjerle would play seven seasons for the Suns, and made three All-Star squads. Mark West would play center for the Suns for seven seasons, Ty Corbin would be with the team for two years, and Kevin Johnson—KJ—would be a Phoenix Sun for ten terrific seasons. He would prove one of the greatest players in not only the history of the Suns, but the history of the league. His career assists-per-game of 9.48 ranks him fourth in NBA annals, behind Oscar Robertson, Magic Johnson, and John Stockton. He is only the twenty-second player to total eleven thousand points and five thousand assists. He is one of only five players to average more than twenty points and more than ten assists in three straight seasons. He is the franchise career playoff leader in eight separate categories: games played, points, steals, assists, field goals attempted and made, free throws attempted and made. He was named to the All-Star team three times.

In addition to these accomplishments, I'd like to mention a couple more. In 1990–91, KJ received the *Sports Illustrated for Kids* Good Sports Award, and the J. Walter Kennedy Good Citizenship Award. *USA Today* selected him as "Most Caring Athlete" in 1995 for his humanitarian efforts and contributions to the community. In 1992, he was chosen as one of President George Bush's "1,000 Points of Light."

But Cotton wasn't done, not even with that blockbuster trade. That summer, the first unrestricted free agent in league history, Tom Chambers, was signed by the Suns. Tom would become a four-time All-Star, in the course of fifteen seasons and counting in the NBA.

Of course, these trades and signings would take a while to jell and have an effect on the court. In the meanwhile, the Suns suffered through a miserable year on the court, finishing 28–54.

The upshot of all this frenzy of player activity was that the Suns went from those twenty-eight victories in 1986 to fifty-five victories in 1987. The team also reached the conference finals. That heralded the start of a ten-year run, during which the club averaged fifty-five wins per season.

But the story was not restricted to what happened on the court. Off the court, we were near the bottom in revenues in the NBA, playing in the nineteenth largest marketplace in the country. That, too, would soon change, and for the better.

Not many franchises can claim to have effected that kind of turnaround that quickly. Particularly not in the teeth of such a bitterly contentious start, not in the face of so much cynicism and opposition.

The lesson was not to be sidetracked, not to allow other people's agenda dissuade you from your goals. I had all the excuses in the world to fail, or not even try. But that kind of thinking was self-defeating. I saw my business, I understood my challenges, I respected my market and my customers, and I set to work.

The rest was irrelevant.

I held a press conference to announce the change in ownership and to announce some of our priorities. Obviously, the first priority was getting the team. Now that that first step had been accomplished, priority two was getting a new arena.

This allusion to an arena was not a casual reference. I stated loud and clear that for the Phoenix Suns to move forward and compete within the NBA, we were going to need a new facility.

In the next breath, I also made it absolutely clear that this declaration was not about trying to gain leverage with the city of Phoenix or the people of Arizona. I was not warning or threatening or hinting that if the Suns did not get a new building, the team would move to friendlier environs. To the contrary: We needed a new facility in Phoenix because the Suns weren't going anywhere. That statement—that promise—was simple and definite. I hadn't raised the money and bought the team to relocate to another city.

Unbeknownst to me, a fellow named Denny Moss was paying attention to what I had to say at the press conference. His attention had special significance, because Denny Moss was in charge of economic development for the city of Phoenix. And Moss thought he had an suggestion he judged worth sharing when I stated that the bottom-line questions had become, How would the Suns get a building, and where would we put it?

Moss called me with a proposition. "What do you think of downtown?" he said.

I didn't need more than a moment to consider his words. I instantly knew that Moss had it right.

"That's where it belongs," I said.

At first glance, downtown Phoenix was an underwhelming choice. Unlike Chicago or New York or San Francisco, or most major cities for that matter, what should have been the thriving business district of Arizona's capital city and most populous metropolis was not much more than a decaying shell.

It hadn't always been that way. Stores and restaurants and hotels had once thrived throughout downtown. However, some forty or so years ago, Phoenix began to spread out and the northern areas of the city started to grow more populated, to the detriment of the downtown district, which had failed to develop and maintain a solid infrastructure of apartment buildings and private homes.

Eventually, this would result in Phoenix emerging, along with Los Angeles and Shanghai, among others, as the prototypical "modern" city, laid out horizontally instead of vertically There are pluses and minuses to vertical rather than horizontal growth, but that discussion belongs in another venue. As far as Phoenix is concerned, this horizontal spread would almost kill downtown, because it essentially rendered it just another city section, instead of the essential section, the central business and meeting place.

The late Senator Barry Goldwater's great-grandfather, along with his brothers, opened a shop in the 1800s that would eventually become a chain of department stores across Arizona, the most important department stores in the state. When the flagship Goldwater store in downtown Phoenix moved to a shopping center to the north in the 1950s, it spelled the beginning of the end for the central city area.

Over the years, as the better establishments departed, the major businesses that remained were some lawyers and accountants and other professionals, whose practices often depended upon the city and state government offices that were clustered downtown. These professionals promptly and without fail fled their offices for more pleasant vistas elsewhere as soon as the work day ended. Finally, scattered around these government and legal offices were the debris and flotsam of any city, including a flophouse hotel, a handful of small shops, and a number of abandoned buildings and vacant lots.

Could a city be great without a central business district, a central cultural district, a central meeting and gathering district? It hardly seemed possible.

A new basketball arena, along with several other projects already undertaken by public and private interests, would go a long way towards revitalizing downtown, towards attracting other businesses to the area.

Over a series of months, a public-private partnership between the city and the Suns was worked out, a partnership that has served as a prototype for other cities and other franchises, a prototype for how a municipality and a sports franchise could put a deal together that would prove a win-win situation for everyone.

A couple of people were especially helpful in putting together the arena deal. In particular, I had read about Sam Katz, who had been down this road before, and, intrigued by his financing deals, retained him as a financial consultant.

In addition, Rich Dozer was a young accountant with Arthur Andersen. As previously noted, Rich's father, Dick Dozer, wrote for the *Tribune* back in Chicago, and even covered me when I was a high school and college athlete. Rich knew Arizona from accompanying his dad to spring training.

He later attended the University of Arizona and stayed in the state upon graduation.

Rich was already working on the Suns' account at Arthur Andersen when I realized he was *that* Dozer.

Legacy or not, I was sufficiently impressed with his work to bring him into our organization as my chief financial officer. He had already proven to be of great assistance when we put the deal together for the purchase of the team, and he would prove equally valuable when we structured the complicated deal to build the arena.

My people were pushing to build 17,000 seats inside. I wanted 19,000, believing that it was better to build it now rather than have to add it later. And I expected to fill up that arena, as many nights as I could.

Our experts figured that building the arena would cost $70 million. That meant that we negotiated a deal with the city to split the construction costs fifty-fifty, capping the city's expense and exposure at $35 million. We created a new legal entity, a shell to represent our organization's interests with regard to the arena, for tax reasons.

When Moss approached me with his idea of locating the arena downtown, he offered, on behalf of the city and the mayor, Terry Goddard, who was a very strong advocate of this notion of a downtown arena, to give the Suns a subsidy to help pay our expenses. However, this subsidy, which was actually in the form of a tax abatement, had a couple of problems. One, it was allowable for only eight years. What happened after that? Two, it was a bad idea from a public relations standpoint. A subsidy was guaranteed to anger the public. It was the wrong word, and even the wrong idea. I didn't like it either. We were looking for a mutually beneficial business relationship, a partnership, not a handout.

Eventually, we arrived at a more creative solution, and a better deal for both the city and the Suns. To begin, the city would raise its share of the costs through a slight increase in the hotel tax and the rental car tax. Mayor Goddard and

Moss asked me to help persuade the city council to pass this measure, which I did. The city contributed the land upon which the arena would be located. When the city ran short of the money needed to purchase this land, it asked us to contribute $500,000. We agreed to this request.

We decided to make the building larger than its original design, and thus more expensive. The Suns paid for those additional costs. We negotiated with Restaura, a restaurant concessionaire experienced in large venues, involved with the concession package. Restaura, incidentally was owned by Dial, our first corporate investor. Concessions are an extremely profitable to both the arena and the concessionaire, and this was a vital agreement. Depending on the deal, the concessionaire can help finance the part of the construction that pertains to its operations, which is referred to as "improvements," and which are usually extensive and expensive. It's a numbers game—if you need the concessionaire's money up-front to help pay for construction, you reduce the percentage on the other end. As with every aspect of this endeavor, I needed to learn something about Restaura's business, so I would know what was reasonable and necessary to ask for.

Construction progressed on a fast track. Our timing was perfect. Business in Phoenix and Arizona was down, as it was throughout the southwest and the country as a whole—particularly in real estate and construction. Every firm associated with construction was eager for a job of this magnitude. Every single bid on each part of the job came in lower than we expected. These savings allowed us to add a lot of bells and whistles to the package.

(Later on, I would discover that the word on this building throughout the land was that we got more bang for our buck than any building constructed in a decade. Of course, just the opposite would be true when we built the baseball stadium. The real estate market was going wild, and new houses and offices buildings were being thrown up all over the valley and the United States. Everything associated with construction, from labor to materials, was at a premium, and we paid very dearly for Bank One Ballpark. Oh, well: timing might be everything, but everything can't wait for the right time.)

The final bill for the America West Arena—which included the cost of land acquisition and all soft (i.e., architectural plans, designs, and so on) and hard (construction) expenses—was $110 million. The Suns paid the difference between the original agreement and the end result.

In the final analysis, after the lawyers and accountants and negotiators were done, the key points underlying the deal weren't difficult to understand: The city owned the arena and the Suns were the exclusive landlords and managers of the property, and in concert we devised a formula to divide the costs and the profits between these public and private centers.

Revenue was generated by tickets and concessions and a variety of marketing gambits and arrangements. Additional revenue was produced by selling the naming rights to the arena to America West Airlines. The Suns received $26 million over thirty years from America West Airlines for those naming rights, as well as additional suite revenue and marketing packages.

But that deal was only the start. By the time America West Arena opened in 1992, it had the second-most signage revenue of any building in the NBA.

The city was to receive as rent $500,000 annually, a figure that would rise 3 percent every year. All the revenues from rent, concessions, signage, suites, and parking, went into a pot, and was divided from there. (Concession revenue was split with Restaura, and parking revenue was relatively negligible, as the garage only housed 1,500 vehicles.)

The only revenues treated differently were those from tickets, which went directly to the franchise. Whatever other revenues from other shows and attractions the organization could draw to the arena went into the general plot.

But that was not the end of it. The Suns were to act as the building's management, so we had to take those revenues and distribute them on behalf of the building. According to a formula negotiated to a satisfactory agreement by both sides, the annual gross revenues would be distributed thusly: First, that the arena would have adequate funds to operate to maximum efficiency; Second, that the arena's $44 million debt would be serviced; Third, that the rent to the city would be paid; Fourth, that the building refurbishing account would be funded, which required approximately $300,000 to $400,000 per year; and fifth and finally, that the franchise would receive its marketing fee. This last would be carried on the books as receivables if no cash was available, after paying off the first four items. In fact, the marketing fees due to the Suns are only beginning to be paid.

The upshot of this deal was that America West Arena was the first venue in the country financed not through collateral or hard cash, but with the promise of sufficient future revenues to pay for the cost of its construction. The deal wasn't based around bricks and mortar, but around the principals involved in the business.

That constituted the basic outline of this revolutionary deal. The Suns were happy and the city was happy, and the arena was built. America West Arena, with over nineteen thousand unobstructed seats, regarded far and wide as the finest basketball venue in the nation, was and continues to be a tremendous success.

Though we had a terrific arena, supported by extensive signage, our work was far from completed. For now we needed to fill up our wonderful venue, even when the Suns weren't playing. One way to do that was to bring in any sort of show that could find an audience in Phoenix. And so today, this September–October, despite the NBA lockout, the Phoenix Coyotes of the National Hockey League are deep in the midst of their campaign, and AWA will host all sorts of shows, from music acts as diverse as country stars LeAnn Rimes and Brian White, rock legends Jimmy Page and Robert Plant, alternative artist Tori Amos, pop diva Celine Dion, Gospel singer Bill Gaither, and rap masters the Beastie Boys. But the shows go beyond music, including everything from the 32d Annual Western States Karate Championship to the Original Coors Rodeo Showdown to a full-slate theatrical production of the animated Nickelodeon series, "Rugrats."

And that's at the tail end of the Arizona summer, which is not exactly the height of the tourist season in Phoenix. Indeed, it is the time when local resorts are still dramatically lowering their prices to attract business, and many valley residents are just returning after fleeing the heat in favor of their mountain retreats in Flagstaff, Sedona, and other more moderate climes, in and out of state.

We work without pause to maximize the arena's resources and capabilities. Once again, this was not something I planned on or thought long and hard about before the arena was built. Instead, it was a natural outgrowth, a logical, virtually unavoidable, extension of our primary business. It must be a blessing to be a visionary, to see things years before even the prospect tangibly materializes. However, as wondrous as that ability, that gift, is, in the world of business, it is almost as valuable—and decidedly more reliable—to be prepared and open to new opportunities as they arise.

That's where I come in. I am always ready to grow my business in any new direction that makes sense. I am not talking about taking a leap of faith into the unknown, risking huge resources on an endeavor that I know nothing about, that has nothing to do with anything my organization understands, that has no relationship to our experience and prime interests.

In large part, I am confident in attempting new ventures because I am confident in our organization. I feel strongly that we've assembled a strong group of people, and it takes people, working together in a directed, determined organization, to make things happen. It also takes leadership, but leadership is not all giving speeches and handing out orders. Leadership is also picking the right people, the people in whom you can place your faith, the people who you can trust with responsibility and independence. One person is linked to the person directly above and below them, but they must also have room to think and try and test, to be bold and be creative, all within the framework of the organization.

Similarly, when growing your business by stepping outside of your core concern to take on other enterprises, it is imperative that one business link up with another in an organic and integrated manner. You see it over and over, as companies take a flier and go far afield to try something removed from their expertise. Most commonly, you find this in the entertainment industry, where a company or even wealthy individual with absolutely no experience in show business will suddenly make a big, splashy investment in films, and then, not too many years later, sulk away after losing his shirt.

This sort of venture has never intrigued me. Whatever we have done, whatever we have invested in, has been a result of careful planning and synergistic logic. A (meaning the Suns) leads to the B (the arena), which leads to C, D, E, F, and so on (traveling circuses, concerts, T-shirts, retail shops, etc.).

Eventually A would lead rather far down the alphabet, all the way to M, and back around again to B—as in MLB, Major League Baseball, and BOB, Bank One Ballpark.

But we'll get to that a bit later. Right now, let's go back to the beginning, to our exploring other ventures, and then incorporating some of them into our operation, sometimes for better and sometimes for worse.

CHAPTER FOUR

Synergy and the Sports Business

So THE DEAL was done. First we had a team, and now we had an arena. And before too long, we would have other teams in other sports playing in America West Arena.

To many people, looking from today's vantage point, it must seem as if the Suns organization had a game plan for procuring other teams, for diving into other businesses.

The fact was, one thing led to another; the process evolved as we developed special needs, learned other businesses, and expanded our capabilities. Long before I put together the group that purchased the team, I knew that I eventually wanted to develop my own advertising and public relations agency. The Suns required the services of advertising and PR pros. Why not set up our own department, allowing us to handle these tasks ourselves? Those were my modest goals for the prospective department.

Ray Artigue was the part-owner of an agency that was handling these tasks for us. I made him an offer and he accepted, and Ray came to work for the Suns in 1991 as our vice president of communications, essentially doing the same job he had been doing. As we started more teams, he and his group worked on those accounts. Artigue did such a fine job with these accounts that the Suns' little agency, named S.R.O. Communications (Standing Room Only), began to attract the attention of other companies who were impressed with our advertising product. In fact, they wanted to hire our department to work on their accounts.

S.R.O. started to take on clients and began to earn money. Today, the agency has three dozen full-time employees and handles not only advertising and PR but also publishing, graphic design, and event planning. The agency bills some $4 million each year, with a client base that includes Pulitzer Radio Group, the Phoenix Open, and KUTP-TV.

I can't claim that this was anything I intended or planned. But it is not crucial in business, or in life, to know exactly the end result of a venture, as long as the conception is sound and it meets a specific need. Bringing the agency in-house met our needs—if it never went further than that, I would have been satisfied. Because the conception was sound and the implementation was exemplary, the agency grew beyond all expectations. That was a bonus, for sure—though not a bonus that was based on pure chance or luck. Even though we didn't plan for it, the expansion of the agency was a reasonable result, one which we were easily able to respond to and incorporate into our larger business.

Piece by piece, we became a full-service organization. The Suns needed to videotape our games, both for internal and external purposes. Instead of paying somebody else to do it, why not set up our own production company?

When we had decided upon the site for the arena, an old building was already located on the property. We did some research and discovered that the building had some historical significance—it was the location of a Chinese settlement earlier in the century—as well as some character. Though we had the right to tear it down, we recognized that this was an important part of Phoenix's heritage and spent approximately $2 million refurbishing the building.

When that was finished, we placed some of our offices in

the building. Even then, we were still left with a lot of extra space. Let the area go to waste? Absolutely not. We put in a state-of-the-art athletic club, not only for our employees, but with membership open to the public.

The current buzz term for this sort of thinking, this melding together of capabilities and interests, is—as anyone who has even glanced at a story about another giant merger in the paper or attended an introductory business school course—*synergy.*

Synergy. A fancy-sounding word to convey a pretty straightforward idea. In any event, we were employing the strategy years before any of us ever heard the word.

Now that we know what to call it, the real synergistic opportunity was not in video production or public relations. Instead, the real thrust of our new business ventures was and remains the other sports we brought to our venue. Arena Football has proved a great success for us, and the story of how the Arizona Rattlers came into being is short and sweet.

I was with Bryan, my son and the general manager of the Suns, in Detroit in 1990 on basketball business. We had some time off and decided to take in the championship Arena Football game between Detroit and Tampa. I had seen a couple of games on late-night cable and was impressed by the enthusiasm of the fans. Still, I had never been to a game before, and was quite intrigued to find out what this sport was really all about. Though I didn't place any specific expectations in this small but growing game, in the back of my mind, I wondered if maybe the sport had something to offer us.

After all, indoor football was played in the summer, when basketball was done and the arena was empty. Additionally, we didn't yet have Major League Baseball in Arizona, so there was a definite pro sports gap in the Phoenix schedule, just waiting to be filled.

I saw less than one quarter of the game and I turned to Bryan and said, "We're in." I liked the sense of the game, I liked the feel of the arena, I liked the feel of the action.

I don't think of myself as an impulsive individual, though it might appear that way to somebody reading about how I embraced this or that on sight—like the downtown venue for the Suns or Arena Football—and went forward with time and money to bring it to fruition. While it may seem that way, it isn't so. Everything I learn—and everything the organization learns—is added to everything we have learned before and is fodder for what we will learn in the future.

Thus, when we recognize that the Suns require a new arena, we know the team's requirements for the players, in the locker room and the practice court and the training room. We know the team's requirements for the fans, in the stands and the concessions, in the bathrooms and the parking lots. We know the facts and figures, so when we are presented with an option—downtown, in this case—we can very rapidly process the information and conclude whether it fits our needs and parameters.

The same with Arena Football. We needed to find attractions that would fill the place. Individual events are terrific, but to find an ongoing enterprise—a "multiple date attraction"—is obviously a more effective and efficient use of our resources. Team sports, circuses, and touring musicals are some examples of the multiple date attraction concept.

Arena Football had the additional virtue of being an attraction that the organization could own and control, as opposed to a show that comes and goes, opening up the possibility of further revenue streams from ancillary product sales.

So when I came upon Arena Football, I already knew, in broad strokes, what we needed, before I had actually seen it.

The game was decidedly a minor sport, struggling to achieve greater popularity and profitability. The commissioner and some of the owners of the Arena Football League were rather eager to have the Phoenix Suns organization sign up to buy a franchise in the indoor football game. They judged having a team in Phoenix—and what they assumed would be a well-run team—would only add to the league, in credibility, exposure, and revenue.

We met with the league and were informed that the price of purchasing a franchise was $500,000. Half a million might not sound like a lot when we talk about money in the sports industry, but in sheer terms, it remains a lot of money—perhaps not more money than the franchise was worth, but more than I was willing to pay. Besides, we weren't merely bringing money to the table, we were bringing our record of experience and success, too. We were bringing real value that could help propel the league to another level, value that was far beyond the numbers quoted as any franchise fee.

In my estimation, the Arena Football League had at least as much to gain by our joining with them as we did by buying into the league. Hence, I took the asking price of $500,000 as exactly that—an asking price. I replied by offering to put up $125,000. We settled on $250,000, half of which I would pay up front, and the other half of which would be paid out of future expansion fees owed to the Suns organization, when and if the league expanded and procured those fees.

The league agreed, approving our formal application on September 11, 1991. This meant that it cost us $125,000 to end up with a franchise, the Arizona Rattlers, that is probably worth $6 million today, based on what we generate in revenues, and what our operation costs us.

Why is the team worth so much? Because once we commit to a sport, we think we know how to run our franchise. One day less than one month later, we hired Danny White as the Rattlers' first general manager and head coach. A local boy and a star at his Mesa high school, Danny then attended Arizona State University and enjoyed a career that marked him as one of college football's greatest quarterbacks ever and a place in the College Hall of Fame. He went on to earn All-

Pro career with the Dallas Cowboys, while leading the team to the NFC East title three times. Sports is about people more than equipment or marketing, or anything else, and given the chance to start the team with a football player of Danny White's caliber was an opportunity too good to pass up.

In addition, the public relations value of associating Danny White with the new team was enormous, granting it immediate local credibility and garnering instant local interest. In many ways, Coach White set the tone not only on the football field for the Rattlers, but, in the minds of many Arizona fans, also off the field.

(Later on, when the Diamondbacks came into being, I would replicate the hiring of a leader for the new team, when one of my first moves was to hire Buck Showalter, the outstanding manager of the New York Yankees, once again setting the stage for excellence.)

Some seven months later, the Rattlers played their first game. It was a preseason contest, and they lost. On June 13, 1992, the Rattlers debuted at home, at America West Arena, taking on the Sacramento Attack before a sellout crowd of 15,505. The arena had officially opened only the previous week, on June 5. The Arena Football League game was the first sporting event in the building.

After losing their first two contests on the road, the Arizona Rattlers won this one, 51–36, and finished the season 4 and 6. The team became the first AFL club to sell out every home game in a season.

(The Sacramento franchise moved the following year to Florida, where they became the Miami Hooters, in homage to their ownership by the restaurant chain of the same name. The Hooters were then sold to another group, which mercifully changed the name to the Florida Bobcats.)

In the course of their brief history, the Rattlers have recorded many notable achievements. By 1993, only two years into this venture, Bryan Colangelo earned the Executive of the Year award, and Danny White has been named Coach of the Year. By 1996, 500,000 fans had watched the team play at home. To reach this mark, the Rattlers enjoyed over 98 percent capacity for five years at home. The franchise received the AFL Commissioners Award an unprecedented two years in a row, in recognition of the best team organization, on and off the field, in the league.

Above and beyond all their other accomplishments, (at least to my way of thinking), the Rattlers have given me one thing that I have not been able to achieve with any other team, in any other sport: they have won a world championship. Two world championships, in fact, in four years.

It is certainly true that, to many people, winning the World Series or the NBA Finals carries considerably more prestige and recognition than winning the Arena Football League title. Nor do these AFL triumphs diminish my hunger to capture those other championships in any way. However, when all is said and done, those truths do not denigrate the effort put forth by the athletes and the organization in attaining a high degree of skill and determination required to consistently win. The athletes in Arena Football are good and tough. They play hard, and they play well. It is not easy to win at any level in organized sports, from high school to college to professional, and anyone or any team that strives and succeeds at being the best in their sport and in their league deserves praise and respect.

So I proudly wear the championship ring the Arizona Rattlers were awarded for winning the Arena Football League championship on September 2, 1994, defeating the Orlando Predators, 36–31, in Arena Bowl VIII. This was the first world championship not only for our organization, but also for the state of Arizona.

Even so, speaking from a business standpoint, it is entirely plausible to suggest that Arena Football may not be a draw in every major market. In fact, in some of the major markets where the league has had franchises, the teams have struggled. In New York City, for instance, the Arena Football

CityHawks have to compete with an exceptionally long list of popular professional teams and leagues competing for the same sports fans: the Yankees and the Mets in MLB; the Giants and the Jets in the NFL; the Knicks and the Nets in the NBA; the Rangers, the Islanders, and the Devils in the NHL. Then there is the WNBA, pro soccer, the U.S. Tennis Open, and the PGA. . . . The amateur list includes the New York Marathon, the Goodwill Games (a toss-up to place in the pro or amateur category), and the college basketball National Invitational Tournament, et cetera, et cetera.

With all that competition, the CityHawks are not the draw that the Rattlers are, nor have they been able to attract and sustain the rabid fan base or entice the constant media attention that the Rattlers have.

Putting aside the fate of both the Rattlers and the City-Hawks, there are more than sufficient markets to make the AFL successful. Some of those markets will be extremely large, with all kinds of entertainment attractions vying for the public's attention and affection, while others will be substantially smaller, with nary a pro franchise of any sort to its name.

So, as with all matters large and small, it comes down to timing and location, to picking your spots and making it work. We needed a summer program to put people in the building and didn't know for sure what would do the job. Arena Football appeared to fit the bill, though there was surely no guarantee that it would catch on. We can never know for certain what will strike people's curiosity, let alone grab them emotionally; in the end, we can only structure our presentations, programs, and sports as attractively as we can; put it out for the public's judgment; and hope for the best.

We give each new sport we buy into three years to prove itself. If it can't find its audience in three years, then it's never going to. Arena Football made it, and a couple of others didn't.

Speaking of those failures, we committed three years to World Team Tennis, from 1992 through 1994. WTT was a new concept for tennis, transforming this individual sport, where one player took on another, or one pair took on another pair, into a more traditional team format, with players shuttling in and out, substituting for one another in the course of a match. We signed tennis great Jimmy Connors to serve as our headliner for the Phoenix Smash, our WTT franchise and help bring in the fans.

Even with a sizable financial investment, and a correspondingly sizable organizational effort, replete with marketing and promotional schemes, the Phoenix Smash and World Team Tennis failed. The market just wasn't there to support the idea.

The same thing happened with the Arizona Sandsharks of the Continental Indoor Soccer League. We thought the league had promise. Soccer was the wave of the future, so some people say. Maybe it is—the game has certainly captured the enthusiasm of the young, as membership in youth soccer leagues explode across the country.

So soccer—the indoor variety for our arena—seemed like a good bet. We formed the Sandsharks in 1993, gave the league three years of our time and money, but it just didn't work. All those soccer kids and soccer moms and dads never showed up.

The CISL didn't work, and we decided to pull out. The league eventually folded.

Nonetheless, after totting up our wins and losses, I have to say that it is fun to grow something from scratch. And when a team takes hold, when a sport works, it is terrific.

The Rattlers, for example, have done so well by presenting an entertaining product, forging intense fan loyalty, that they've created a very solid niche. I have no doubt that there's a niche for our newest team, the Phoenix Mercury of the WNBA. After just one season under our belts, (as well as the league's belt), the women's basketball league already proved its athletic excitement and its fan appeal.

The Phoenix Mercury gained a winning record the team's

first season in 1997, with sixteen victories and twelve losses. Following in our organization's tradition of hiring the best coach around when beginning a new club, we hired Cheryl Miller. Cheryl led USC to consecutive national titles in 1983 and 1984, garnering All-American honors four years in a row. For the last three years of her college career, she was the national College Player of the Year. Miller led the U.S. women to their first gold medal at the 1984 Summer Olympics and was voted ESPN Woman Athlete of the Year in 1985 and 1986.

Cheryl became the head coach at USC in 1993, scored a forty-four and fourteen record in two seasons, and won the Pacific-10 Conference title.

Miller was the best we could find—the best we could imagine. She rewarded our faith in her ability and leadership by molding her players into a smart, aggressive team that reached the playoffs in the league's first year. She was also a terrific public spokeswoman, embodying the style and spirit of the Mercury for the media and the fans.

Cheryl and her team did such an excellent job, playing enthusiastically and terrifically, with style and élan, that by the end of the season the Mercury had developed a deeply loyal fan base.

Of course, the marketing departments for the team and the arena both had a hand in creating an exciting product. Anyone who has ever attended a Phoenix Mercury game at America West Arena will immediately know what I'm talking about.

June 14, 1998. The Mercury are about to take on the Los Angeles Sparks at 1 P.M. It is a very busy day in downtown Phoenix, for just a couple of blocks away, the Diamondbacks are preparing to battle the St. Louis Cardinals, who are led by Mark McGwire, chasing Roger Maris's home run record.

The baseball crowd, as befits the difference in venue size, is much larger. Not only larger, it also appears to be a slightly different sort of crowd. Take a look at the people gathering

outside America West Arena before the basketball game begins. Compared to the baseball game at Bank One Ballpark,
there are an unusual number of young girls and grown women
waiting to attend this sports event—a majority of this crowd,
in fact. Take notice of how many little girls are wearing Mercury game jerseys, and how many adults are garbed in Mercury T-shirts. Artists in booths are busy painting many of the
girls' faces in Mercury red and yellow, adorned with stars and
suns and maybe the number of their favorite players: number
7 for Michelle Timms, 32 for Bridget Pettis, 22 for Jennifer
Gillom, 0 for Toni Foster.

Inside the arena, the team shop is humming with busy
customers, as many who don't already own Mercury gear
check out the full array of souvenirs, from clothes to all sorts
of trinkets.

Around the concourse encircling the court are the many
concession stands—hot dogs, lemonade, ice cream, pizza,
more souvenirs. A table set up by the Phoenix Mercury Charities is selling raffle tickets to benefit a shelter for abused
women and children.

The action is building as game time nears. Music is
loudly playing, the rock drumbeat urging on the happy crowd
to take their seats and get ready. Pregame television interviews
are being conducted on the court, with Coach Miller and
some of the players.

The arena is jumping as the fans, which have pretty much
filled every seat in the place, clap their hands and bang their
feet in time with the music, which must be almost as loud as
the system, and human ears, can go.

Terry Alice from En Vogue in a short, shimmering dress
sings the national anthem in grand style, reaching up, octave
after octave. The crowd cheers as fireworks explode, red
bombs bursting. The energy is tremendous, the fans are ready.

Suddenly Danny Manning, the star forward from the
Suns, appears on the video screen high in the arena. "Hey,
Coach Miller," he says. "Who's your sixth man?"

The lights go out, the music is turned up still louder, and spotlights and even more dramatic explosions light up the room. The "sixth man" to whom Danny is referring is the crowd, all the fans together, who respond with unbridled and joyful shouts and cries and applause.

It's time to play.

This enthusiasm on the part of franchise and fans translated into hard numbers and increased ticket sales for the Mercury: in the second year, we doubled our season ticket base, which guaranteed that we would have an outstanding year off the court as well as on, where the Mercury made it into the playoffs once again, reaching the 1998 Finals.

The Mercury have exposed a hitherto largely disinterested, or at least neglected, audience—that, of course, being the female audience—to the wonderful game of basketball. In doing so, the Mercury have built up a fan base that is separate and distinct from the fan bases of other sports and other teams—even distinct from the fans of the Suns, the "other" basketball club in town. That must be the goal of every franchise, especially those outside the four major team sports. The Rattlers have accomplished a similar feat, creating their own base of committed fans

In a remarkably short time, the Phoenix Mercury have staked their claim in the sports world, and the team and the WNBA are definitely here to stay.

Phoenix is one of only eleven cities with franchises in all four major league sports—baseball, football, basketball, and hockey. That has prompted some people to argue that the Phoenix marketplace is saturated with sports franchises, that no room exists for all these teams, as well as other pro franchises, like the Rattlers and the Mercury. And if you rely on population figures and expendable dollars per family, or whatever criteria economists prefer, then, yes, Phoenix is saturated.

Of course, if you just go by the numbers, then Green Bay, Wisconsin, with a population that barely breaks six figures, shouldn't be able to support its lone team, the storied Packers of the NFL. And the Packers are supported very well indeed, with perhaps the most devoted fans in football, and a fistful of world championships to their credit.

Numbers are important. Facts and figures are important. But numbers and facts and figures don't tell the whole story, not always, maybe not ever. To my mind, the fact that we've become such a saturated sports marketplace, a marketplace for teams that are supported, is evidence that if you stick to your policies and your beliefs and your standards on how to promote and package and a present a product—and that product is what the public wants—there will be room for perhaps even more clubs than the economists contend is conceivable.

In addition, I think that a certain amount of our success has to do with the reputation that our organization has earned in Phoenix. You see, if people come to trust you and expect that you will present a good product, there is a reasonable possibility that they will support you. Not necessarily in all things, as I have found out, but at the start, the public might be willing to give you the opening and the opportunity. They will give you the opportunity if you are willing to take a risk and try something new.

Phoenix has not only exploded as a marketplace; the city, the entire valley, has become known as a sports mecca. So despite the studies, despite the economists who talk about such pessimistic concepts as "recycled leisure dollars," also known as "expendable income" (the notion that consumers only have so much money to spend on sports and movies and carnivals, and adding a new sports team in a town only causes people to redirect their funds away from the movies and carnivals and to the new team, thereby increasing leisure spending not one whit), the fact remains that we are succeeding in Phoenix to bring new teams and new sports to a receptive public.

With the success of the Suns and our other franchises, we recognized another marketing outlet, one directly tied to our teams. We started by selling novelties out of our ticket office and did so well that we decided to go into the retail business. We grossed more than $7 million dollars in sales this last year, and, with the addition of the Diamondbacks, will probably double that in one year. We hired some very good people and have retail locations in malls and in our own facilities. It's a big business.

And that's not all. To employ a fancy term of our own, there's some horizontal development and expansion. With the Diamondbacks and Bank One Ballpark, for example, we've entered into joint ventures with the restaurant corporations like TGIF's and giant conglomerates like the Miller Brewing Company. The key is that all these joint ventures stem out of our main businesses.

For many reasons, it makes sense to stay close to those main businesses. By staying in the areas where you possess some expertise, your expertise can help build something new and related, even if that new enterprise is only peripherally related. I believe in taking risks, but when you stray too far from your core, from your center of experience and knowledge, the risks can quickly spiral out of your control.

Not only does this make sense from the business perspective, but it also makes sense in conducting your personal life, too. Stay true to who you are, to where you came from, to what you believe and know. Then, no matter what life throws you—and life has a tendency to throw some pretty stunning curves—you will be able to maintain your balance, your emotional and spiritual equilibrium. You will be able to persevere and fight your way through all obstacles, and emerge sane and whole and triumphant in the end.

In this conversation about synergy, I'd like to mention a word about my son Bryan. There is synergy in business, and then there is a profoundly more personal form of synergy, the synergy of bringing selected members of your family into your business.

By the time he reached high school, Bryan had emerged as an excellent athlete, earning a spot on Arizona's All-State basketball squad. At the same time, I was well aware that being the son of a person involved in local public affairs—very public affairs—and the attendant media attention could not always be easy on a young man.

With that in mind, it made sense for Bryan to spend his college years out of town, allowing him to spread his wings and find out on his own who he was, what was important to him, and start to decide what he wanted to accomplish with his life. Bryan spent four years at Cornell in upstate New York and did quite well, learning, maturing, growing.

Like any father, I held within me a certain hope that one day my son would become involved in my business. And through letters, phone calls, and visits, Bryan remained well informed of the ups and downs in the Suns' fortunes. Still, I was careful to keep my hope in the background, letting Bryan discover his own path.

During our time of greatest travail, as the drug scandal was gathering steam and the situation was becoming quite unpleasant and ugly, I received a letter from Bryan. He said I should keep doing what I believed in, what I believed was right. That simple formula had worked for me throughout my career and would help me overcome this trouble. He said I had his support and his love.

The letter moved me to tears. It also showed me how far Bryan had come, how he had matured into an impressive young man.

Upon graduation, Bryan went to work in New York City for a commercial real estate firm. The real estate market was depressed at the time, and it was a baptism by fire in the business world. Regardless, Bryan did very well and thrived for several years in this most competitive industry, in that most competitive city.

When he could, I also had him doing some part-time scouting for the Suns, which helped to keep his hand in the game. After a few years, I called Bryan and told him I'd like to have him consider coming back to Phoenix to work for the organization. I made it clear that it would be a difficult situation in some ways, that many people would dismiss him as the boss's son. He would have to start on the bottom and would advance only as his merit warranted it. I told him to take some time and think about it.

Bryan chose to return to Phoenix. From almost the moment he started working with the Suns, I felt that it was the correct decision. He fit right in, quickly gaining the friendship and confidence of his fellow workers. Bryan was willing to do whatever he had to do to succeed at his appointed tasks. He refused to be outworked by anyone and showed that he was his own man, not Jerry's boy.

I had always had confidence in his abilities and had taught him that you don't demand respect, you earn it. I was able to give him the opportunity to succeed with the franchise, but only he could prove to others that he deserved their attention and regard.

Today, Bryan is one of the most esteemed general managers in the NBA, clearly respected by his peers in the league. Personally and professionally, he has become the man I always hoped he would be.

This brief discussion centered about synergy and sports would not be complete without a look at the television and radio industries. TV and radio have a singularly strong symbiotic relationship to sports. The media devour product as the channels and stations transmit twenty-four hours a day, every day of the year. That means that the media need the entertainment value that sports bring, and the guaranteed endless supply of entertainment. And so the networks have paid handsomely to obtain those many, many games from a multitude of sports.

At the same time, the sports business needs the media, needs the exposure and the excitement and the rights fees the networks pay. Thus, it might seem to make obvious sense for our organization to purchase our own media outlet.

Some of the smartest people in business, who control some exceptionally huge corporations, have embraced that position with a passion—a profitable passion at that. Ted Turner has made his Atlanta Braves into a terrifically profitable and winning team by broadcasting their games on his national cable system, Turner Broadcasting System—simultaneously generating tremendous revenue for TBS. In this manner, each component—the team and the cable system—creates profits for the other, resulting in an entirely win-win situation for Turner.

Taking the same idea to another level is Rupert Murdoch and his Fox Network. For years, Fox has delved deeper and deeper into the sports broadcasting business—buying the rights to the NFL's NFC games, televising MLB games, establishing a series of regional sports networks, which concentrate on local professional and other contests. Now Murdoch has purchased the Los Angeles Dodgers, one of the most fabled franchises in any sport. Apart from owning this immensely successful franchise, Murdoch might very well be planning to bring the team to a global audience through Fox's worldwide television reach.

If that should happen (and I have no inside information, one way or the other), watch the synergy at work: Fox builds a new worldwide base of fans, perhaps broadcasting Dodger games not only in North America, but also to baseball hot spots such as Japan and Latin America, creating a new market for not only additional TV advertising revenue but also Dodger souvenirs. Can you imagine how many Dodger caps the franchise will sell once the team goes planetary?

The more revenue the network earns, the more sports and

games it can bid on for broadcast, producing more revenue. The more revenue the team receives, the more aggressive it can be in signing high-priced stars, outbidding teams without national (let alone international) support. Thus, the cycle continues, more revenue buying a better team, which in turn produces more revenue for the franchise, allowing it to buy more stellar athletes, the cycle effortlessly spinning round and round.

That is synergy on a grand scale. For both Turner and Murdoch, of course, sports might be regarded as a secondary business—maybe even tertiary. The same is true today for many of the owners of the professional franchises in any sport.

Whether, in the long run, having these corporate owners is the best for basketball or baseball or football remains an open question—though there is no question that the phenomenal costs associated with professional sports ownership have rendered the individual owner virtually extinct. I believe, as we will discuss in detail a bit later, that this will prove not only inevitable but beneficial for the sports industry.

This assumes that these conglomerates will prove to be intelligent, responsible stewards of the teams they purchase. However, if it should turn out that the corporations care more for the bottom line than for the team and the players and the fans—or conversely, think too little about their financial position and recklessly overspend—then problems will surely arise. Once the game—any game—simply becomes a commodity, it ceases to be a game in any meaningful or even interesting sense. Why should any fan care what happens to its hometown team when it is apparent that the team itself, as embodied by the owners and management, and maybe its extremely well-paid players, too, regard the team as only another line on an accounting sheet?

We have seen both sides of this problem—reckless overspending and then bottom-line accounting and slashing—come to life in Miami. Although a very young major league franchise, the decision was made to spend great sums to sign all-star free agents in order to garner fan support. Though the Marlins won the World Series, the fan support didn't material-ize—at least not the amount of fan support required to pay those huge player paychecks. Dissatisfied with the return on its investment, the ownership decided to cut its losses and rid itself of its high-priced stars, trading them away in return for young prospects. This rather shocking turn-about—from World Series champions one year to a team with the worst record in baseball the next—left the fans disillusioned and disgusted, and they have stayed away in droves.

Of course, it need not be that way. The rush to win on the field and profit off it pushed the Marlins into a problematic strategy. A more sensible strategy for long-term stability and growth, and one that the Diamondbacks have pursued, is to build a farm system that will develop the young talent that will provide the major-league club with a progression of trained, skilled players, year after year.

I believe, and have always believed, that owning a profes-sional sports team is a privilege, not a right. And that same sense of privilege should be felt and honored at every level of pro sports, from the owners to the management to the players.

That, returning to the main point, is one reason we have stayed with the businesses we knew and understood and en-joyed. Getting back to the media, we looked at buying into TV or radio, but decided the cost was prohibitive. Even if we raised the necessary funding, the effort and money expended would distract us from our prime business, and eventually de-tract from that business.

Meanwhile, we feel we have as good a situation as we could without controlling a media outlet, because we control the inventory, the games, the product. It comes down to what your play is, what your point is, what you want to do with your life and in what business you want to be.

With that in forefront of our corporate consciousness, packaging our product is as important as anything we do. We maintain control of our destiny by controlling our rights. Additionally, by owning so many teams, so many products, so many assets, we have extra leverage with the media.

And the media is the gateway for the sponsors and advertisers. So by packaging all these rights into one bundle—entering into exclusive or semi-exclusive arrangements combining television, radio, signage, tickets, and other promotional and marketing opportunities—you can maximize the value of those rights.

When you're in a small market, or even a relatively small market compared to the majors, it is not possible to sell your rights for enough to compete with the bigger markets. You can be competitive only by being better—which translates into being more creative and more aggressive—at packaging than anyone else. And in sports, marketing is not simply a matter of earning profits for the franchise; rather, marketing is a primary means by which you fund the salaries of your players, and the improvements in your training and other facilities. Thus, marketing helps ensure the competitiveness on the court of your team. And our marketing success has helped the Suns remain one of the NBA's better teams, year in, year out.

When America West Arena opened in 1992–93, the Phoenix Suns, located in what was then the nineteenth-largest television market in the country, led the NBA in revenues. We did not accomplish this by having the highest ticket prices in the league. To the contrary: our tickets rank somewhere near the middle of the pack in cost. So tickets didn't do it for us.

Marketing did. A potential sponsor couldn't buy signage in the arena or any association with the team in lone purchases, or by consulting the advertising rate card. He had to buy the entire package, soup to nuts. We raised the marketing bar in this way and got more for both our sponsors and for the franchise.

This approach, which was so stunningly successful, had two significant results. First, we transformed the many local and national companies who worked with us into more than just advertisers or sponsors—we made them part of our team, part of our experience, which resulted in them wanting to do more to support both their efforts and ours. Second, on the heels of our success, other people and other franchises began to alter their business philosophies and adopted ours. Along with the many new buildings going up around the league, our revenue lead vanished very quickly. Today, the Knicks, for example, enjoy ticket revenues that are twice that of the Suns.

So our challenge is to stay ahead of the curve and continue to be a little bit more creative and aggressive than anyone else.

All in all, when considering the direction of our operations, the structure of our investments, the course of our business, I am fairly well satisfied with the situation the way it is. That's not to say that I won't change my mind sometime in the future and look for new opportunities.

It could happen. We're always growing and changing. We've grown from twenty-five employees to five hundred full-time employees and a couple of thousand part-timers. We will surely continue to grow; the question is how and in what direction.

Whatever we do, maintaining a synergistic relationship with our key businesses is paramount. I am in the sports business; that is the business I aspired to enter, once I was presented with the chance. This is where I intend to stay.

CHAPTER FIVE

Character and Characters

THE MOST VOLATILE and fundamental relationship management can have is with its work force. If you're in the car business and you're running General Motors, that means the men and women assembling the cars on the factory floor. If you're in the basketball business and you're running the Phoenix Suns and Phoenix Mercury, that means the men and women executing the plays on the hardwood floor.

And whether in the automobile or the sports business, it is important that a degree of mutual respect exists between the workers and management. We can't take the analogy between any industry and sports too far, because in sports, the players constitute even more than the work force, they represent and embody the game to the fans. The consumers don't care who builds their Chevrolet Cavaliers, as long as they run well. The fans most certainly care who's playing for their favorite teams; they know the players' names and stats and probably who they're dating. Hence, in a very real sense, the players are the lifeblood of the industry.

As a former player, I have never viewed the athletes as mere pieces in the corporate puzzle, as cogs in a machine. I have always worked hard to develop and maintain good relationships with my players, as well as with players around the league. My concept of a good relationship means being open and fair and honest. Though openness, fairness, and honesty aren't complicated or unusual notions, they sometimes seem that way when big money and big pressure are involved.

I believe that my work in this area has paid off for our teams. Forbes magazine made note of this when, in 1994, all-star Danny Manning accepted $1 million and a one-year contract from the Suns over a seven-year contract from the Atlanta Hawks, worth $35 million. "This is everything I wanted," Manning said, referring to the Suns, "except the money. I've played around the league, and I've never heard one negative thing about Mr. Colangelo. That's pretty impressive in this cutthroat business."

Danny understood that, under the salary cap, which restricts the total amount that each team can spend on its payroll, the Suns only had $1 million left to pay him. After that season, the salary cap loosened, and we rewarded Manning's loyalty and desire to play for Phoenix with a $40 million, six-year contract.

I don't think anyone can doubt that it creates quite a statement that players are willing to risk losing multimillions of dollars for the chance to play in Phoenix. By no means am I claiming that whatever reputation I have earned in the NBA is sufficient to cause an athlete to forgo millions of dollars just to sign a contract, any contract, with the Suns. Along with how we do business, we are situated in a great city, with great living conditions and great weather, and play in what very well may be the "finest indoor sports facility in America," to quote the *Boston Globe*. Not only is America West Arena singularly fan friendly, with its intimate seating, unobstructed views, and multiple choices of concessions, it is outstandingly player friendly, with our own game-quality practice facilities, clubhouse, and many other amenities. Both the arena and the organization have been fashioned in such a manner that the players know that they will be taken care of by the organization, from start to finish, as long as they give 100 percent effort to their jobs and the team.

There are many other wonderful cities, many other dedicated organizations, and many other concerned owners in professional sports. And these wonderful cities, dedicated organizations, and concerned owners have taken years, just as we have, to build the types of interconnected, overlapping, solid relationships and reputations that speak volumes to players. We in Phoenix have put in those years and that work, particularly with the Suns, our first and oldest team, and our efforts have paid tangible dividends for us.

In fact, our work at being a most attractive site for pro basketball players has had definite side benefits in another sport. As we were starting to seek out players for the first time for the Arizona Diamondbacks, we had no track record and no tradition that would attract players and tell them what kind of organization they were joining. We didn't even have a stadium—though we did have one in the works.

Nonetheless, while the Diamondbacks didn't have a reputation, the Suns certainly did, and that reputation counted for enough that it even managed to jump sports. *Baseball Weekly* took note some months ago when it ran an article ranking the most attractive places to play in baseball. Phoenix was rated number two, right behind Atlanta. Now Atlanta, a fine city in its own right, had a couple of advantages over us— primarily a venerable baseball club with a winning record that pegged them as one of the very best teams in baseball through the entire Nineties.

Personally, I recently tested Danny Manning's words about my alleged standing as a fairly decent fellow in the basketball game. We were in the midst of a collective bargaining session this year. Patrick Ewing, the veteran center of the Knicks and the president of the player's union, was in attendance, along with several others players and maybe half a dozen owners.

The subject at hand was the deep distrust that exists

between players and owners. Patrick was talking, and he was talking at length about what he felt were the players' legitimate grievances against the owners, about all the things owners did that damaged the game and the players.

Ewing finally finished, and I leaned over and said, "Patrick, I'm curious. Is that what you really think of me?"

And Patrick said, "Oh, no. You're an exception. You're different. All the guys know that."

The bottom line in this business is putting a competitive product on the court. The bottom line is winning. All the things we do off the court—providing excellent training facilities, the best physical therapists, smooth transport from home to airport to hotel to arena—all of it is useful and helpful and important, but none of it dribbles or shoots or scores.

It comes down to the players. And that means you have to be very selective in deciding who you put in your uniforms. In deciding who will represent the team.

Most of the time, when you gamble on a player of dubious character, when you take that risk, you get burned. The best way to eliminate the risk, or take a more calculated and reasonable risk when that red flag goes up in the scouting process, is to do your homework.

This goes to behavior both on and off the court. While this certainly isn't true in all cases, it is far from uncommon that one's behavior off the playing field will point to how he will act on the field—whether he'll hang tough, whether he'll prove a good teammate or whether he'll be selfish, disruptive, and ultimately destructive to himself and the club.

You see, the question is not only whether a guy can play or not, but whether he can play in those crucial moments when the game's on the line. It doesn't take a genius to see how he reacts in the heat of the battle, whether he's crushed or rises to a new level when things go against him. We watch everything: body language and eye contact with his coach during a game, his communicative skills, his practice habits, his relationships with his coaches and teammates, his relationships with opposing players and coaches. For a pro player, we already know much of this information. For a college player entering the draft, we get into all his friends and activities off the court, and we go into depth, interviewing family, friends, neighbors. You go back, as far back as deemed necessary, to check whether he's clean.

That takes investigative work, and there are services available that professional leagues employ that carry out these assignments. The stakes are so high today that you better know who you're picking.

Forewarned is forearmed.

Of course, it wasn't always like this. For decades, the major professional sports constituted a part-time profession for the players. Few athletes could support themselves and their families—never mind guaranteeing a secure postplaying future—on what they earned on the field. Players, even great players, were not assured of a spot with the team until they had fought for and won it, again and again. In many ways, this system made them a more mature lot.

This is not to suggest that the past was some golden era with regard to athletes. More often than not, the public didn't know about some athletes' less glorious behavior and attitudes. The newspapers didn't write it, and the teams certainly didn't publicize it. More "colorful" episodes were kept quiet, as the press and the teams collaborated on protecting the games and protecting their own interests.

Obviously, it's completely different today. As a result of widespread television coverage of college basketball, many, or perhaps most, of the young players entering the NBA have already garnered a measure of media attention and reached a certain level of fame. This media spotlight, and the attendant praise and rewards, psychic and material, that often come with fame, can lead them to believe that, simply stated, they are entitled to whatever they can get, and then some.

At the same time, athletes increasingly view themselves as profit centers, rather than just as athletes. They have limited years to make as much money as they can, and frequently the market shows that they can earn even more money off the court than on it. From shoe contracts to movie roles to personal appearances to an infinite assortment of other endorsement deals and work opportunities, the player with a distinctive image and the right agent (and all-star status doesn't hurt either), can earn an astonishing amount of money in short order.

Consider Dennis Rodman. Though one of the greatest rebounders the game has ever seen, that skill alone would not have made Rodman the household name that he has become. It was Rodman's basketball skills plus his singular personality, unmistakable style, and unsurpassed willingness to promote himself that has brought him the platform which has led to a bestselling book, a starring part in a big-budget action movie, a television series on MTV, guest-starring bouts with the pro wrestling tour, romances with other pop celebs, numberless media interviews and talk show appearances, on and on, his fifteen minutes of fame extending well into a half-hour, with no end in sight.

Athletes are stars, and stars, as is the current fashion, are accorded the latitude, the unique freedom, to behave as they see fit, to do whatever they want. That doesn't mean that they have to act in such rare fashion as Rodman. To take the foremost example of another sort of behavior, Michael Jordan is a superstar who has always conducted himself with class. You will not find another athlete who has demonstrated, game in, game out, such a fierce competitive desire. He wills his team to win, outside of his own performance. What is truly amazing is how that competitive fire is always burning, on the practice floor, in the locker room, every single day. To me, that's the ultimate, for a professional athlete. Jordan's attitude and conduct raise everyone around him to a higher level.

Off the court, Jordan is a loving family man, a smart businessman, and an unfailingly articulate spokesman for basketball.

That combination—his behavior on and off the court—sets Michael Jordan in a class by himself.

On the other hand, if you have a star who insists on staying separate from the team, and separate from society's norms, you have a different situation. You have a star who can't be a leader, because it's hard to be a leader, as a player or as a person, when you're being pursued by the police or the paparazzi or a paternity suit. Oh, they might have their moments, and they might still be great players, but being a great player with great individual statistics doesn't invariably mean you're helping the team win.

There have been exceptions, but it usually catches up with you. The true test of a player is not what he does in one season or even two, but how he performs over a sustained period, through the course of his career.

I will acknowledge that I probably place more importance on the character of an individual than any owner, and maybe most people in sports. Part of my motivation is that I believe in character, just as I believe in ethics and morality and family—those concepts are integral to the essence of my being.

Another part of my motivation is that I've been burned a few times in this business by athletes I've trusted. I've used this expression on more than one occasion when talking to the press, in explaining the role of a professional franchise in relation to its players, and I'm going to do it again: We are not in the rehabilitation business.

Young athletes are basically shaped by two factors: their upbringing and the system that sees them through their athletic development. The first part of that equation—first their parents, then other family, friends, and school—has to provide the intellectual and moral framework that will give that person the ideas and ideals required to lead a good, productive, responsible life. It is more than unfortunate, it is tragic, both for the individuals and for society, that so many young people today are not provided with that sort of framework. The breakup of the family, the fragmentation of society, the disintegration and decay of our leading institutions, from government to education to social to religious, all have contributed to young athletes set adrift, without the safe harbors of tradition, example, and mentors who give tangible shape and living form to values and beliefs.

There is nothing we in the professional sports industry can do about those incredibly important and powerful issues facing society. Repairing our national community woes is indubitably far beyond any sports league's scope or ability.

However, the second part of that equation is not absolutely beyond our scope or ability. The system that nurtures and shepherds athletes from youth to the pro ranks is full of potholes and roadblocks. It is an informal system, as we all know, a series of people and institutions dedicated to extracting what they can, materially and emotionally, with regard to the native talents of athletes. This could mean a major university using a star halfback to entice alumni to donate money for a new weight room, or a small-town banker chauffeuring an out-of-town teenage tennis star during a local tournament in order to show off his prize to his friends. It could mean money under the table; passing grades for college courses not taken; well-paid, no-show, ghost jobs. It could mean ignoring dangerous injuries and promoting equally dangerous drug use.

This system is something we can address. This system we must address, even if only for our economic well-being. By allowing the bending of rules, the system is delivering young men who are not interested in understanding their roles as the custodians of sport, as the next generation to protect and cherish their game, as examples and heroes and models for those even younger, and still impressionable. Instead, these are far too frequently young men who are only interested in their huge pay checks and endorsement deals and individual status.

We must fix the system because it is too late by the time we get them. After all, when basketball teams draft a young man out of college, we're drafting a young man who is twenty-one or twenty-two years old. And now we're taking them even younger, as they join the pro ranks right out of high school. Football still uses the colleges as its minor-league system, while many baseball players sign minor-league contracts and become professionals right after high school. Tennis players keep getting younger, joining gymnasts and skaters as games for very young people.

In any event, whether seventeen or twenty-one, we are basically getting a finished product. We know that these people are set in their ways, that their value systems are also pretty well set, and what you see is what you'll get.

This is not to indict all schools or the NCAA. Most schools follow the rules. The NCAA, led by its president, Cedric Dempsey, assiduously polices the system. Dempsey, a former athletic director at the University of Arizona and a former professor of mine at the University of Illinois, is a terrifically capable and concerned administrator who is well aware of the problems and working hard to effect changes. But regardless of his efforts, and regardless of the efforts of all the dedicated professionals at the NCAA, the pressure to win is so heavy that it takes its toll, and you see people bending the rules, and you see things happening that shouldn't take place.

Many coaches are well aware of the problem. Bobby Knight, the Indiana coach, has long been one of the most successful and respected leaders and teachers in the college game. My relationship with Bobby goes back to my University of Illinois days, when he was playing at Ohio State with Jerry Lucas, John Havlicek, Larry Siegfried, and Mel Nowell, and we competed against one another. Our relationship was rekindled during my first few years in pro ball, starting in

Chicago and moving on to Phoenix. In fact, we offered Bobby the head coaching job with the Suns in the early Seventies.

Bobby has never broken the rules, and I've always admired his steadfastness in maintaining his high standards. And yet it has been one of the most frustrating things with which he has ever had to deal, keeping to the straight and narrow while being acutely aware of the many schools and coaches who have done anything and everything to win, including bending and breaking the rules.

Competition to win on the professional level is one matter. That is the reason athletes play the game—to win. There is no other motivation that comes close, not for pros. Winning brings the fans. Winning brings tangible rewards. Winning sells.

College sports are supposed to be a different subject. Collegiate athletics are supposed to be about good, clean fun; they're supposed to be about building character, winning a varsity letter, cheerleaders, pep rallies, and all those wholesome things that are part and parcel of the college experience.

Well, okay. I know as well as anyone that though that characterization may still apply to badminton and cricket, in certain sports in certain universities—in many sports in many universities—the fun has been replaced by business, character building has been replaced by mind-numbing, cold competition.

The pressure on coaches and athletes to win at any cost is tremendous, and the pressure comes from the administration, the alumni, the fans, and the media. The administration wants the full stadiums and TV contracts a winning team can bring, and also the alumni contributions, while the alumni and the fans want the prestige, the bragging rights, of a winning team, and the media wants a winning team to write about, a team that the fans will want to read about.

That's a lot of people, a lot of different constituencies, who want the same thing, albeit for different reasons. And that's a lot of pressure bearing down on the coaches, and the athletes, some of whom have responded by bending the rules.

My solution to this overarching problem is four-fold. I must begin by admitting that college sports are too big, too popular, and too profitable for the clock to be turned back. We must deal with reality, and work within its constraints. With that in mind, I offer the following ideas:

1. I would give college coaches tenure, just like any university professors. This would remove the win-or-die burden weighing heavily on every coach's shoulders. Tenure will allow the coaches to do what they believe is right and proper, both for their team and their athletes, without having to worry about being second-guessed at every juncture. This innovation will allow sports to flourish in the same uninhibited atmosphere that encourages the flowering of intellectual disciplines. Tenure has worked for professors and students; I think it would also work for coaches and athletes.

2. I would hold university and college presidents accountable for any misdeeds that occur under their administration. Currently, when something goes amiss, the coaches and their staffs go (assuming anyone goes). Of course, if the coaches are to blame, even simply by their lax watch, they should be censured or fired. However, given the importance of sports in higher education, and the pressure placed by administrations upon their athletic programs, the leaders of the universities and colleges must take a more publicly active role—a public acknowledgment, really—of their responsibility in creating and policing the system.

3. Student/athletes should not be forced to carry a full load of courses when working within the sports profit center. For many sports, not just football and basketball and other major sports, athletes are expected to practice two, three, four, or even more, hours every day. With that sort of schedule, it can be very difficult for most athletes to dedicate the same sort of attention to their classes that other students can give.

In recognition of this, I say that student/athletes should

be permitted to take fewer courses per semester than other students and to extend the term of his college career. This proposal is not to degrade the importance of the athlete's education. Rather, just the opposite is intended: I seek to ensure that all athletes are guaranteed their full education, no matter how long it takes them to complete their schooling and earn their degrees.

Again, this would not apply to every athlete. Many manage both sports and school, same as other students manage to work long hours to earn money to pay for their schooling. Still, too many athletes at too many colleges end up leaving without getting their degrees. This is simply wrong, and something must be done.

4. Student/athletes should be paid. In essence, they work long hours on behalf of the university, which frequently reaps enormous profits off their sweat. I'm not talking about paying these young people the kind of money that would allow them to buy sports cars and Caribbean vacations. I'm talking about the sort of pocket money that so many college students earn, to pay for clothes and books and dates and other incidentals.

While these proposals won't stop illegal offers, nor will they stop those who welcome illegal offers from accepting them, they will go a long way towards blunting illicit behavior.

Once again, the key to any meaningful reformation of the system is approaching the thrust, the accelerating direction, of college sports realistically, looking beyond the frequently overheated rhetoric, past the controversy, and seeing the situation for what it really is. This huge system will not be dismantled. It cannot be, nor should it be.

Those are four proposals. Certainly more ideas could be added to my list, and many knowledgeable people have offered their own proposals and ideas.

Still, I might have one advantage over some of the other experts in pondering this situation. You see, I speak as a product of the system.

In my youth.

A musical career that was not to be.

A teenager, fifteen or sixteen years old, playing for my American Legion team, the Military Order of the Purple Heart. I am standing right in the middle.

Striking a pose at the University of Illinois, 1962.

The birth of the Bulls, 1966—I am on the left, with coach Johnny Kerr, and owner Dick Klein, all in cowboy hats and accompanying a formidable bull, which was led down Michigan Avenue in the first promotion for the new team.

Yes, Virginia, fashion once meant checked pants and white shoes.

The new general manager, 28 years old, 1968.

Announcing new coach Bill van Breda Kolff before 1972-73 season. Unfortunately Bill would be fired before too long, I coached for the reminder of the season.

Coaching, 1972-73.

During the 1974-75 season, I announced that I would give any season ticket holder a half-hour to tell me how to run the team. More than half of the 2,000 holders showed up.

Serving coffee and donuts to fans who spent the night outside the Suns' office in order to get on line for NBA play-off tickets, 1976.

Mandie and dad intently watching during the 1976 play-offs.

On occasion of Wilt scoring his 30,000 point. Connie Hawkins goaltended on the spot. With Wilt and Lakers coach Bull Sharman.

Connie Hawkins' number retirement celebration.

Honoring John Havlicek as he passed through Phoenix during his final season, 1977-78.

The sky darkens, the rain falls, and the Coliseum leaks . . . Announcing the cancellation of a pre-season game in 1978, and how refunds will be distributed. One more reason the Sun needed a new arena.

Draft day, 1984. Seated beside me is John MacLeod, the coach.

Receiving the Executive of the Year award from NBA Commissioner Lawrence O'Brien.

Frank Sinatra visiting with me at the America West Arena.

The street on which I lived . . . Now named Jerry Colangelo Way.

Charles Barkley, with something to say.

Standing up for the Suns.

Bryan and I at AWA.

With the family at the National Italian American Foundation dinner, honoring me, in 1996. From left to right—daughters Kristin, Kathy, and Mandie, joined by Joan and son Bryan.

With my mom at the dedication of the Jerry Colangelo Gymnasium in Chicago Heights, November 10, 1996.

Generation to generation: While Bryan watches the Diamondbacks, son Mattia looks to grandpa, causing my sister Rosemary great amusement.

Signing Buck, November 15, 1995: The team has a manager, twenty-eight months before the Diamondbacks will play their first game.

Hall of Famer Frank Robinson conducting the coin toss at the expansion draft, November 13, 1997, to determine whether Arizona or Tampa Bay would chose first. I called it right.

BOB, in all its roof-opened glory.

With Joe DiMaggio and Senator Carol Moseley Braun at the dedication of the new National Italian American Sports Hall of Fame, September 26, 1998.

Opening Day—March 31, 1998—With Len Coleman and Mrs. Jackie Robinson, presenting Jackie's retired number, which will never be worn by a Diamondback player, and which is emblazoned on the left field wall in BOB.

Opening night ceremonies.

When I received those sixty-six college scholarship offers, based upon my basketball acumen, I also received a number of illegal inducements as well. The propositions ranged from well-paying, no-show jobs to free transportation for family and friends to visit me during the school year to a smorgasbord of other illicit proposals.

I remember one situation in particular, where I was introduced to a wealthy alumnus of one university—the college team's sugar daddy—who told me I could look forward to getting a check once a month from him, and with a special incentive program built in, meaning if I accomplished certain goals on the court, I would receive bonuses.

I think I will leave that school unnamed and do the same for all the others who offered their own incentive programs.

I was a seventeen-year-old kid who didn't know much and didn't have much guidance. I thought this was the way things were done, that it was all part of the package, part of the deal of being a young athlete. This is not to make excuses for myself; obviously, I was aware that this was not quite on the up-and-up, that these matters and these arrangements were private, albeit accepted. I understood what I wanted to understand, and especially understood that I didn't have a lot of money to pay for college or for anything else, and so justified my actions on those terms.

Though it is true that what other students and I were offered in those days was small potatoes compared to what athletes are routinely receiving today—a reflection of how the stakes have grown, thanks to the fees winning universities can expect for television coverage of their contests, can expect in increased sales of their merchandise, can expect in enormous contributions from happy alumni—that in no way excused my actions. Nor do I seek to excuse myself. The point is, I have learned quite a lot about myself since those days, and about the world, and about right and wrong, and consequences and principles and values. And so when I look at the system, and offer some suggestions, I tell you that I know from whence I speak.

Thus, we return to the essential questions. For example: how many accomplished and pursued young athletes choose where to go to school based on the math department's reputation, as opposed to the record of the football team? With dreams of athletic glory swirling through their heads, scholastics are a throw-in, if not a nuisance, for too many athletes, as they load up on nonsense courses designed to get them through school quickly and painlessly.

We must change this. We must give the students and the schools the mechanisms by which each can get the best from the other.

That, of course, is all speculation. Today we face a situation where some athletes come to the pros with, at best, questionable personal habits and problematic attitudes, or, at worst, prison records. And that has serious consequences for professional franchises. At the bottom line: If you take too many risks with guys already adorned with less-than-stellar reputations, or too many raps against them, then there's a good chance you're going to get burned. In fact, I would bet almost any time, you will get burned. It's just too hard to make someone over, to fix perhaps a decade's worth of individual bad behavior, or two decade's worth of societal neglect. A professional sports team is an integrated, sophisticated, responsive, organic unit. For that team to perform at its best, its members must be mature and determined, and effortlessly and willingly fit into the larger scheme.

That is not an easy task by any stretch of the imagination, which is why teams endlessly practice and prepare, and coaches endlessly scout and plan, and general managers endlessly analyze and review.

And even then, there's usually not enough time to do

everything that the conscientious player and coach and general manager want to do to be ready, to be better—to win.

And that's why I say: We are not in the rehabilitation business.

The most famous player ever to wear the uniform of the Phoenix Suns was Charles Barkley. He was also probably the best player, and perhaps the most difficult, the Suns ever had.

The Barkley story is fairly well documented but bears repeating, in light of this chapter's discussion.

We had a good team stocked with a lot of good players prior to Barkley's arrival. The Suns had won more than fifty games each of the last four years, giving them the fifth best record in the NBA over that span. In 1991–92, the team went 53–29 and made it to the second round of the playoffs before succumbing to the Portland Trailblazers.

Even with this success, in our opinion, we had gone about as far as we could go with our roster at that time. In other words, we were good, but not good enough to win a championship.

At the same time, Barkley was rather outspoken about his desire to be traded from the Philadelphia 76ers. However, because so many teams were already at or close to their salary cap limits, there were precious few teams around the league who could make a deal with Philadelphia because the numbers had to precisely fit.

We happened to be one of those few teams, and we offered a three-player trade. Philadelphia accepted, and the deal was done. We gave up forward Tim Perry, center Andrew Lang, and guard Jeff Hornacek (who made the all-star team for the first time that year), for Charles.

Barkley had established himself as one of the premier players in the game. He also had established himself as one of the most opinionated players, always ready with a comment, quip, or criticism.

To be more specific, Barkley's reputation was that he could be very, very difficult to coach. You'd have a lot of disappointments because of his attitude, disappointments not restricted to the court.

Regardless, no one doubted that Barkley, as the phrase goes, came to play every night. You could count on him to give his all, everything he had, once he hit the court. In truth, he has proven to be one of the most extraordinary guys ever to play the game. Not especially big for someone at the forward position, the plays he could make, on both the offensive and defensive ends of the court, were nothing short of incredible.

We knew what we were doing, we knew who we were getting. When we pulled the trigger on the trade, it was a group call on the part of our basketball staff, which included coach Paul Westphal, director of player personnel Cotton Fitzsimmons, scouts Bryan Colangelo and Dick Van Arsdale, and myself.

We all knew Barkley was a risk, but the potential upside was tremendous.

After the trade was announced, I received a call from Billy Cunningham. Though at that time he was one of the owners of the Miami Heat (along with Lew Schaffel, a friend of mine of long standing), Billy had been the coach of the 76ers, and thus Charles's former coach. He was also my friend.

"I wish we had spoken in advance," Billy said.

I wondered why.

"I'm afraid he's going to come in," Billy said, "and give you a great year, and then he's going to break your heart."

Looking back, I have to say that sounds pretty prophetic.

Cotton had gotten to know Charles pretty well as he made his way to Phoenix. Cotton picked Barkley up at the airport, to the accompaniment of media and fan frenzy.

It was June of 1992, and we had just opened America West Arena. Charles walked into my office and gave me a little hug, thanking me for bringing him to Arizona.

"Charles," I said, "I just want you to know that we're happy to have you. I want you to know that we don't need you to sell one ticket. Every ticket is sold. This is a great facility. You're here to help us put a banner in the rafters."

Charles appeared to truly appreciate my words, and seemed to be very, very committed to winning that championship. And Charles went out and played terrifically. He had a fabulous year. He was the MVP in the league, and the Suns had the best record in basketball.

Accolades were due all around. Paul Westphal, a four-time all-star guard who had taken over the coaching post that year, won more games than any other rookie coach in NBA history. Along with Barkley, guard/forward Dan Majerle was also named to the All-Star team. I was fortunate to be selected as the NBA Executive of the Year for a fourth time.

The Suns had a scare in the first round of the play-offs against Los Angeles. We lost the first two games of the five-game series, and then roared back to take three in a row, the first team in league history to come back from such a daunting deficit.

The Suns next beat the San Antonio Spurs, and then defeated Seattle in a seven-game series. We had fought our way into the Finals.

The Chicago Bulls were waiting. They beat us in the first two games on our own court. We won two of the next three in Chicago. Game Three was a classic. It took three overtimes to settle the issue, during which Majerle tied an NBA Finals record with six three-pointers, and Kevin Johnson set the Finals record with sixty-two minutes played. The Suns eventually won, 129–121.

Despite the team's heroics, the Bulls captured the championship in the sixth game, when Chicago's John Paxson hit a three-pointer to win the game with 3.9 seconds left.

Despite our defeat, it was a fantastic year. The club's performance brought an amazing amount of attention, both nationally and internationally, to the Suns, to Phoenix, and to Arizona. It also provided the opportunity to demonstrate, in the most glorious way, how deeply the fans appreciated the effort put forth by the team, and what sort of an impact the Suns had made on the community.

A parade was schedule for downtown Phoenix a few days after the Finals ended, so the Suns could show their gratitude for the fans' support. However, expectations for the size of the crowd were limited when the day started out hot and soon became much hotter, the hottest of the year to date. The temperature would top out at 114 degrees, the kind of temperature that not only melted asphalt but also the enthusiasm of men and women to stand out on the street for untold hours.

It didn't matter. Nothing seemed to matter, except getting downtown to cheer the Suns. Three hundred thousand people jammed the streets and flooded the hotels and office buildings to see the players and yell and scream and applaud. The police were overwhelmed, but there were no serious problems other than dozens of medical cases that were the result of the heat. Unlike what has happened in some other cities where the people have taken to the streets to celebrate their sports heroes, there were no overturned cars or broken store windows or mini-riots. It was, to use an expression from the Sixties, a love-in.

And that's basically what I told the crowd. "I just want to tell you that I love you!" I shouted from the podium erected near the arena.

Charles Barkley had abandoned any attempt to ride through the mass of humanity in a convertible, retreating on foot to the arena. He now stood before the crowd and proclaimed, "We didn't come here to be runners-up! Wait 'til next year!"

The cheers that greeted his declaration were deafening.

Fans are often fickle, and there is good reason why. After all, sports are entertainment, often a welcome distraction from the hard realities of daily life. When life is hard, when people are struggling, it is fun to forget all the problems for a while and jump on the bandwagon and get behind a winner. Conversely, when the team loses, many fans view the team as merely another expired hope, another aggravation—and in a world filled with aggravations, who needs to take on another, entirely voluntary aggravation?

We had lost, but we had given our fans a great ride and they stayed with us. And our fans would stay with us, through winning seasons and not-such-winning seasons. Because some teams can make that leap from mere sideshow, sometimes winning and sometimes aggravating, they become part of the fabric of the community. Those teams never lose their fans, because those teams mean more than any seasonal record they achieve, even more than any championships they win. Those teams become flesh-and-blood. Those teams become family.

I believe the Suns have become part of the community, even part of the family for many, many people.

It was a great day. One that I will never forget. One that promised many more exciting days to come.

So though we were ultimately denied our goal, though we suffered disappointment, the future looked not merely bright but assured, with more championship runs—and hopefully a championship or two—surely in the offing.

But it was not to be. We lost in the playoffs the next two years to the Houston Rockets, who went on to win back-to-back championships.

I remember a conversation I had with Charles early on in his Phoenix career. I told him I really didn't care about the past, his reputation for being difficult, all that. What was important to me was the relationship that we developed, and how we worked together into the future.

I said that I knew who Charles was, and that he lived his life as he chose. He prided himself on saying and doing exactly what he felt like saying and doing. That was a given. Regardless, I said that he had the unique opportunity to write his own ticket in this town, because the fans were so happy that he was with the Suns, so eager for him to lead and succeed. I told him that he could finish his career in a blaze of glory, and be a positive force for basketball and for Phoenix.

I told him it was all up to him.

Charles chose to have a great first year and then chose to make things more and more unpleasant and difficult. Everything started off on as positive a note as imaginable and over a period of time deteriorated.

The end of the story is very simply this: He gave us a tremendous first year. And he did break my heart.

Contrary to what you might have heard, Charles was not simply dealt to another team. He wanted to leave, decided to leave, and we accommodated him. And so Charles Barkley left Phoenix for what he hoped would be greener pastures in Houston.

Among others, here's one lesson I learned: Next time, I'll call Billy before I make a really big trade.

It's one small, specific lesson that probably won't be of much use to *you*.

My exposure in the pro ranks has primarily been to basketball players. I've had some experience with hockey players, and a little with football players, and now, with the Diamondbacks, I'm getting to know baseball players.

My early look at baseball is encouraging. I see athletes who overwhelmingly have a solid work ethic, who are totally committed to their game. The star syndrome, the Hollywood attitude, hasn't taken hold to the extent that it has in the NBA.

The possible reasons are many. First and foremost, perhaps the baseball season, the longest season of the four major team sports, is just too long and too grueling for most players to adopt difficult attitudes and still maintain their day in, day out, edge.

However baseball has evolved, there is no doubt that the situation is not the same in the NBA. For the most part, we have a lot of great athletes who are also great guys. There are some exceptions. These players are often members of what you could call the new breed, young men who have been stars since their schoolyard or college days, and land in the NBA with exorbitant demands to match their exorbitant contracts.

Basketball is different from baseball in so many ways, ways that are significant to the celebrity status of the athletes. Basketball not only has fewer players engaged in the action at any one time, but basketball players are also more continually involved in the action than in baseball. In other words, aside from the pitcher, the audience generally focuses on each player mainly when he's at bat. In basketball, all players are always in the mix, thus giving the fans more of a chance to familiarize themselves with the player, from talent to attitude—not to mention with their bodies, given their relatively revealing out-fits and the proximity of the court to the seats.

All that renders basketball players easier to recognize and thus easier to make famous.

Of course, there's more to it than that. Baseball players are different from their basketball counterparts in other ways as well. Baseball players rarely jump from school to stardom and untold riches. They labor in the minors, traveling from town to town by perhaps the least glamorous means of trans-portation known to modern man—by bus. They work long and hard, unheralded and unpampered. They have neither the time nor the means to become too spoiled, too soon.

Back to basketball, I don't know if we could have done anything differently, let alone better. We've brought a league that was a mom-and-pop business to a new maturity, and it's fared extremely well in a very competitive business atmo-sphere.

Now that the NBA has evolved as a major player and

leader in professional sports, and the sports industry is such a vital part of the larger entertainment industry, that system can produce athletes who have been affected, for better or worse, as they succeed and earn more and more money and act in movies, perform on records, date supermodels, and become part and parcel of the American celebrity machine.

Every sport, including baseball, has its own set of problems to deal with, including the conduct of its players, and a lot of those problems revolve around money, with regard to the players, with regard to the owners.

I wouldn't dare ascribe all the problems of the sports industry to the players. Ownership and management must certainly accept part of the responsibility with their relationships with both players and fans. Ownership and management should never lose sight of the fact that communicating with both players and fans is of the utmost importance. Our organization, same as the overwhelming majority of organizations in our industry, has treated fans with unconditional respect, because we appreciate that the fans are our very lifeblood.

Nevertheless, I will tell you categorically that as the stakes have increased in sports, and more opportunities have popped up for people in every segment of the industry to bend the rules, to take shortcuts, the ethics of the business have deteriorated. The business seemed not only more innocent in its earlier days but also more ethical.

Maybe it wasn't. Maybe *I* was more innocent, and just didn't see the truth. I don't think so. My reasoning is fairly simple and entirely personal: Back then, we could compete in the front offices, we could beat each other's brains out, and then go out together and have a beer afterward. That's what I saw. And I miss it.

We live in a much more permissive society than we did thirty years ago, when people were more prone to do the right thing, both inside the business world and out. Thirty years ago, there weren't any books about business ethics. None that I knew about. Today, business books explaining ethics are all over the place. Why? Because today it's a problem, a big problem, that has created its own self-help, advice-strewn, book category.

Anyone who has been in the sports business aspires to win a championship. Yet there have been some terrific players who have enjoyed careers of which they can be most proud and have never experienced that victory, that moment, that joy. In fact, they have never had the opportunity to get close to that experience. Likewise, there are coaches and general managers who are in the same unenviable position.

On the other hand, other players—untried rookies— have stepped into a winning situation and been swept along to sip the champagne of a championship year.

That's the way the ball bounces. It may be in the stars and then again, it may not be. My attitude, after all these years of working and trying, is this: If you have a team that you have built and trained and now has a legitimate chance, the rest of it is out of your control.

So the measuring stick for the Suns is that they possess the third- or fourth-best record in the history of the NBA. And we've made all these play-off appearances, we've won all these western conference titles, and we've been to the Finals. And we've come close.

And I'm thankful for all those regular season and play-off victories. It's been terrific and a great run. But . . . Still . . . We're missing that elusive championship ring. And I'm hopeful that someday I might enjoy it.

The thrill of the chase is important. Every year you hear people talking about trades, and hope springs eternal. Most of the time, though, in professional sports, in professional leagues, the truth is the same teams win and the same teams lose, again and again. The excitement is the challenge of redoing a ball team, of rebuilding, of restructuring. And I've gone through maybe three cycles of redoing and rebuilding and restructuring, of putting together a group and taking a run, and failing, and starting again.

That's why I wear that Rattlers ring. They've done it. Twice. And I always wear their ring. The franchise's triumph has been an exciting gift.

C H A P T E R   S I X

Thinking Baseball

I HAD BEEN in the baseball business a couple of years (though still before the Arizona Diamondbacks had taken the field for the first time), when the *Rocky Mountain News* asked Bowie Kuhn and me to each write a column answering the question, Is corporate ownership good for baseball? Bowie, the commissioner of Major League Baseball from 1969 to 1984, supported the negative position, while I championed the affirmative.

The former commissioner argued that the integrity of the game demanded a reverence for its history and traditions, to a degree unique among sports. Baseball fans were the most conservative of fans, and their love of baseball's remarkably rich past obligated the game's caretakers to not carelessly fiddle with the rules and manners of the sport in the name of profit.

Thus, it was only logical to conclude that individual owners, in the business for the love of the game, were more apt to choose tradition over balance sheets, than a faceless, bloodless corporation in the game for the love of business. Wrote Kuhn:

I'm not criticizing corporate ownership, but more often than not, corporate owners are driven more by the profit motive.

For instance, to them, interleague play is good because it means we can sell more widgets, not necessarily because it's good for the fans.

What we're going to see if corporate ownership continues to grow is that baseball will be converted into a new kind of game. It will be highly successful, and it will draw numbers in the future that you can scarcely imagine today. It will be internationalized, and the marketing will be intense. But somewhere down the line, there may be a fatal flaw. The traditional values may be put aside, and I see signs of that already.

It was not easy to argue with someone who had spent so many years in MLB's top job. Bowie certainly knew his game, the game he loved and served.

Still, I viewed professional baseball and its future through my own perspective, based on my own observations and experience. I entitled my rejoinder, "Mom-and-Pop Era Is Over," and tried to get to the essential point as succinctly as I could:

First, there is a tremendous investment needed to buy in. Second, there is tremendous cost, in terms of operating and other commitments, such as facilities, just to be in the business today. These things make it almost beyond the means of any individual.

The Arizona Diamondbacks have invested $325 million in this expansion franchise: $155 million as it relates to franchise cost—the $130 million expansion fee plus $25 million in future television revenue that we're not going to get—plus $60 million start-up costs and $110 million in the ballpark.

All that is kind of kind of pricey for any individual. What we see are corporate partnerships. The way we're constructed is that almost every corporation in Arizona is a limited partner with me.

You see conglomerates, like those in the cable-television industries, making purchases for various reasons but, first and foremost, for programming. So we see these conglomerates like Rupert Murdoch and Ted Turner. You see people who recognize professional sports as much more than sport. They're part of the entertainment world, and it's just another piece of the puzzle. . . .

With his knowledge and love of the game, Bowie made a compelling case, though perhaps based more on emotion than facts. In contrast, I think I had the facts on my side. The numbers and statistics were neither nostalgic nor lovely, but they were what they were, and nothing could change their stark reality. And the numbers and statistics computed to an unalterable conclusion: Only by assembling enormous financial forces and marketing baseball's best features in an economically viable package could America's National Pastime successfully compete with other exciting major league sports.

For somebody who had once been a baseball prospect, I had fallen pretty far from this important part of my roots. I had gotten involved with the NBA more than three decades before, and basketball had consumed my professional life. Oh, I still followed baseball, but only as a casual fan. I wasn't around it—after all, we didn't have a team in Phoenix—and I certainly wasn't involved in any business way.

However, being in professional sports, I naturally followed how other leagues were doing. Baseball, as well as other major league sports, has had more than its share of troubles, starting with the Curt Flood case in 1970, and going through all the labor problems, culminating with the strike in the middle of the 1994 season, an absolutely ruinous strike from which baseball is just beginning to recover.

I've already recounted how I attended a game in Wrigley back in 1993, in the midst of a Suns play-off series with the Bulls, and how I thought about how great it would be to see something like this in Phoenix. To see a wonderful ballpark, filled with people, watching Arizona's own team.

It was a thrilling notion, but it came and went in a moment, and I returned to my own reality. But the play-offs ended, and two weeks later I was visited in my office on a hot summer day by Jim Bruner, of the Maricopa County Board of Supervisors, and Joe Garagiola, Jr., an attorney in town.

These two men wanted to talk about bringing Major League Baseball to Phoenix. They had neither arrived at this conclusion casually nor were they entirely powerless to effect the course of such an undertaking. The board of supervisors is the most powerful government body overseeing the political and economic affairs of Maricopa County, which encompasses the city of Phoenix, the neighboring cities and towns, and the outlying rural area. That adds up to three million people living in a county the size of New Jersey. Jim Bruner was one of five elected supervisors.

Joe Garagiola Jr. was the son of the renowned former catcher of the same name. He had also worked as general counsel and assistant to the president of the New York Yankees. After moving to Phoenix, he had concentrated on sports law and got involved in a series of commissions and foundations that were dedicated to fostering the development of sports in Arizona.

Others had tried to entice MLB to locate a franchise in Phoenix. For one reason or another, those efforts had always fallen short. The money for the fee and the team wasn't in place; the business community wasn't vigorously supporting the effort; the political leadership wasn't effectively supporting the effort; no adequate stadium existed in the city; no adequate stadium was under construction.

To make matters more difficult, other cities and states were vastly more committed and more prepared to acquire major league franchises. That was why Colorado and Florida beat out Arizona for the new expansion clubs in 1990.

For a time, it appeared that MLB was done expanding at least for the rest of the century. Then, rather surprisingly, the media reported that professional baseball was interested in adding a couple of more teams. Tampa–St. Petersburg was definitely in the running, and, so went the rumor, so was Phoenix. But Phoenix was hardly a shoo-in—the money had to be in the bank for both a team and a new stadium, the management had to be impressive, every "t" had to be crossed and every "i" dotted.

There was no room for mistakes, no room for stumbling. Individuals and groups representing Phoenix had done enough of that, and the result was that although new franchises were granted from the east to the west, no MLB club called Phoenix home.

This could prove to be Phoenix's last chance for perhaps decades to come to secure a baseball franchise, because no one really knew what MLB's long-terms plans were.

Bruner and Garagiola sat in my office for well over an hour and explained the entire situation, as they saw it. In their joint opinion, I was the guy who could make it happen, who could lead a successful effort to win a franchise for Arizona.

My initial reaction was not particularly positive. I wasn't an expert, but I had considered the state of baseball long enough to believe that the game faced many tough problems, from restructuring the relationship between players and owners, to competing with other pro leagues which were doing better jobs of promotion and marketing, to revitalizing and expanding the fan base for MLB, problem after problem, issue after issue.

My visitors reminded me of the tax incentive that had

been put on the books by the state legislature, an incentive that would guarantee that a stadium would be built, utilizing taxpayer funds.

Though many people will find this hard to believe—and others will simply refuse to believe it, no matter what—I couldn't recall anything about any tax.

Bruner and Garagiola explained the matter to me. A couple of years before, a legislator who also happened to be a diehard baseball fan had examined the issue of MLB's reluctance to settle in Phoenix in detail. He had arrived at the conclusion that nothing would ever change until the mechanism for ensuring the construction of a new stadium—a stadium worthy of a major league franchise—was in place.

This was not an inconsequential point. A modern stadium, an enticing venue to attract fans, was central to any franchise's ability to be competitive, by helping it recoup its investment and then earn a profit. A modern stadium was also enormously expensive and increasingly difficult to fund, out of reach of private investors, reliant upon government intervention and assistance.

That diehard fan was Chris Herstam, and he was the Republican majority whip of the Arizona House of Representatives. Preparing to retire from electoral politics, he offered a bill which basically authorized the Maricopa County Board of Supervisors to formally act as a county stadium district, with the authority to levy a quarter-cent sales tax to raise funds to assist in building a stadium.

There were a few other provisions. The stadium would have to be completely new, not a renovated venue, and it would have to be devoted to baseball, and not constructed as a multi-use stadium offering baseball one season, football the next.

The bill was a clever device. In essence, its existence opened the door to MLB. If a franchise was awarded to Phoenix, the county could authorize a bill that would fund a stadium. Not a dime of public money had to be spent, not an ounce of energy wasted, until a team was pledged to Phoenix.

This arrangement was quite different from the situation in Tampa, where a stadium had been built with taxpayer money in the hope that it would propel the baseball powers to award the city a team. The team had not been forthcoming, and the stadium stayed empty, year after year, a gigantic, aging white elephant.

Republican Herstam's bill was supported by Democrat governor Rose Mofford. The bill passed rather handily, thirty-five to twenty in the Arizona House, and eighteen to ten in the Senate.

Many myths have sprung up around Chris Herstam's bill. Some politicians have alleged, in interviews and speeches years after the vote, that they didn't know what they were voting for, that the bill was somehow sneaked into law past their watchful eyes, that the dirty deed was accomplished in the middle of a black, forbidding night.

Some journalists have abetted these politicians by giving credence to these allegations. To take just one example: HBO's "Inside Sports," the cable network's sports magazine news series, proclaimed in a story about the building of Bank One Ballpark that added to this cacophony of nonsense by stating that the measure was passed "in the dead of night." HBO made this assertion without offering any evidence or supporting material.

HBO was sloppy and biased and flat-out wrong. HBO clearly wanted a scandalous story, and it presented one, even if the facts didn't come close to supporting their allegations.

Why did so many politicians deny their positions and their votes, changing their tune in such a transparent, even embarrassing manner? And their denials are transparent and embarrassing, the former because the facts are so easy to check, and the latter because what kind of mature, responsible legislator loudly proclaims that they voted for something and then later claims they didn't understand it?

They denied it because the conception of a new stadium, so enticing at the beginning, before Phoenix had a team, clashed with the reality of using taxpayer money to actually fulfill this vision. And that clash resulted in many citizens rising in anger over taxes being collected for the stadium, and some of the media rising to exploit this issue. And that anger and that exploitation was twisted and pushed and provoked to irrational heights, causing the further spread of more disinformation and anger.

This is a short, interesting tale for anyone working to build or produce something that will have a public impact on society, because it is also a cautionary tale of how the intersection between business and government and the media really operates.

You see, it begins with politics. Chris Herstam had a grand notion, and enough legislators agreed to pass his bill. It didn't allocate the expenditure of any funds, but it granted the right to the Maricopa County governing board to levy a tax if and when the county desired to help construct a stadium for a professional baseball team. The bill was restricted to Maricopa County, because only Maricopa, encompassing Phoenix, the capital and largest city in Arizona, held the potential in the Grand Canyon State to host a MLB franchise.

So now the legislation was in place. You might have noticed that I have yet to mention my role in all this. The reason for that is simple: I did not have a role. I had nothing to do with Herstam's measure, or the legislature's approval of the bill. I was not involved in baseball and had no plans to become involved. The year was 1990. I was pretty much between my purchase of the Suns following the drug scandal of 1986–87, and the opening of America West Arena in 1992. We were working hard to reestablish the good name of the franchise in the public's eyes, while ensuring that the new arena would set a standard for the entire NBA to follow. Everything, as usual, was in flux, complicated, and undecided.

In other words, I was very, very busy. The machinations of the state legislature regarding a nonexistent stadium for a nonexistent franchise—a franchise which others in business and government were assiduously pursuing—was not at the top of my concerns.

Now several years had passed. The Suns were back on track. America West Arena was flourishing. And still there was no baseball team in Arizona.

I didn't really know if I was interested. More precisely, my emotions were engaged, but whether the prospects for baseball, both in Phoenix and throughout the country, warranted the sort of immense effort it would require to bring a team home was unclear. I needed to think about if I could marshal the local forces, in government and business, required to pull off the undertaking. I needed to think about what it would require from the organization and from me personally.

I would not go into this with any illusions. It would be a long, hard struggle to win and create a major league franchise. I needed to think about whether I really wanted to do this, if this task was worth what it would take, if it was worth it to Phoenix, to Arizona, and to me.

I don't mean to sound like this was entirely altruistic. Obviously, if the team succeeded, so would I. If the team made money, so would I. And there was nothing wrong with that, that was why people worked and created and built and sweated and sacrificed—to earn that reward.

But other rewards were also important. To put it bluntly, I already ran an exciting, successful franchise, as well as some ancillary smaller teams and businesses, too. I wasn't just starting out in life. I didn't need to find myself a job.

But then, even if I didn't need a job, we all need challenges. Building a baseball franchise, and all that could go along with that, was a considerable challenge. I had no doubt that a team could bring remarkable benefits to Phoenix and Arizona, some immediate and apparent, and others that no one could yet fully anticipate.

It is only fair and reasonable to note that this was not a risk-free situation for our organization. Time constraints existed that demanded action, specifically the time constraints with the stadium tax. The taxing mechanism that the state legislature had passed was not an open-ended measure—in other words, if the Maricopa Country board of supervisors didn't implement the measure by a certain date, the measure would expire and the county would no longer have the right to execute any tax.

It was clear that we would have to go forward with attempting to secure the franchise, and also prepare to build a stadium before the county decided upon the fate of any tax. This translated into the Phoenix Suns organization having to spend about $3 million to be in position to not only gain the MLB franchise, but also to have the stadium ready to go, if and when MLB granted the team, and if and when the county passed the tax.

Here was a unique situation: one professional sports franchise putting up a considerable sum at risk to bring another professional sports franchise to town.

As I stated, here was a situation worth noting.

Other factors weighed heavily as we considered what to do. In addition to the millions already mentioned at risk before anything was decided, once we got the franchise, the costs would immediately and dramatically escalate. The price of an expansion franchise, including entry fee, and start-up and ongoing expenses, was sure to be sky-high. The stadium presented its own special set of problems. Stadiums took a long time to build, and they took a longer time to recoup their investments. They had to be built before any team could play, before any fans could cheer, before any restaurants or hotels could open nearby, before any of the other business opportunities could develop. They were phenomenally expensive and getting more so each day. The cost of building both a team and a stadium was far beyond my reach, and the reach of any group I could put together.

And without the guarantee of a new stadium, with luxury boxes and concessions and a multitude of other attractions, all of which rendered it possible to recoup the initial expense of construction, there could be no major league team in Arizona.

It was far from uncommon for municipalities and states

to partially or completely subsidize new stadiums. Denver, our neighbor to the north, which had become an MLB town in the last expansion, had garnered a team and then invested in a terrific facility. In return for the stadium, the Rockies' ownership sold the naming rights to Coors Brewing Company for a very handsome sum. At the same time, the Rockies would occupy the building rent-free for five years, a token amount after that, while keeping all the revenue from luxury boxes, concessions, parking, and advertising. The franchise would also keep all moneys derived from nonbaseball activities, such as concerts and meetings.

It would seem apparent that the Rockies had made an exceptionally advantageous deal with Denver. Nonetheless, the deal had proven well worth the investment to Denver, for Coors Field had led to the revitalization of the downtown area, which had been virtually moribund prior to the arrival of baseball.

In our own valley, taxes and city expenditures had helped pay for new stadiums for Cactus League teams. New venues had become a necessity, if Arizona was going to keep MLB clubs in the state for spring training. So Maricopa County and the city of Peoria, in the northwest section of the valley, had dropped $32 million into a fine new spring training stadium for the Seattle Mariners and the San Diego Padres. Scottsdale, Mesa, Phoenix, and Tucson invested another $200 million in new ballparks, in order to keep franchises from moving to Florida, which was attempting to woo all of baseball to join its Grapefruit League.

These facilities were paid for and built with taxpayer dollars, an allocation that sparked no widespread protests, no loud objections. Keeping spring training in Arizona, and the hundreds of millions of dollars it annually brought to the valley, was an obviously sound economic decision.

According to the Cactus League Baseball Association, total attendance for the 1998 Cactus League season was over 900,000, of whom 58 percent were visitors from other states who spent an average of 5.4 nights in Arizona, at an average cost of $200 per day. Of these visitors, a survey revealed that 94 percent said that spring training played a role in their decision to journey to Phoenix and/or Tucson, while fully 80 percent declared that it was the "primary/major" reason for their sojourn in the Grand Canyon State.

Adding up the numbers, total direct spending was more than $108 million—and we're talking about a season that lasts just one month.

Thus, it only made sense to many people that spending some money to bring a big league franchise to Phoenix would also garner wide public support.

It was not to be. A legend arose, stoked by antitax activists and some opportunists in politics and the media, that this deal was somehow different, in some way dark and disquieting. The politicians had to be in on it, because they passed the bill—except those who had been somehow duped—and a semisinister conspiracy must have been working, so neither the media nor the public were alerted to the ongoing shenanigans.

And, so this line of reasoning naturally continued, this conspiracy required—demanded—a star conspirator. Because, in the popular culture, a conspiracy couldn't exist without a central figure—from Sherlock Holmes's nemesis, Professor Moriarity; to Ian Fleming's roll call of villains, including Goldfinger and Dr. No and SMERSH's Number 1; to Cancer Man in the *X Files*—silently, almost magically, manipulating events from behind the scenes, leaving nary a fingerprint, invisible to all except the initiated.

Conspiracies are easy to believe in and strangely comforting to many people. They help explain a frequently confusing, frightening, frustrating world to those who seek explanation, without actually explaining anything.

In this manner, the events that led up to the tax couldn't have simply been the result of one legislator having a notion, convincing others that it made sense, including a couple of people who understood how to best employ the tax to achieve the desired result—an MLB franchise—and pressing hard to accomplish it, recruiting me in the process.

And nobody started objecting until talk of obtaining the franchise, and all that it required, was gathering steam, coming closer to reality. And then it was difficult to turn back the clock, to envision how we could get a team without the money that the tax would provide.

No, instead, it was easier for some to believe that I had wanted a team, that I therefore got the legislature to do my bidding, and that I was now poised to take advantage of the tax by having a stadium built on my behalf.

The only problem was, it just wasn't anywhere close to reality.

Many people wanted MLB baseball to come to Arizona, and not only during spring training. Some of those people—like Joe Garagiola and Jim Bruner, as well as scores of others—had labored for years, trying to figure out a way to make the dream a reality, trying and failing, and trying and failing again. Now Herstam had opened a door for them, and they rushed through, ready to give it another go. They found me, and I put the money together, realizing that this was possible only because the mechanism for constructing a terrific, modern stadium was in place.

It's not as exciting a story as a conspiracy, but it does have the virtue of being true.

There are many facts that have been conveniently neglected by the critics of this process. One example: Some have claimed that the state bill resulted in a de facto, underhanded tax authorization, practically propelling the board of supervisors towards the implementing the tax. Wrong. The law authorizing the Maricopa County Board of Supervisors to exact the tax did not forbid the board from putting the measure to a vote of the county. The members of the board chose not to go this route, relying on their own judgment to decide what to do. The state legislature did not offer an opinion one way or the other.

Hence, first the state legislators decided what was in the best interests of the state and their constituents. Then the county board of supervisors decided what was in the best interests of the county and their constituents. Then, and only then, still without the absolute assurance that the tax would be implemented and collected, I decided what was in the best interests of my organization and my community.

I feel compelled to talk about this at some length because of the tremendous and often unrelenting heat I've taken on this issue. I did not ask for the tax; I did not campaign for the tax; but I certainly embraced the tax as the only road to securing major league baseball in Phoenix.

I am a businessman. I seek out opportunities to expand my business. This was an opportunity.

I am a concerned citizen. I seek out opportunities to make my community a more prosperous, more stimulating, more interesting place to live. This was an opportunity.

Those twin interests, twin motivations, made going after a major league franchise the right decision.

However, in today's business climate, anyone stepping into the public arena, working in a business that directly has an impact upon the public, interacts with government, or interests the media, must anticipate the possibility of a sudden, adverse reaction from the public, the government and/or the media—warranted or not.

I had experienced the displeasure of the public and the media before, during the Suns scandal. As unpleasant as that had been, it was small change compared to the uproar over the stadium tax. I found, and continue to find, one particular aspect of this entire episode especially galling. I have built a career upon being honest and forthright, on, simply stated, telling the truth. In 1998, *Sports Illustrated* sought to rank the best and worst NBA front-office bosses by polling basketball executives and agents. Jerry West, the vice president of the Lakers, justly received the number one spot. I was gratified to come in tied for second, a rating that was accompanied by the comment: "His word is gold. One of the few."

It took years in the business to earn that reputation. To have it tarnished by unfounded rumor and innuendo has been deeply upsetting.

The amount, incidentally, that the supervisors agreed upon was a quarter-cent sales tax, in operation only until $238 million was raised. That taxing cap was absolute. No matter how much the stadium costs rose—and the costs rose quite a bit—$238 million was all the county would contribute.

The franchise would receive a $15 million loan from the county, which, as with any loan, would have to be repaid. Based on the first estimate of the construction costs, which were placed at some $279 million, we would have been on the hook for $41 million. In my mind, virtually from the start, I thought the construction would end up costing around $300 million, so I knew we would have to contribute roughly $50 million.

As the actual stadium cost rose, and rose, the Diamondbacks would pick up the additional tab, eventually to the tune of $100 million. The tax itself was collected in only two and half years, six months ahead of projections. Once it was collected, the tax was over. Unlike so many other taxes, the county could not keep collecting the tax and use the proceeds for purposes different from its original intent. This unambiguous, definite end to the tax, a fairly unusual stipulation in taxing measures, is called the "Sunset Provision."

In January 1994, a local polling firm asked the citizenry if it supported the stadium tax. Given the opportunity, 59 percent of valley residents said they would vote against it, 30 percent favored it, and 11 percent had no opinion. Party affiliation made no difference in an individual's stance, the results splitting evenly along party lines. Perhaps the board should have taken the bill to the people for a vote. Perhaps they did the right thing by accepting their responsibility as elected officials and deciding among themselves. I cannot say for sure either way. That was not my call to make, and no one asked my opinion.

Eventually, as the community saw the stadium rising from the ground, was invited to tour the finished product, and then experienced the excitement of the action, either in person or through television, as well as the action of the bars and restaurants springing up around the stadium, it is my anecdotal experience that opinion turned more than a bit about the value of implementing the tax and erecting the building.

Careers were won and lost because of the tax. Jim Bruner, who had done so much to bring baseball to Phoenix, badly lost his bid to gain the Republican nomination for a seat in the U.S. Congress. This was a race that, before the tax controversy, he had been heavily favored to win. Another supervisor, Ed King, failed to win the Republican renomination to the Maricopa County board.

The investment tax will be repaid many times over, and the county will reap profit for years to come. The investment in the stadium is already proving a great success.

With the first season completed, the numbers are in. Not long ago, The Downtown Phoenix Partnership hired independent experts to compile and evaluate the 1998 data, and compare the facts with our economic estimates from the feasibility study we conducted back in 1993 when we supported the public's investment in downtown. Though feasibility studies are a common enough tactic to build backing for a project, rarely do the supporters of that study return to reveal whether the promises actually bore any fruit for the community.

In the case of Bank One Ballpark, we discovered that the reality far exceeded the hopes in every category. To begin, our estimate was that 3,101 jobs would be created, directly or indirectly, during the construction phase of the endeavor. In fact, the construction of the stadium produced exactly 4,626 new jobs.

Once construction was done, it was expected that 340 individuals would find work inside the stadium. That figure was off by more than half, as 738 positions needed filling. But that's only the tip of the iceberg; in total, directly and indirectly, 4,110 new jobs now exist owing to stadium operations.

In 1993, direct revenues inside the stadium were projected at $81.9 million, while those revenues were actually $129 million. Similarly, spending outside the stadium was more than anticipated—$38.1 million versus $34.5 million—leaving the projection of the total impact of stadium operations of $221.2 million woefully behind the actual output of $319.5 million.

The revenue streams are in a state of evolution. For example, the city of Phoenix recorded that restaurant sales, just from March through June, increased by $14.7 million over the same period for the previous year. At the same time, 94 percent of that increase was directly accountable to BOB and its related restaurants. Experience with new ballparks and venues has demonstrated that it takes time for people to spread out beyond the immediate area of the venue, after they have sampled the ballpark's fare and wares, and after they have familiarized themselves with parking and the area, and begin to more widely patronize the neighborhood's other establishments, from restaurants to parks, museums to movies, and so on.

Thus, with time, it is only logical to conclude that the figures will continue to increase, and the benefits spread more widely throughout the community.

Leaving the stadium, let's shift back to the issue of the franchise itself, and Bruner and Garagiola's visit to my office. When they were finished, I said I'd have to consider the idea before getting back to them. I said they'd hear from me after Labor Day.

I began conducting my own investigation of the franchise. I read some of the literature on baseball, learning about the financial state of the game, the dynamics of its structure, and the hopes and ideas underlying its history and future.

I also spoke to people in baseball, people like Jerry Reinsdorf, my old friend and the owner of both the Chicago Bulls and the Chicago White Sox; and Bud Selig, another friend, the owner of the Milwaukee Brewers and at that time the acting commissioner of MLB, subsequently named full-time commissioner. I also spoke with Don Fehr, the head of the players' union.

I was literally attempting to educate myself as to why baseball was in the less-than-stellar shape it currently found itself. I studied the twenty-five year history of collective bargaining, which was at the core of baseball's problems. I discovered that baseball's recent past resembled a pendulum: prior to the landmark Curt Flood case, players were held in virtual economic bondage. Essentially, for the entire duration of their careers, they were the property of their team, which held the absolute right as to the disposition of each and every one of their players—whether to keep or trade or send them down to the minors. In other words, when a player signed a pro contract, it was for life. The mechanism in every player's contract that spelled out this contractual arrangement was called the reserve clause.

In 1970, all-star outfielder Curt Flood of the St. Louis Cardinals sued for the right to determine his own future, at least to some degree. The case went all the way to the Supreme Court. Though Flood lost, and the reserve clause remained in effect, his case hastened the unraveling of the owners' absolute hold on the players. In 1972, a thirteen-day strike by the players delayed the opening of the season, and three years later, arbitrator Peter Seitz ruled in the Messersmith-McNally case that the players had the right to establish a claim to free agency by playing out their option years without a signed contract. Thus, step by step, the players were gaining their freedom. This process was accelerated as the owners made mistake after mistake in collective bargaining for the next two and half decades.

The pendulum, which had started all the way over on the owners' side, had swung in the other direction in dramatic fashion, eventually flipping over to the players' side as completely as it had previously been on the owners'. Now the players were in charge, and they were reaping huge rewards, signing increasingly large contracts, shifting teams as they saw fit.

Not surprisingly, the owners didn't like it. The owners said, in effect, Hey, fellows, the system isn't working. We have to change things.

Again, not too surprisingly, the players had an opposite point of view. No, they replied, it took us all this time to get you where we have you. We're not interested in sending that pendulum back your way again.

This tug-of-war between labor and management had led down a road that was frequently contentious and ugly. This union-ownership struggle caused some bitterness among the fans, caused many of them to turn away from the game altogether. The damage done to the game was not easily repaired and was made worse many times over by the events of 1994. Disappointment turned to disgust during that strike-interrupted season, when an exciting season, filled with thrilling pennant races and outstanding individual performances, was abruptly cut short by the athletes themselves. Hitler and World War II couldn't stop the World Series, but the players and owners could, and for the first time since 1904, the series was canceled. This argument between "millionaires and billionaires," as a popular phrase had it, endeared neither the players nor the owners to a public utterly disinterested in either side's grievances.

Simply put, it was difficult for fans (and many in the game as well) to comprehend why successful owners and well-paid athletes couldn't meet at the bargaining table and come to an agreement that was beneficial for their own interests, and good for the game.

Nor, finally, and perhaps most crucially, was baseball an essential service. Sports was entertainment, nothing more, nothing less; if baseball went on strike, people could still eat and get medical care and work and play, and lead perfectly full, happy lives. If baseball—not the game of baseball, but the business of professional baseball—was going to cause people aggravation, then people would turn away from the game and discover new outlets for their time and money and affection.

The strike was eventually settled, and the following year Major League Baseball returned to the action on the field, instead of in the courtroom. The fans hadn't rushed back to the bleachers and boxes, and attendance remained down, far below prestrike levels. Slowly, however, the great game began to lure the fans back. The 1998 season, with two new teams, incredible performances by teams like the Yankees, and individuals like Mark McGwire and Sammy Sosa, the resurgence in fan interest has swelled to tremendous proportions, and baseball is really, finally coming back.

Of course, baseball's revival was still in the future when I was first presented with the option of getting in the business. After considering baseball from as many angles as possible, my read on the situation was that the game's problems might have bottomed out. Baseball's financial pendulum appeared to be set somewhere in the middle of the two sides, both stunned by the public's dismissive response to their internal warring. At the same time, though very slowly, baseball was staging a comeback, as the game's native appeal, the heroics of its athletes, and fierce competition between teams, lured more and more fans back to the stands.

By the end of the summer, I felt comfortable in saying that if we could acquire a franchise, we could be successful. As much as anything else, I based this feeling on our organization's track record, and our ability to implement the same formula, the same techniques and tactics, again.

Step one was raising the equity necessary to buy the franchise. Step two was believing in the strength of our marketplace. A key part of calculating that market was adding up the number of television households in the valley and determining whether that total represented sufficient homes to ensure a substantial advertising base.

Step three was ascertaining our ability to appeal to that market. I had no doubt that we could maximize this opportunity, based upon our organization's performance with other sports.

Taking all those steps together, this confluence of elements, I felt we had a great chance to succeed. We could handle our part of the equation. Having reached that conclusion, the focus now shifted to what would prove the more intriguing question: What was Major League Baseball, as an industry, going to do? Would the owners offer Phoenix a franchise, and on what terms? Would they welcome us to the game?

Those few questions might be overstating the drama of the issue. I had talked to enough people to know that MLB wanted Phoenix as much Phoenix wanted MLB. Otherwise, I wouldn't have gone about the process of putting together a game plan, of preparing to build and run a new franchise.

I set about the task of raising the money. I contacted many of the same people and corporations that had invested in the Suns. When looking for money, it only makes sense to go back to those with whom you have happily and profitably already done business. Those who had invested with me in the Suns when I had first gotten control of the team had seen their money returned in four years, and is now worth six times over that initial investment.

I employed the same legal structure I had used for the

Suns. I formed a limited partnership, in which investors could purchase a unit. Thirty units were available, at $5 million each. I went back to John Teets at the Viad Corporation. Viad bought two units, thus contributing $10 million to the baseball war chest. Later, Viad would purchase one more unit. (Viad was the result of Dial splitting into two components. Dial would keep the consumer products, while Viad would retain the investment in the Suns and Diamondbacks, and also keep the Restaura business.)

Selling all the units, as we eventually did, would mean that we had raised $150 million.

America West Airlines, Bank America, Wells Fargo, Arizona Public Service, Bank One, Circle K, Finova, Phelps Dodge, and a myriad of other companies and individuals purchased one unit each.

Individuals brought along other individuals to the table. Especially noteworthy: Jimmy Walker, a close friend and top insurance expert and executive who frequently dealt with sports and entertainment types, was responsible for a number of people investing, as were my long-time business partners Mel Schultz and Eddie Lynch.

I cannot stress how different an experience it was raising money this time around, as compared to my trials and tribulations with the Suns. One example: I was introduced to a fellow named Dale Jensen. Dale had been employed by a bank back in his hometown of Lincoln, Nebraska. In his spare time, working out of his garage, Dale and another bank employee had come up with an ingenious banking software program. They had offered it to the bank, but the bank had rejected their program. Dale and his friend had decided to go into business for themselves, selling their software. Not too many years thereafter, they had sold their little start-up business for about $500 million.

Dale had moved to Scottsdale, and started to involve himself in the community. To further that aim, he was looking to invest in a few local businesses. As an avid sports fan, the

Diamondbacks looked like an intriguing place to park some money.

We met in my office. Dale said he had heard good things about me and how I did business from this one and that, and he wanted to invest. In fact, he had $20 million looking for a new home.

To cut to the chase, I didn't accept his offer on that day. I said I liked to do business with people I knew, and I needed to get to know him better before I accepted his proposal. Over some time, Dale and I became better acquainted, and I soon learned that he was a terrific person, who would surely make a terrific partner. I offered Dale two units in the team. I was also able to offer a $3 million piece of the Suns that had suddenly become available. Dale accepted both propositions. I didn't offer him more than two units because I had more potential investors than units on the books, and I wanted to make sure everybody who wanted to had the opportunity to buy into the franchise.

There had been a time, not very long before, when I would have walked across the desert barefoot to find an investor with Dale's kind of money, and his kind of faith in our plans and our ability to execute those plans. I had almost lost the Suns because it was no easy task to convince investors that we could make a long-term success of this basketball team, a team that had already enjoyed great triumphs, including a trip to the NBA Finals. Now corporations and people were rushing forward with their checkbooks, eager to invest in a team that didn't exist, that had no record, that had no name, in fact.

What a difference a decade makes.

All in all, we raised a lot of money, assuming that the expansion fee required by MLB would be in the $115–125 million range. Just a few years before, Colorado and Florida had each put up $95 million for their teams. That was a lot of money, but inflation was extraordinary when it came to sports, and those figures were no longer operative.

Of course, I did not base that figure simply on inflation. I spent considerable time before we bid for the team visiting with people in baseball. I traveled to their ballparks, I watched their games, I sat in their offices.

In the wake of my journeys and meetings, I believed that I had a pretty good feel—as did Vincent Naimoli and his group in Tampa, which was also bidding for a team for their state—as to where we thought the expansion fee price would land.

In fact, it was more than a belief. It was a firm conviction based upon what I was led to believe by those who would vote and decide.

The owners' meeting in early March 1995 would decide whether the groups from Arizona and Florida would receive franchises. I flew to Palm Beach with some of our key personnel to present our case and wait for the vote.

The press was swarming over the hotel, anticipating the announcement of the awarding of the franchises. I really didn't have much to say—except that we wanted and expected to be placed in the National League. Even before we got the official nod, I was lobbying for our team to be in the NL West. I had no doubt that it was the right spot for us because of the natural, geographic rivalries with the Colorado Rockies, the Los Angeles Dodgers, the San Francisco Giants, and the San Diego Padres that awaited exploitation.

Regardless of my preferences, we first had to be asked to join the MLB club and work out our arrangements—particularly our financial arrangements.

Shortly after I reached the hotel, I began to get the feeling that something was up. Actually, I couldn't take all the credit for my intuitive antenna rising; rather, I was pretty well led to this realization by conversations I began in the hotel, and carried on till four in the morning, with a series of owners and other baseball types.

The expansion fee was looking like it was heading higher. Some of the owners thought they could get more money out of us, and they appeared determined to try.

This was not good. This was not right. This wasn't a definite, this wasn't certain, this wasn't a done deal, but this was not good. I got a little sleep, as much as I could, and waited for tomorrow.

The expansion committee, which consisted of franchise owners and presidents—John Harrington of the Boston Red Sox and chairman of the committee, Jerry Reinsdorf of the Chicago White Sox (and the Chicago Bulls), George Steinbrenner of the New York Yankees, Richard Jacobs of the Cleveland Indians, Stan Kasten of the Atlanta Braves, and Bill Giles of the Philadelphia Phillies—was meeting in one of the hotel's conference rooms. That left me in the lobby with my Arizona cohorts, the group from Tampa, the media, and assorted tourists enjoying the Florida winter.

In the midst of the hubbub, who should walk into the hotel but none other than Jim Bouton, my old high school teammate and former Yankee pitcher. Jim was in town on another matter and stopped by to say hello and to tell the press that Jerry Colangelo was going to make a fine addition to MLB. I truly appreciated the gesture from someone who knew the game as well as Jim did.

I sat down with Vince Naimoli to talk over my suspicions. He had done his homework and agreed with my price evaluation. Neither of us was happy with this turn of events— with this potential turn of events, because, after all, nobody had actually told us that the price was rising. Now, at this moment, after all our work and preparation, we had nothing left to do but sit and cool our heels.

I had expected that our two groups would go into the expansion meeting together. However, when the time came,

Vince was called in first and alone. The committee seemed to be employing the old strategy of Divide and Conquer.

Vince emerged from his meeting, having accepted the deal. He was now a baseball owner. He wasn't necessarily happy about the all the arrangements, but he was happy to be in the game.

The committee summoned me and I went into the meeting. In short order, they spelled out the terms. The price was $130 million, a jump that was nothing other than astonishing.

Astonished and infuriated, I told the assembled members of the committee what they could do with their offer. I think they were a bit surprised by my reaction. I left the room.

Not only have I been in the sports business a long time, I have been involved in expansion deals before. In fact, I served as chairman of the expansion committee in the NBA and was primarily responsible for setting the expansion price for the new franchises. In addition, it was my initiative that caused the NBA's expansion to incorporate not just the Toronto franchise but also a franchise in Vancouver.

In other words, I have been on the other side of the expansion business.

And let's not forget, I had been in a similar situation before, almost thirty years before, with the Bulls. As you might recall, just before the deal had closed, the NBA owners had raised the price from $750,000 to $1.25 million. In fact, percentage-wise, that jump had been a more dramatic increase than what MLB was proposing. On the other hand, the NBA owners had given Dick Klein more notice before jumping the price. Their MLB counterparts had waited until I had left home and was in their hotel meeting room.

Of course, there were differences between those two deals. Unlike with Klein and the NBA, MLB never actually committed to a number for the expansion fee. They didn't tell us the official price until the very last minute. It was true that no official personage had stepped forward and announced to us the definitive, absolute, final fee.

On the other hand, and putting all business considerations aside, I was surprised by the manner and timing of this demand from my prospective fellow owners. I hadn't spent months talking to everybody I could corner in baseball as a casual exercise. We had determined exactly how much money we needed to raise, and gone out and raised it, because of what we had been told by those occupying the positions of power and influence in MLB.

Well, right or wrong, good or bad, that was the situation that was presented to me, and that was the situation with which we had to deal. I'm not making excuses, and I hope I'm not complaining too much. I'm a big boy—I've been in the business a long time, and I understand how business is done, for better and worse. I didn't like what happened, but once I had gotten past the initial surprise, I accepted it and tried to deal with it, as rationally as possible.

We came close to walking. Very close. I turned it over in my head, and in my heart, wondering, questioning, considering, over and over, through a long night. Finally, it boiled down to one idea: I had put all this time and work into starting this team because I had internally and publicly asserted my belief that this was a constructive, productive, good thing to do, for Phoenix and Arizona, for reasons tangible and intangible, economic and inspirational. So the question now stood, Did I really believe in all the things I said I believed in?

Yes, I did. I most surely did.

I wanted to do this because I was convinced it would be great to have an MLB team in Phoenix. I was convinced it would add to the quality of life of the people of Arizona. New businesses and new jobs would be created. The economic impact would be significant. We would generate vast new sales tax dollars, as the team would stimulate its own economic boom.

Those were the reasons. Yes, if we were successful, I would benefit financially. Absolutely. I am in business, and that is what business persons work to achieve, both for themselves and their companies and organizations. But that was not substantial enough motivation for me to undertake this arduous task. And so I had to believe that baseball could mean something interesting, important and vital, to the people of Phoenix and Arizona, for us to press forward, regardless.

So I bit the bullet and went ahead with the franchise, and accepted MLB's terms and conditions.

And then it was done.

We had our team.

The bottom line: We had our team.

CHAPTER SEVEN

Protecting Your Investment

As THE NEW kid on the baseball block, my intentions were to be quiet and listen and learn. I had employed the same technique at the start of my career with the Bulls, and it had served me very well. Listen and learn—and then decide and act.

At the same time, this go-round was different. When I started with the Bulls, I was completely new to the sports industry. Now I had almost three decades of experience under my belt. Not that professional baseball mirrored professional basketball in every regard, either as a game or a business. And that was why I intended to keep quiet when appropriate—and speak up when it was necessary.

When entering any new venture, it is important to understand the lay of the land, with regard to both the overall business atmosphere and also to the strengths and weaknesses within your own group or organization.

Organizationally, sports offers unique challenges. When I started in professional basketball, the franchises were mom-and-pop operations—both in the structure and operation of the teams and the front offices. In the beginning, there was a great deal of musical chairs in terms of filling positions, again both on the teams and in the offices, as needs changed and structured matured and the franchises and league grew.

As the NBA expanded and became wealthier and more successful, this changed dramatically. Not necessarily on the court or on the sidelines, because coaches and assistant coaches constituted a tight fraternity, and they had a tendency to shuffle among teams. A similar situation existed for general managers; finding GMs with experience was difficult, so they also seemed to land with another team after being cut loose by their employers. Still, even with that static situation, the larger organization just beneath the top was a continual swirl of people coming and going, moving into the industry and then leaving to seek opportunities elsewhere.

That has not been the case in Phoenix. We have developed an organization that is dissimilar from most others in that we have very little turnover, at any position. The reasons are several.

To begin, ownership in sports—in all sports—changes quite often. In fact, in the Arizona Diamondbacks' first season in the National League West Division, which included the San Francisco Giants, the San Diego Padres, the Colorado Rockies, and the Los Angeles Dodgers, the owner with the most seniority in the group was Jerry McMorris of the Rockies, the youngest club in the division after the Diamondbacks.

When ownership changes, so do many jobs, as the new decision makers bring in their own friends and allies. Of course, I have always remained in charge of the Suns, even before the original owners sold out. In our thirty-year history, we've had people who have been with us fifteen years, twenty, twenty-five—even the whole way, from the very start, such as Ruthie Dryjanski, my exceptional assistant, and Joe Proski, our outstanding head trainer, who has been named "NBA Athletic Trainer of the Year" and served as trainer at four All-Star games, among other honors and awards. As we've gotten bigger and taken on more teams and businesses and more people, an unusually high percentage of our people has stayed with the organization. In the sports industry, such longevity is a distinct anomaly.

Stagnation is always a problem, with any company in any business. The leadership of the organization must be cognizant of that potential problem, because nothing can be more ruinous than your work force becoming bored, uninterested, restless. It is imperative that as the organization grows and changes, and the leadership grows and changes, so must the rest of your people be encouraged to grow and change, too.

Of course, with five hundred full-time employees and more than a couple thousand part-timers, it's not possible to be in constant touch with everyone in the business. There are simply too many people for that. It's not possible to have your hands on all the buttons, to be totally aware of what's happening throughout your organization. You must rely on your managers throughout your organization to not only perform their functions but also keep those in their departments motivated on a daily basis.

I have always enjoyed the changes in my own job description, as I moved from scout to general manager to managing partner, from basketball to arena football to hockey to tennis to indoor soccer to baseball. I enjoy the fact that in the course of the day I'm dealing with many issues on different teams, different problems, different subject matters.

And so this business is never mundane to me. There are a lot of deals waiting to be made, there is an unending whirl of activity. The business keeps me moving, keeps me thinking. I believe that organizationally, when people at the top show that kind of active leadership, it funnels down, and sets the right example.

In truth, I don't think we've ever had a problem with trying to keep people happy or interested. We have accomplished this through several approaches. We care about our people. We try to instill the idea that they are not merely competent workers, but valued co-workers, valued men and women, valued friends, valued members of our small community.

This notion of community is more than just high-minded pabulum, a sop to what is politically correct these days. I hold certain ideas, perhaps a certain vision, of what our teams and our organization can achieve, what it can mean to Phoenix and Arizona. It only makes good business sense to let your employees become as close to those ideas and that vision as possible, so they can feel they're working for more than wages, for a real purpose. It is better for the employees, and better for the organization.

Community is one manner of keeping employees happy and motivated. In addition—and perhaps more pertinent—they're well compensated. The sports business is a high-profile business. There are many perks associated with it—games to attend, logo-laden products to receive, championships, and fellowship to relish.

There are many reasons someone might not be in a hurry to leave our industry and our organization.

We're always seeking to promote from within, to reward the people who have helped make our business what it is. Of course, we do post opportunities outside the organization, and we hire from outside, but we do what we can to start from within.

When we won our baseball franchise, the Diamondbacks needed to jump-start an organization from scratch. My first requirement was that the first place we would look to fill the jobs was from our other teams. We shifted people over from the basketball operation, and from other operations, and gave them a chance to move up the ladder. There can be no better worker than someone who has put in his time, and has done a good job, and who is then rewarded—and not only with compensation but also with more responsibility. Though many companies like to use fancy titles to bolster their employees' morale, I'm not really impressed with that sort of thing. In the end, it means nothing. Having rows of vice presidents, and junior vice presidents and senior vice presidents and assistant vice presidents and first vice presidents and executive vice presidents—you get the idea—doesn't help the corporation be more efficient, doesn't help the employee be more effective.

Responsibility is what counts, and I like to give people a lot of rope to do what they need to do to run their areas. Sometimes I pull the rope and sometimes I give them more rope. It depends on the person and how he performs.

Reward, compensation, community, opportunity, responsibility: I hope you can understand why someone would be prone to stay.

Much of our organization's work off the playing fields revolves around marketing, and so I will specifically address that. We have a strong reputation for marketing and receive more than our share of applications from capable, promising applicants. Many people start in entry-level positions in marketing, and they get a pretty good education for a couple of years. They learn about the business in an exciting environment and have a tremendous amount of fun while doing so.

We have many young people who come here for a couple of years and then move on to something else, to another company, another industry. And many of them have done very well someplace else. We've proven to be a pretty good training ground.

Those who stay, those who we want to stay, are moved into teams. Because there are only so many management positions, we keep adding teams and setting these teams to distinct, different tasks.

In this way, we keep our people active and alert, intrigued and interested. And the proof that our management style works is our exceedingly low turnover.

At the same time, if anyone feels tapped out by the work, or bored with sports, or frustrated about the pace of advancement, then he or she should leave. And when someone does leave, I'm happy to help them. I wish them well. The more people who are former employees of mine who are out there being successful, the more positive a statement that is about our organization.

But that doesn't happen all that often.

In starting our new organization, I took into account baseball's traditions and manners. While I respected what was important and special to baseball, such respect did not mean that I was intent on merely following the norm. I had to combine traditional values with my own, with my own experience and instincts and knowledge. We had succeeded in other endeavors by doing things our way, within the bounds of the league's norms and traditions, and we would continue to act in a similar manner.

This combination of interests and imperatives added up to one simple realization: Everything counts. No doubt, some things count more than others, but everything counts. And to complicate matters just a bit, you can't always be sure what will count the most.

One thing that I knew that counted was assembling the leadership of the new organization.

With that perspective, it only made sense to begin by tapping into the Suns' hierarchy for Diamondback prospects. I called in Rich Dozer and asked him if he'd like to transfer from the basketball operation to the new baseball group. Rich answered that he'd go wherever I thought he would be most useful. I called in Bryan and posed the same question. Bryan replied that he wanted to stay with basketball.

Rich became the president of the Diamondbacks. Bryan stayed on as the vice president and general manager of the Suns.

Their dissimilar responses made sense. Bryan had "grown up" in basketball, spending considerable time in America West Arena and other basketball venues, watching the team practice, watching the team play. He had been a basketball player himself. He understood the game inside and out, loved it, loved working the trades, loved dealing with the players, loved being part of the franchise. He belonged in basketball.

Rich, on the other hand, had come to our organization from an accounting agency. It wasn't overstating the case to say that he was very, very happy to be in the sports industry. Since he had entered the sports business from the outside, his allegiance was not to a particular sport so much as to the organization. Thus, it didn't matter so much to Rich were he worked, basketball or baseball, as long as it made sense in the larger scheme.

Both responses were reasonable and appropriate.

I asked Joe Garagiola, Jr., to be the Diamondbacks' general manager and vice president. Joe was thrilled. He had been around baseball his whole life, first as the son of a player, and then as a lawyer working for the Yankees, and then different athletes and groups. He had worked for some time to bring MLB to Arizona, and of course had been a prime mover in starting me down the road towards acquiring a franchise.

Joe was ready to take on a big challenge. I thought he would work harder than anyone to become a success at his new post.

Neither hire fit any traditional notion of who a general manager or a president of a club should be. Neither Rich nor Joe was a tried-and-true baseball man, a survivor of pennant races and management-union wars and media assaults. However, they were smart and eager, and knew negotiating and contracts and business.

I had no doubt that they would learn and work and grow, and perform as well as anyone in the league at their new jobs.

At the same time, I wanted a baseball man in the front office. And not just any baseball man, but one of the best baseball men around. And we were lucky enough to find him.

Roland Hemond has been in the game since 1951, when he joined the front office of the Eastern League's Hartford Chiefs. Roland moved up the ladder to the major league Boston Braves, then accompanied the franchise in its move to Milwaukee. His next stop was Los Angeles, where he was the scouting and farm director for the expansion Angels. The Chicago White Sox named Hemond their director of major league player personnel. Roland stayed with the Sox for fifteen campaigns, ending up as the executive vice president of baseball operations. From there, it was on to a two-year stint in the MLB commissioner's office, and then to the Orioles.

In the course of this distinguished career, Roland won three Executive of the Year awards.

Now word had it that the Orioles were thinking about a change at the top. I contacted Roland and we sat down and spent some time together. In fact, we talked until midnight. Roland was an impressive fellow, personally and professionally, and I asked him to join our club as our senior executive vice president. By the end of our long night together, he had made his decision to join our organization. In addition to working to build the team that would take the field, one of his responsibilities would be to help Joe become the best general manager in professional baseball.

The way I had imagined our organization, the front office would essentially take care of business, in all its ramifications, and the baseball management would take care of baseball decisions.

There would be other hires, more front office people, many more baseball people. But this was a very good start.

From the beginning, I looked at the Diamondbacks as the end result of all the things that we've done well. And if the Diamondbacks were the end result, then it all began with the Suns. I am incessantly telling people that if it had not been for the success of the basketball franchise, which began as a little mom-and-pop operation many years ago, which through adversity and victory and prosperity has grown into a large organization, with a fan base with an awful lot of support, there would be nothing, no other teams, no arena, no stadium.

The Phoenix Suns are the motherlode.

Now, with the Diamondbacks, we've attempted to take our success to another level.

And so to baseball.

For example: The new team would need a name and a logo. Nothing extraordinary about that, but it still required creativity and deliberation and, ultimately, a decision. To choose these, I set up a committee of several of my leading people, including Rich Dozer, Joe Garagiola, Jr., and Scott Brubaker.

Scott had come to the Suns in 1986, just out of college. He was eager and smart, and we put him to work as a sales and marketing representative. He labored in a variety of positions for a number of sports and teams and events, from the aforementioned Suns to the Rattlers to hockey to boxing to all sorts of shows. He worked and apprenticed under the tutelage of Harvey Shank, one of the most creative and productive marketing pros in the business. Along the way, he married my daughter Kriss.

Harvey Shank joined the California Angels organization as a pitcher upon graduation from Stanford University in 1968. After four years in baseball, he signed up with the Suns as a salesman, worked his way up to director of marketing, and then to vice president of marketing. His leadership has helped fashion the Suns into one of the most successful franchises not only in the NBA but in all of professional sports.

Scott learned so well from Harvey that when the time came to select someone to head up the new baseball team's sales and marketing department, Scott emerged as the obvious choice.

In addition to the little group that was going to help choose a name for the new club, we also had some professional help, in the form of Campbell Fisher Ditka Design, a top-flight design firm based in Phoenix.

It seemed like a simple chore, and it basically was. The leading choices were Rattlers, Scorpions, and Diamondbacks—all desert denizens, all Arizona residents, all obvious and worthy names. We talked among ourselves, we solicited the public for its favorite choices, we turned over the names and logos and designs over and over.

The evident simplicity of this decision was counterbalanced by the stakes involved. The name, the logo, the colors, the design of the caps and uniforms, souvenir pennants, and all the rest, these would help determine the profitability of the entire enterprise. Selling the team's merchandise had become an incredibly large part of every franchise's prime business in the sports industry. Millions of dollars were at stake, and a winning team was not enough to guarantee a reasonable percentage of consumer expenditures.

Why people have become so devoted to wearing logos on their clothes—and not only team logos, but also designer logos, brand logos, special event logos, et cetera—is not exactly clear, and I will leave it to others more sociologically inclined to speculate and analyze the underlying causes behind our growing societal need to publicly show this commercial allegiance. Surely, in the case of sports teams, there is no real secret: fans wish to express their loyalty to their favorite franchises and demonstrate their solidarity to those franchises.

With that in mind, I assembled the core team and asked them not only for their opinions, but finally for their votes. Rattlers was already firmly identified with our Arena Football team, and so it came down to Scorpions and Diamondbacks. The ballot was secret, and I made it clear to all of the participants in the deliberations that though everybody would cast one ballot, my ballot would weigh a bit heavier than the others—than all the others put together, in fact.

I contend that this was more than mere hubris on my part, more than just another boss flexing his muscles. This was not a decision that could be based upon numbers and left to the bean counters, nor was it a decision that could really be settled by any analytical method. This final result would be a mixture of survey (via asking the public), opinion, and intuition.

That meant I would have one of three choices. One, I could leave the decision to the design firm. This was not an unreasonable alternative, given their expertise, but it was also unacceptable. This was our baseball team, and it had to be our decision. Two, I could rely on the committee's judgment. This too made sense; after all, these were some of the key people who would be involved with the club.

Still, I wasn't uncomfortable with this scenario either. I had been in the sports business a long time, and a lot longer than any of my cohorts. I had marketed players and teams, and believed I had a pretty good handle on what worked, and what didn't, and I knew that Diamondbacks worked better than Scorpions. The "diamond" in Diamondbacks was reminiscent of the baseball field. Aside from that obvious identification, I judged that the name was stronger and more memorable than Scorpions.

With such unmitigated conviction, I would have been amiss in my responsibility—because, as the managing general partner, the responsibility was ultimately mine—if I had not gone with my gut. So it was Diamondbacks.

Incidentally, only Joe Garagiola, Jr., voted for Diamondbacks. Everyone else, including the design experts, voted for Scorpions.

As the first season ended, the Arizona Diamondbacks stood at fifth in merchandising sales among all the teams in MLB.

I think it is fair to say that, so far, "Diamondbacks" has worked out just fine.

Choosing a name required a definite decision, one with ramifications that would permanently affect the franchise. Another situation arose that also required a similar decisive action, again with long-lasting repercussions. This time, however, the time frame was compressed more so than with the name question, and it involved a person and not a logo, rendering the whole process much more fluid and potentially problematic.

Buck Showalter had spent his entire career with the New York Yankees organization. In fact, Buck had never held any job outside the organization in his entire adult life. He spent seven years with the Yankees as a minor league player. In 1985, at the age of twenty-eight, he moved over to the managerial side, leading the Yankees' Class A club in Oneonta, New York.

Buck worked his way up to the big leagues, by virtue of his baseball savvy and his renowned, round-the-clock work habits. By 1994, he was named Manager of the Year. Unfortunately, the strike cut short the season, depriving Buck of the opportunity to lead his first-place team into the play-offs. The following year, the Bronx Bombers were once again a terrific team, and Buck had them in the play-offs for the first time in fourteen years. The Yankees were knocked out of the post-season by their cross-continental rivals, the Seattle Mariners, in a tough, close, five-game series.

By the age of thirty-nine, Buck Showalter had clearly established himself as one of the finest managers in the game. The casual observer might have assumed that he would be the Yankees manager for a very long time. The casual observer would have been wrong.

As was his wont, George Steinbrenner, the principal owner of the Yankees, decided he wanted to make a few changes. And, to cut to the chase, that would leave Buck out of a job.

I hadn't intended to hire a manager until after the expansion draft in November 1997—there didn't seem to be much of a need for one until then—but this was too good an opportunity to pass up. I had spoken to a lot of people in baseball about the man and liked everything I heard.

Of course, it was against the rules to contact a manager while he was under contract, so I had to wait. Buck's contract expired at midnight, November 1, 1995. No more than two minutes after midnight, I called Buck at home, and invited him down to Arizona to talk.

He agreed to a visit, and, I took him to the Phoenix Suns home opener on November 5. We talked, and I was impressed by his intelligence and his integrity. One more, very key thing: We discovered that we saw eye-to-eye on our desire to win, and our desire to totally commit ourselves to that objective.

Other franchises wanted Buck, franchises that were already fielding teams, playing in the bigs, but I made an offer, a seven-year offer, because I saw that bringing Buck on board this early could allow one of the best minds in the game to become involved in every aspect of the development of the franchise. I hadn't planned this, but I reacted to the opportunity, and tried to react as fast as possible.

It was a seven-year offer, and that demonstrated my commitment to Buck, to hand him the reins and trust him to guide us over the long haul, from start to hopefully a championship.

Buck quickly accepted, and on November 15, just ten days after that Suns home opener, he signed a contract to lead the Arizona Diamondbacks well into the next century.

Selecting a manager was a vitally important decision for any club, and one I had not expected to make for quite some time. But when the right opportunity presents itself, the conscientious administrator must be ready to act, and act boldly and decisively. That action must be the end result of preparation, of gathering together whatever facts are available and evaluating them, understanding them. Information is power, and power must be used skillfully and wisely.

In other words, when need be, damn the schedule, full speed ahead!

That's what it means to be in charge. Whether selecting administrators and aides, or keeping the organization engaged and excited, or choosing a logo or a baseball manager, the challenge is basically the same: to learn more efficiently, to consider more judiciously, to react more quickly, to act more decisively. The process never stops, the education never ends.

Improving your business or organization should be sufficient motivation. If it isn't, remember, that the competition is also working to gain the same information, the same edge, the same opportunities, as you.

In sports, only one franchise can win it all. That's not true in most businesses—General Motors, Ford, Toyota, and all the others can each grab a piece of the whole market and do very well for themselves—but it might not be a bad way to approach, at least conceptually, your business.

CHAPTER   EIGHT

The Stadium

TRAVELING AROUND THE country to visit the venues in baseball, I continually picked up on clever innovations, as well as unfortunate mistakes. The end result of these journeys was that in building our ballpark, we were flying neither blind nor solo. Others had traveled this road before—after all, stadiums large and small dotted the land. One of our primary tasks in imagining our venue was to take all that had come before and improve upon it. There is never a reason to reinvent the wheel, in any aspect of business, but there is always a reason to pause and search for something that will render that wheel smoother or shinier, more efficient or more appealing.

The path to the final design of our ballpark was uneven and rocky and littered with examples of stadiums we did not want to emulate. Baseball had evolved from rudimentary wooden grandstands surrounding unenclosed fields, to more elaborate wooden structures, to mammoth concrete and steel monuments. It required almost a year—May 5, 1922 to April 18, 1923—for Yankee Stadium to rise to completion, and when the ballpark was done, with its white facade and three concrete decks extending from behind home plate to each corner, the House That Ruth Built established a new standard for elegance and grace that has yet to be bested.

Other classically handsome parks soon followed, including Boston's Fenway Park, Detroit's Tiger Stadium, Cincinnati's Crosley Field, Chicago's Wrigley Field, and Brooklyn's Ebbets Field. After that, starting in the 1950s, multipurpose stadiums became something of the rage, employed for both baseball and football, while truly satisfying the demands of neither. Examples of multi-use venues include County Stadium in Milwaukee, Three Rivers Stadium in Pittsburgh, Oakland-Alameda County Coliseum in Oakland, and Joe Robbie Stadium in Miami.

More recent days have seen a move back to the classic styles, with their natural grass and asymmetrical lines and intimate settings. Baltimore's Camden Yards Stadium and Texas's Ballpark at Arlington and Cleveland's Jacobs Field and Denver's Coors Field are outstanding examples of these stadiums.

We intended to follow this retro trend, and add a few special wrinkles of our own.

One already existing innovation that I appreciated could be found in Camden Yards, set along the city's sparkling new waterfront. When Baltimore put in the seats, the franchise and the builders discovered that if the seats along the left and right field lines were turned towards home plate, consumers in those seats would have a markedly improved angle on the action.

Once conceived, this innovation might seem obvious. Of course! Why should a seat between third base and the outfield wall face the left fielder and the outfield grass, when the majority of the game is played far to the right? Why force the fan to twist his body and head to see what is happening? Why not simply turn the seats and provide everyone with a good view?

It also made sense from a business standpoint: by rendering the experience more accessible and more enjoyable, the ballpark would be a more inviting place to which to return. Of course.

Obvious, yes, but only once stated, as proven by the failure of every stadium in every sport in every city for decades to give this a try. Don't judge stadium owners and designers too harshly for their inability to hit this nail on the head. Gravity seems obvious now, as does a round rather than flat world—everything is obvious once somebody else figures it out. ⌁

The same is true of stadiums and seats.

When Camden Yards turned their seats, they lost a few of them, owing to additional space requirements caused by the angle alteration. That was fine by me; my goal was to make our ballpark the most comfortable building of its kind ever constructed. In Bank One Ballpark, you can go all the way down the line and the seats are turned, facing home plate.

Along with the angle, I wanted to ensure that the fans had adequate room for their legs and arms and trunks, so we spaced our seats further apart than the norm. In the same vein, we opened up the concourse inside and around the stadium, so people could comfortably walk and browse and shop, and simultaneously watch the action on the field. In everything we did, we took the fans into consideration, because they came first. They were the reason we needed a ballpark, they were the audience who would fill it, they were the fans who would give the building life and emotion and purpose.

We examined the capacities of all the ballparks in MLB in determining how many seats we should have. Some of the "modern" stadiums, particularly the multipurpose stadiums, bolted in as many chairs and rows and bleachers as they could cram into their facilities. The trend, however, in the most recently built parks, the "new classic" parks, is friendlier, with fewer seats, and thus fewer fans. Where the multipurpose parks can have room for 50,000 to 60,000 customers, the new classic parks restrict themselves to the 40,000 to 50,000 range.

Of course, there exists a tension—not only in the sports business, but in so many areas of virtually all businesses—between providing a service and earning a profit. Services cost money, whether you are preparing a meal or preparing a tax return, whether you are drilling a tooth or drilling for oil, whether you are designing a dress or designing a stadium. The more you spend on your services, the less profit you can extract—assuming your ability to charge for your product is relatively fixed, as is the case with any leisure, nonessential activity such as sports.

Of course, prices aren't all that fixed. Some large market teams have at times raised the pricing bar under the argument that it costs more to operate a franchise in major markets. Those actions have been one contributing factor in the creeping rise in consumer costs. Additionally, the proliferation of agents and the empowerment of the union, along with increased television revenue, have resulted in the dramatic rise of player salaries. Strikes and shutdowns in sports have also had tremendous impacts upon ticket prices.

I can state unequivocally that there is great sensitivity to what has happened to consumer prices in all major league front offices. The escalating pricing hike is one of the key reasons why the owners in the NBA determined that the cost structure in the league, the cost structure between the players and the owners, had to be reevaluated and restructured.

Regardless, one point must be made. Critics often contend that ordinary, middle-class fans have been pushed out of the seats in professional sporting events by fat cats and corporations buying up all the seats. This is simply not true. What is true is that luxury boxes and club seats are expensive and designed to extract maximum profit, necessary profit, to help the team compete. When people say they can't afford to go to the game, what they are really saying is that they can't sit behind home plate. In Bank One Ballpark, ticket prices start at one dollar. We set a one-dollar price, covering 350 seats, to ensure that just about any and everyone in Phoenix could afford to see the Diamondbacks play. Other seats cost $3.50 and $5.50. In fact, of the almost 50,000 seats in the ballpark, fully seventeen thousand seats, more than a third of the total, are priced at nine dollars or less.

With all our teams, we set our prices by first comparing our rates to the rates set by the competition in other cities. Then we compare that to the rates for entertainment in our own market. You do market research, you talk to your people, and you arrive at the figures you think are appropriate.

I've always said that we would never have the top-priced ticket to any of our games, in any of our sports. That's a personal decision. It's an interesting dilemma, when you're competing franchise to franchise, small city to mid-sized city to megalopolis. In 1992–93, as has been previously stated, the opening of America West Arena brought the Suns a brief, shining moment—we were the star for a day—and we led the NBA in revenues. At the same time, we were somewhere between seventh and tenth in ticket prices. We achieved this success through focusing on marketing, and developing a very strong promotion package.

Regardless, despite our concentrated efforts, despite our fantastic arena, just a few years later, the New York Knicks are today outgrossing us in ticket revenue approximately two to one. Phoenix might be a big city and getting bigger all the time, but no sports team in town (and no business of any kind, most probably) can compete with the ability of New York sports teams (and restaurants, clothing stores, and movie theaters), to charge higher prices. When our top ticket is $300 and New York's is $1,350, then the Knicks have a lot more money to spend on resigning their own free agents at however much it takes, as allowed under the Larry Bird rule.

And if that disparity holds true for the sixth-largest city in the nation, imagine how much worse, how much more difficult it is for franchises in smaller communities to earn enough money to compete.

Putting all the economics and comparisons and intra-league competition aside, I've developed and held to a philos-

ophy about pricing: It's not so much what the market will
bear—it's also what's fair. And that's a philosophy I've followed in my thirty-two years in the sports business.

With the Suns, we settled on a price range of thirteen
dollars to eighty dollars, with the relatively few floor seats going for three hundred dollars. In contrast, we set the Rattlers'
ticket prices lower, in accord with the nature of the game and
the fan base, from a low of nine dollars to a high of thirty-
nine dollars.

Now, with the Diamondbacks, we sought to locate ourselves in the middle of the pack, with some interesting extras.

To begin, we first decided on our ballpark's capacity. We
played around with different numbers and different seating arrangements, considering 42,000 to 50,000. We finally settled
on 48,500.

(Incidentally, that doesn't mean we can't fit more people
into the stadium. We have movable seats, party suites, and
other places and ways to easily fit more people inside the park.
On many nights we have over 50,000 fans in Bank One Ballpark. Nonetheless, every stadium must have a set number by
which the venue's managers can determine and declare a sell-
out.)

Returning to the issue of the stadium's design, I already
mentioned the influence Camden Yards had on our thinking.
Baltimore was my first stop on my national ballpark tour. My
appreciation for Camden Yards went far beyond the angled
seats. I found Baltimore's intimacy enthralling, its old-
fashioned look with the newest innovations. I liked the picnic
area in the outfield, and having the club seats and the suite
seats on the same level, so as not to isolate either group in its
own small, separate section. I admired the view of Baltimore's
skyline from the seats inside the stadium. I loved the red brick
and green steel that Baltimore's architects had incorporated
into their building (just as had the designers of Denver's Coors
Field), clearly borrowing the idea from the look of many of
the older stadiums.

Another terrific innovation: outside the stadium, beyond right field, on Eutaw Street, stood an old warehouse that had been turned into a series of retail shops. Not only was it a prime retail location, the area functioned as a gathering spot for fans and friends.

From the large to the small: I liked the finishing touches in the building. The wall and floor coverings, the endless number of fixtures, the variety of brick and stone that were used— the care taken to select all these was evident. The scoreboard in the outfield and the signage around the stadium were also impressive.

We would incorporate parts of all of these designs into Bank One Ballpark. We made extensive use of our shades of red brick and green steel throughout the stadium. We built the venue so that, with the roof open, part of Phoenix's skyline is visible to the fans. We placed the club seats and the suite seats on one level. We made a deal with Miller Brewing to use one of their subsidiaries, Leinenkugel's, as the brand name to adorn a large restaurant/bar on the plaza outside the stadium, near the ticket booths and ticket gates, to serve as a prime gathering place for not only our fans, but for all of downtown Phoenix.

In Cleveland, a fine dining facility was built inside the new Jacobs Field, down the left field line. Season club seat holders had their own, reserved restaurant on the other side of the ballpark.

We sufficiently appreciated these ideas to use them ourselves, locating rather good restaurants in various places in the park, usually designed for specific audiences. The Arizona Baseball Club on the suite/club seat level, provided a restaurant just for those customers. One level up, two beer gardens, sponsored by Miller Lite and each one 6000 square feet in size, is open to all fans.

At the new home for the Rangers in Arlington, Texas, ethnic food stations, with unusual items on the menus (unusual for baseball, that is), were situated around the concourses. The national restaurant chain TGIF ran an eatery, named Front Row, inside the ballpark. We checked, and the stadium restaurant was one of the highest grossing in the entire chain. The stadium also had a Hall of Fame, with different exhibits extolling the game's illustrious history, which was associated with Cooperstown.

We favored each of these features. We assembled many different food concessions into the ballpark, from Garcia's Mexican fare to Ben & Jerry's Ice Cream, to Little Caesar's pizza, to Blimpie's sandwiches. The gamut ran as wide as could be imagined, from vegetable stands called Fielder's Choice, where fresh celery, carrot sticks, and other farm produce waited in plastic bags, laid out on a bed of ice; to one of the most ubiquitous symbols of the American fast-food culture, the Golden Arches of McDonald's, the only MLB stadium in the country to welcome Mickey D's indoors. We also brought TGIF into the building, which opened its Front Row Sports Grill overlooking left field. In addition to the regular restaurant and bar enticements, the Front Row came equipped with indoor and outdoor seating, all the better to watch the game.

We built the Cox Clubhouse beyond center field, near the picnic area, which consists of several rows of tables, primarily intended for families to sit and watch the game while eating. The clubhouse is also a family attraction, with interactive games for the kids and a baseball museum for everyone. Many of the exhibits in the museum have been lent to the Diamondbacks by the National Museum of Baseball in Cooperstown, New York.

In this way, we are seeking to render a visit to the ballpark a total experience, with something for everyone, beyond watching the game. That is the nature of baseball. The games generally take longer and are paced more leisurely than basketball or football. No clock forces or stops the action. Baseball progress at its own pace. People come and go, walking from their seats to the concessions. Some are more intent on following the action than others, marking down each pitch, while their companions are more interested in getting a hot dog and soda. This unique pacing is part of baseball's sum and substance, as are the eighty-one home games each team hosts, so many more than in any other sport. The challenge for the marketing end of a franchise, the business end, is to take greatest advantage of that pacing, and all those games, and make the most of the opportunities it presents. We have sought to do this—and so have all the new venues under construction—by enlarging the experience, by making it as interesting and as diverse as possible, so people, beyond those dedicated fans diligently marking their scorecards, will keep coming back.

Continuing with our travels through MLB, and what we learned: Cleveland's Jacobs Field was located downtown, next to the basketball arena. Bank One Ballpark was constructed one city block from America West Arena. We also followed in the footsteps of Baltimore's Camden Yards and Denver's Coors Field, both of which were placed in the city's warehouse district. So was Bank One Ballpark.

One of the advantages to being located downtown was that a restaurant like the Front Row could remain open even when no game waited on the schedule and still pack them in. And the Front Row has quickly established itself as a prime downtown meeting spot, with or without baseball.

Coors Field, as befitted its namesake, had its brewery inside the park. We went outside with our version, the Leinenkugel's Ballyard Brewery, 20,000 square feet enclosed in two stories. Even though Leinenkugel's would be located on the plaza along Fourth Street, the restaurant featured items that were specifically intended to be eaten by hand, without utensils, so they could be carried into the stadium.

I also noted a few things I didn't like. The concessions at Camden Yards were on the outside ring of the interior concourse. This meant that fans would be facing away from the field when they waited to purchase food and drink, thus miss-

ing the action. We placed as many of our concessions as possible on the inside of the concourse. With our concourse's
wide-open design, granting a frequently unobstructed view of
the field from inside the park, the fan can stand in line, waiting
to order his beer or taco or strawberries and cream, and not
miss a strike or double play or home run.

In Cleveland, suites were arrayed right behind home
plate, on the field level. Since Jacobs Field was the first ballpark to employ this idea, I was especially intrigued. The sight
line from the suites placed the ballplayers almost at eye level,
giving an effect that reminded me a bit of a bunker. Though we
didn't copy this design, out of that concept came the notion of
putting a big lounge beneath and behind home plate, surrounded by our club seats, which would have exclusive access
to the lounge. The club seats have ended up generating more
revenue for us than any comparable number of suites could
have in that same space.

In a statement that will come as a surprise to no one,
all these improvements cost money, huge piles of money. The
average amount spent in the newer parks to build in the multiple concession improvements is around $12 to 15 million.
Jacobs Field topped the list, with a bill that totaled $23 mil-
lion. We beat that by a mile, spending some $30 million. It
was a lot of money, but (a) it provided us with the foundation
to service our fans to an exceptional degree, and (b) which in
turn was sure to return our investment by increasing our
points of sales, and by fulfilling (a).

In addition to all these things, we needed a retractable
roof. The roof made baseball in Phoenix in the summer possible; the promise of the roof was a factor in MLB granting
Arizona a franchise. After all, summer temperatures routinely
reached 110 degrees and more, day after day, week after week.
Not only was that kind of weather unhealthy for human beings playing ball in polyester uniforms and wool caps, it was
positively murder for grass. And I wanted natural grass, real

grass, not some synthetic substitute. It looked better, it played better, it was baseball's essential, intended home.

Despite the engineering complications presented by building a retractable roof on the top of the stadium, it did necessarily steer us towards our desire to construct an intimate setting. Rather than build our rows and levels outward, as has been the case with so many arenas, causing fans to be pushed further and further away from the action, the need to keep the roof within manageable dimensions forced a more upright edifice.

Intimacy sells in sports. America West Arena has been judged far and wide as the most intimate venue of its size in basketball. We sought to do the same with Bank One Ballpark, to build an intimate stadium from all vantage points. We employed tight foul lines on both sides, and the pool area overlooking right/center field is right against the outfield wall.

We also take a close look at the amenities provided our season ticket holders, as well as our other higher priced and special customers. The club seat/suite concourse, one up from the main concourse, is adorned with the best materials and touches we could afford. We put up a garage for the season ticket and suite holders next to the stadium and built a walkway from the garage right to that second-story concourse.

We saved a few spaces that could have been used for these corporate suites and turned them into party suites. We already had sixty-nine suites, which were rented by corporations for an average fee of $100,000 per year, which used them as an extension of their business, entertaining clients and so on. The party suites, on the other hand, were available for renting on a day-to-day basis, allowing individuals and small companies to get in on the fun.

The essence of marketing is to take your product—whatever your product—and make the most of it. In this regard, we took the main concourse and created DiamondTown, more formally known as Fox Sports Arizona DiamondTown.

In most stadiums, the concourse is no more than a concrete thoroughfare, getting from one place to another, with a series of concession stands and bathrooms along the way. We thought we could make better use of the space.

We divided the concourse into ten zones, each 120 feet in length. Each zone was then structured around a message, with the result that the entire concourse consists of ten different themed areas, all brought to life through video walls, three-dimensional exhibits, and a graphic timeline, revealing some of baseball's greatest moments and heroes. By creating these zones, we created a new experience that would educate and entertain the fans and also lead to new marketing opportunities to which sponsors have eagerly responded

A similar situation existed with the rotunda, which is inside the plaza and past the ticket-takers and is the single, central meeting place for everyone entering the stadium. Escalators lead to the upper levels, while to one side is the team shop, and straight ahead are the doors to the main concourse.

On the floor of the rotunda is a map of Arizona with the names of the state's leading fifty cities emblazoned on and around it. On the bottom level of the rounded wall leading to the top of the stadium, we had a mural painted which depicted the history of sport. On the higher levels of the rotunda's walls, the murals change to a beautiful series of pictorials displaying some of the wondrous sites of the Grand Canyon State.

When I first heard about the architects' plans for the rotunda, I questioned the point of the rotunda. But then I realized that this was exactly what Bank One Ballpark was all about, to act as a unifying place for Arizonans to meet and to celebrate their stadium and their state, their past and their future.

In the course of our travels and studies, we learned what to do, both in terms of design and operation, and what not to do. Much of what we picked up was through simple observation. Anyone standing outside the bathrooms in any ballpark, movie house, or bar, knows that women are invariably waiting on line to get inside while the men stroll in and out, quick as a breeze. Why? Because designers, in the interests of fairness or simply out of laziness, unthinkingly put in an equal number of male and female facilities, ignoring the reality that women need more time. It's not exactly a secret. We sought to remedy this distressing situation by building substantially more toilets for women than for men: 340 versus 276. And from opening day, those numbers have made a dent in that line.

On the other hand, we did not learn everything by mere observation; rather, all the franchises we visited were extraordinarily open and frank with us, explaining the ins and outs of their management and maintenance. We have tried to be just as open and as frank with those who have called on us for opinions and assistance as they plan their new venues. As a result of this cooperation, perhaps unprecedented in big business, every new building in baseball, as well as other sports, has a real chance to be better, in some ways, than all those that have come before.

We fixed a goal to lead the league in terms of season ticket sales. And we reached our goal. We sold 36,000 season tickets, a record for Major League Baseball. We pushed hard to sell those tickets, throwing our marketing muscle into the effort.

Still, marketing was not primarily responsible for our success. Selling those tickets was not an isolated undertaking, separate and removed from our other tasks and from our history.

In truth, I can't say that we did anything especially innovative or different in the course of this labor. Instead, this was just a continuation of our ongoing work, a part of the whole. When we decided to go forward with baseball, our record in basketball and other sports spoke for us—and spoke well.

Many people in town, and across the state, wanted to be involved in baseball and wanted to be part of our venture.

We offered tickets to Suns' season ticket holders, as well as those who had season tickets to our other teams. We moved on to season ticket holders for the Phoenix Firebirds and the Tucson Toros, Arizona's minor league teams.

We sought to get as many commitments as early as we could, and spread the word through the media and through individual contacts that we would do everything possible to service season ticket holders.

I cannot stress this enough, and this commitment to service should certainly apply to any business. I regard my organization as a sort of extended family, and the organization regards season ticket holders as a further extension of that. Why? Because season ticket holders are the lifeblood of any franchise. They are the solid base, who will be there through victories and defeats. They carry the franchise through the ups and downs inevitable in any sport and with any team.

We cherish our relationship with our season ticket holders, and treat them with the respect that they deserve. This starts by communicating with them on a regular basis via the mail and the telephone, and by responding to their questions and requests with alacrity.

When it came time for the Diamondbacks' new season ticket holders to choose their seats, we had every individual who wished to (in the order based upon a lottery we held), walk into our office, examine the model of the yet-to-be constructed stadium, and select the seat he wanted. This contact allowed us to meet our new fans and begin developing a one-on-one relationship with each one.

So we set a target and hit the mark. Thirty-six thousand season tickets. What that means is that we have the base on which to build our franchise, to develop the type of relationship with our fans and customers that will sustain us through our early years as we work to become better and more competitive, and win more games, always aiming towards a division title, then the pennant, then the World Series.

Is it realistic to assume that the fans will grant us this grace period while we labor towards a winning record? Look at Colorado for an indicator: the Rockies' honeymoon has lasted five years, supporting them through good times and not such good times. If we can do as well as that, I have absolutely no doubt that we will be presenting a vastly improved team on the field before too long, a playoff-bound team.

So the secret to season ticket holders is not only getting them, but keeping them. It's no different in any other business—a car dealer wants to keep customers coming back, trading in their old autos for new ones; a real estate agent wants to sell a client a house, and then list that house when the client moves, and then sell that client his or her next house. Renewals are the key, and absolutely so in the sports business.

In our marketplace, we know that if people respect what you are doing and believe in what you are doing, you are halfway home. Then, if tickets are affordable, and they feel they're are getting their money's worth, they'll stick with you all the way.

Once we bought the Suns, we found that the fans supported us, even as our fortunes rose and dipped. Today, the waiting list for Suns' season tickets numbers in the thousands. We are doing whatever we can to make the Diamondbacks' season tickets equally precious.

So far we've done extremely well. While final figures are not yet in, it appears that the Diamondbacks should end up tenth in revenue in our first season playing in Major League Baseball. That is a good start. A very good start indeed.

Regardless, just as the true mark of a player or a team cannot be judged by the results of only one season, the same is true for a franchise and a stadium.

If we continue to service our fans through the years with the enthusiasm we displayed in the very beginning, if we continue to pay attention to the details, if we continue to maintain the highest standards for our organization, if we continue to innovate and improve the stadium as opportunities arise, then we should be able to retain and even increase the loyalty and affection and business of our fans.

And if all that comes to pass, then we'll know we have done it right.

CHAPTER NINE

Basketball Faces New Challenges

I HAVE BEEN part of the National Basketball Association for so many years that I now hold the distinction of having served the league longer than anyone currently in the game except Abe Pollin, the owner of the Washington Wizards, formerly the Washington Bullets.

Accordingly, it should come as no surprise that I have seen a lot during that tenure. I have been involved in all sorts of negotiations, all sorts of deals, all sorts of problems and opportunities. I have traveled all over the world to help both my franchise and the league prosper and grow. I have dealt with players, owners, general managers, agents, reporters, and government officials. In furtherance of my work, I have been gained a perspective that encompasses a vast store of experience, and remains all my own.

For example: back in the mid-Eighties, I received a call from Dick Percudani in Europe. "Perc" had been an influential coach on the New York City high school basketball scene before becoming the first American head coach in the Italian Pro Leagues. Perc was an immediate hit: in 1966, he was named Coach of the Year with Milan.

Eventually, he moved over to become a scout for the

Suns. He phoned because he had seen a player the Suns had to sign. The fellow's name was Georgi Glouchkov, and he was a six-foot-eight, 235-pound forward-center from Bulgaria. Along with the majority of Americans, I didn't know much about Bulgaria, which, along with half of Europe, was still under communism's dictatorial grip.

No NBA club had ever signed a player from behind the Iron Curtain. There weren't many players who had the tools, and there wasn't much known about them anyway. I didn't spend a great deal of time worrying about basketball, communist-style.

Still, Perc knew basketball, over here or over there, and so when he said this Glouchkov was our guy, that meant he was our guy. I flew over to make the deal.

The deal would be with Glouchkov's agent: the Bulgarian government, and specifically the Ministry of Sports. And the bureaucrats weren't interested in any 10 percent—oh no, they were going to cash our check and pay Glouchkov some kind of salary.

So I packed my bags and flew to Munich, then to Sofia, the Bulgarian capital.

We landed in the dead of winter, a typically cold winter. Perc and I were met by a full, official delegation on the runway. So far, so good. But then we hit a small snag. For some reason, we were detained at the airport, despite our official delegation, and our luggage was thoroughly searched.

Oh, and while we're cooling our heels, a man sidled up to me and whispered that he needed to talk to me. Alone. Someplace else.

And then he slinked away.

Eventually, our bags were returned, and we left the airport. But this offered the first hint that perhaps everything was not perfectly all right.

Our escorts took us to our hotel. We were given rooms on the top floor, and by now I had decided that our accommodations were par for the course. From everything I had seen in my brief Bulgarian sojourn, gray was the dominant local color. The people were gray, the buildings were gray, the sky was gray. My room was the same—dilapidated and depressing—and had the additional distinction of being incredibly overheated, as the hotel's antiquated heating system pumped out moist, hot air, which all rose to the top floor, enough to broil a roast.

From there, we piled back into the official car and drove to the Sports Ministry.

We were shown to a conference room, where eight Bulgarian officials were seated on one side of the table, leaving the other side for Perc and me. Protocol demanded that we toast each other—each and every one of us, in fact, which meant ten toasts. The Bulgarians provided local whiskey for the main course and Coca-Cola as the chaser.

Everybody was having a fine old time, and the Bulgarians were being so agreeable to our suggestions and ideas about how to complete this deal. In fact, I was beginning to think that the comrades were far too agreeable, and this was much too easy.

By the time we finished, and had the outline of the deal in place, it was close to midnight. Just when I thought we were done, the Bulgarians announced that we were heading out to dine.

As we were at the mercy of our hosts, we smiled and got back in the car and drove off. We drove for quite a while, until we were suddenly pulled over at a police checkpoint. Despite being accompanied by all these high-ranking officials, we had our credentials examined and questioned. I took this as an attempt to intimidate us, though exactly for what reason I wasn't sure. We weren't arms negotiators, we weren't spies, we weren't journalists, we were simply a couple of guys trying to sign a basketball player for our basketball team.

In due course, the cops let us go, and our motorcade drove off. Finally, we reached a mountain, somewhere in the middle of nowhere, and we headed to its top, where a restaurant was situated. Aside from our party, the other diners were Russian tourists, who were brought in by the busloads.

It was around two in the morning when I asked myself, What am I doing here?

I got to bed about four in the morning, exhausted but at least satisfied that we had settled the deal that had prompted my very far journey.

We convened once again with the Bulgarians at nine the next morning, back in their conference room at the ministry. I had assumed we had gathered together to sum up, to shake hands on what we had already agreed.

Unfortunately, the Bulgarians had other notions. They were no longer smiling and acted as though our discussions the previous day had never occurred.

We started all over, and to make a long story short, inked the deal. We left on the next flight out of town, though the Bulgarians got in their last shot: They stuck us with the hotel bill, though they had originally promised to pick up our expenses.

One last note: after all that effort, Glouchkov didn't work out for us, in large measure because of his newfound, unabashed love of American candy, as well as American women, neither of which proved the best route for getting into NBA shape. Finally, he seemed to lose a great deal of muscle very quickly. Given the well-known regard in Eastern Europe for steroids, it was far from inconceivable that Glouchkov had bulked up through chemicals, and now, with his supply cut off, he was heading back to his normal size, a size unfortunately augmented by the addition of nonathletic fat.

Though we had signed him to a two-year deal, after the first year we sent him back to Europe.

Live and learn.

Bulgaria hasn't been the only stop on my NBA travels. I've toured the world as the Suns played in Israel and Italy, Japan and Puerto Rico, Mexico and Spain, Hawaii and Alaska. As I stated, I've met world leaders, business leaders, and every U.S. President who has held office since 1976—Carter, Reagan, Bush, and Clinton. I've learned how sports, business, and community meet and meld together. And I've learned what we have done well, and what we have done not so well.

Most of the knowledge I've accumulated in the course of my career has been hard-earned. And not everyone has always appreciated the breadth and depth of my acquired wisdom. Back in the early Seventies, when I was still fairly new to the basketball business, the general managers got together and decided that we needed to organize. Compared to other GMs in other sports, and compared to the deals the players were making, we felt that we deserved a more equitable package and also greater participation in helping determine the direction of the NBA.

I was selected by my fellow GMs as the chairman of our group, which meant I would represent the GMs with the owners. Under those auspices, I attended the next owners' meeting. I appeared before the owners and gave a little talk about how the GMs collectively had more to offer the owners and the league in terms of becoming more involved in the NBA's decision-making process.

This seemed like not only a reasonable proposition, but a generous one as well. I should say it seemed this way to me, at least.

Ned Irish was one of the original NBA men, one of the celebrated founders of the league. Now he ran Madison Square Garden, and also the New York Knicks and the Rangers. And now Ned rose after I spoke, and Ned was mad.

"Who the hell do you think you are?" thundered Irish. "Coming in and telling us how to run our business?"

Ned's ire notwithstanding, the general managers and the owners worked out an accord. I wound up serving as the chairman of the GM group for years. I also served on many other NBA committees over time, in my capacity as both general manager and owner: the competition and rules committee, the advisory finance committee, the long-range planning committee, chairman of the expansion committee. In the Eighties, when the NBA was going through some tough times, I was asked to chair a committee (of which I was the only member who was not an owner), to investigate what we could do differently.

In that capacity, I responded to the media's questions on behalf of the league at a press conference after we made the announcement. When queried on the fundamental points, I provided rather direct answers. Why did we expand not only the number of teams, but also the number of teams that could make the play-offs? Because we needed the additional revenue—new teams meant expansion fees, more teams in the play-offs meant more games on the schedule, and more excitement for the fans. Why did we tighten the rules regarding draft picks and how they could be traded? Because we wanted to ensure that teams didn't trade away their futures by giving away their young players to pursue immediate success with veterans.

I've been involved in a number of key moments in recent NBA history. In 1976, I chaired the committee that dealt with the issues that confronted us when we absorbed the ABA. Because some teams would be coming into the league, while others would be disbanded, and their players available to other teams, one of our primary tasks was to place some sort of value on the many players who were about to enter the league, deciding how all these players would be incorporated into the NBA. I have also given my time to related boards, such as the Board of Trustees of the Naismith Hall of Fame, representing the NBA.

In the nineties, I was a member of the expansion committee which decided to grant Toronto and Vancouver new franchises. Today, I'm on the labor relations committee, which is deeply embroiled in the controversy between players and management, the controversy which, at this writing, threatens to cancel the 1998–99 season.

Whether doing business for my own team or for the NBA, I've always been a strong league man, an advocate for protecting and strengthening the league. It is obviously not enough to develop a winning, profitable franchise. Every franchise only wins and profits within the league structure, and if that league is not a dynamic, successful entity, then it will eventually fail, and all the league's franchises will tumble along with it.

Being a league advocate means being an advocate for the people who make up the league, including the coaches and the players. Coaches and players not only plan and play the game, they embody the NBA to the public. Consequently, it only behooves the industry, and the owners, to include the coaches and the players in the major decisions affecting the league, whenever appropriate. Of course, many issues and problems that face the owners and management must be handled within the confines of that group, because certain issues and problems are the sole province of that group. In the end, primary responsibility of the players is to take care of business on the court—the primary responsibility of the owners is to take care of the business of basketball. And though both sides have a financial stake in the management of the NBA and the future of the industry, the owners are the ones who are monetarily on the line, with their continual, enormous investment in their franchises.

Still, when it makes sense—and it frequently does—all the parties who constitute the league—owners, management, players, coaches—should be heard when discussing the future of the NBA, because that future is the concern of everyone working in the league.

Just as I am an advocate of the league, and take an inclusive approach to league business, so I am a similar sort of strong advocate for Phoenix and Arizona. Our organization seeks to promote our community and works with both the political and business leaders of our community in pursuing this objective.

In today's world, with increasingly close ties, intentional or otherwise, between business, media, and government, working to support and promote the league and the community, be it the NBA or MLB, or Phoenix or Arizona, necessarily works to support and promote our organization and our franchises.

I'd like to briefly return to the pressing problem of the impasse between NBA players and owners, because it is symptomatic of the fundamental problem facing all sports.

David Stern became commissioner of the NBA in the Eighties at a most auspicious time. Stern had entered the NBA as a young lawyer, became an expert in the new technology of cable television, and also educated himself in the ways of marketing. The combination of his skills and experience made David the right guy to take over the leadership of the league when Lawrence O'Brien's tenure expired.

I must admit that my name was mentioned for the job. Though flattered, I wasn't particularly interested. I had no intention of leaving either Phoenix or the Suns for another position, or for any reason.

Besides, I supported David Stern, and my faith in him, and also everyone else's faith in him, has been rewarded many times over. David took over at a time when technology and the league were changing, and changing fast. Television, in all its forms, was bringing sports to new audiences, at home and around the world, while giant athletic clothing and equipment corporations were starting to pour huge, unprecedented sums into athletes and sports in order to garner as much publicity and marketing from those relationships, altering the very nature of the industry itself. Agents were becoming more powerful and influential than ever. Professional sports were exploding across the landscape, becoming a more consequential and pervasive part of our culture.

This was a time of extraordinary opportunity, and David positioned the league to exploit every potential business opening. He led the NBA into new, immensely profitable ventures in marketing the game around the planet. Taking the league worldwide, playing exhibitions overseas, meant creating new markets to sell television rights and merchandise. Every sport has its great athletes and great personalities, but the NBA was uniquely successful in taking several of those individuals— most prominently, Michael Jordan, Magic Johnson, and Larry Bird—and promoting them in such a manner that they became global ambassadors of the game.

In so many ways, the modern NBA is a reflection of David Stern's vision and efforts. He deserves tremendous credit for leading the league to a new level of glory and success, nationally and internationally.

All this success has not only changed the NBA, but also spawned new problems, problems that every major sport already has or inevitably will encounter. While it has been a wondrous journey for me to be part of this evolution, I have great concern for the industry.

NBA athletes are, on the average, the highest-paid of all professional athletes. In addition, many have enjoyed enormous incomes off the court, in part because of the league's marketing strategy, focusing on individuals as stars, and in part because of the nature of the game, which has so many players constantly in on the action, performing their amazing acrobatics so close to the sidelines and to the fans.

The salary cap was put into place to attempt to bring some parity to the league, regardless of each team's market size. In response to the salary cap, the Larry Bird Rule was inaugurated, providing an exception to the cap, allowing each team to pay its own free agents whatever the team chose to pay them regardless of the cap. The efficacy of this exception, along with other exceptions relating to term of service and other factors, is a debatable subject.

What is certainly clear, along with the certainty for the need for some financial parity among teams, is that too much movement by the players from city to city, team to team, is not in the best interest of the NBA, or any league. Fans root for teams, that is to be sure, but players are also the manifest embodiment of that team. And though players come and go, either through trade or retirement, the core has always remained solid, a majority of players staying with one franchise, a continuum of faces and names for the fans to know and support.

The public has no illusions that athletes play solely for the love of the game, that sports are anything other than big business, and that many professional athletes literally earn more in one season than most Americans earn in the course of their entire careers. The public knows all that, and still pro sports are more popular than ever.

However, there are limits, and if the day should arrive when professional athletes are viewed only as mercenaries, with no interest in any team or city, or in the fortunes of that team or city, beyond that year's paycheck, that will herald a sad day for both the fans and the industry.

So it is imperative that we all work together, in the NBA, in MLB, in every sport, to ensure that sport's continued good fortune. In every industry, tension exists between labor and management, tension over money and benefits and working conditions, and sometimes that tension boils over and problems ensue. Of course, both sides must remember that destroying the other side is ultimately not in the best interest of their mutual business and mutual future.

So it is in sports. Larry Fleisher ran the players' union for twenty-seven years until his untimely death in 1989. Fleisher fought tooth-and-nail for his players, but he also knew when to stop and cut a deal. Larry helped make the NBA, and his athletes, so very successful, and the players owe him a great debt.

Since his death, the union has had several different men at the top, and this lack of stability has not proved advantageous to either the union or the league. The missing leadership at the union has only strengthened the hands of the agents, and agents, who are not responsible to the league but to their clients, cannot be given charge of the NBA's future through the de facto abdication by more appropriate authorities.

In the NBA, the players and their representatives have no choice but to realize that their futures are tied to controlling the league's spiraling costs. We cannot have situations, as has already happened with Kevin Garnett in Minnesota, where the existing system forced an untenable situation upon the franchise and the owner. The threat of losing a future star like Garnett, combined with the impossibility, under the legal threat of collusion, of inquiring as to what other teams were offering the young player, caused the Timberwolves to offer a contract that was literally worth more than the value of the entire franchise.

At the same time, the owners cannot simply blame the players and be done with it. After all, the owners are the ones paying the salaries. When all is said and done, it is unreasonable to expect economic self-discipline on either side to substitute for rules—not in a competitive situation—and thus the rules must be improved and strengthened.

The pressure on owners to win—from the fans, from the media, from seemingly everyone in their lives—is incredibly intense. The pressures are so great that some individuals are overpaid, for fear that stars will be lost to another team through free agency. As a result of the strict prohibitions against collusion, which do not simply forbid teams from colluding on deals and salaries—a sensible, legal restriction—but deny teams from gathering any information, including discovery of other offers a player might receive—a restriction that causes ill-considered and often unnecessary counter-offers—salaries and expenses have jumped unreasonably. We need to reform the system, and include, for instance, the right of first refusal, meaning the right to match another team's offer, for at least some of a team's players.

These and other proposals will build some logic and order into the league. Put aside the talk of the salary cap, a term which has gained some notoriety in some quarters—instead, call it a need for reasonable cost certainty.

A house divided against itself cannot stand. That's true for nations, for industries, and even for pro sports leagues.

I'm a strong believer in partnerships, including the partnership between labor and management, or, in sports terms, players and owners. Part of our new partnership must include a fresh realization of our obligation to individually and collectively act as role models.

We can no longer afford to ignore anyone's misdeeds simply because he is a great athlete or lauded coach or clever general manager or powerful owner. Obviously, this admonition relates primarily to the players, who constitute the NBA's most visible and important asset. Players must be held accountable for their actions, right or wrong.

Our increasingly permissive society has blurred the lines between good and bad, right and wrong, virtually denied that some behavior is appropriate and acceptable and some behavior is inappropriate and unacceptable. The NBA, and professional sports in general, can no longer be a sanctuary of lax personal standards. We must have a drug policy that is consistent and specific and tough. We must not condone actions on the court that would not be tolerated in any civilized company off the court. Similarly, we must not condone actions off the court that would not be tolerated by any individual, aside from the those few individuals who are members of our privileged, protected celebrity caste.

Being a role model—representing a handful of basic and decent values, giving something back to a society that has given us so much—is part and parcel of being a member of the NBA, and all other sports, too. This does not preclude anyone from being an individual, and from expressing that individuality in different ways, even if some of those ways are far from the norm. Regardless, some values and virtues are so basic that we must all must embrace and champion them.

In my opinion, if an athlete refuses to accept this responsibility, so fundamental and so simple, then he should find another line of work.

CHAPTER   TEN

Community Service

I OVERSEE AN organization, which runs a business—several businesses, in fact—and how to most successfully operate in the business world has been the largest component of this book. However, we have also discussed other issues—the relationship of the company to the employee, of the organization to the community, of the business to government. Now we will take on another aspect of business—of our business—and discuss charity, and working to better not only the company, but also the world in which it thrives.

The Bible tells us, "For what is a man profited, if he shall gain the whole world, and lose his own soul?" In our society, those timeless words are equally applicable to both the individual and the corporation. What measure of satisfaction would our organization really derive from a Suns championship if by our actions, or lack of actions, the franchise had alienated the community, and no one in Phoenix and Arizona shared our joy?

Of course, the point of doing good work is not to bask in the gratitude and applause, and that was not my point either. Rather, I was trying to stress that the Suns, or any other team, are nothing without the community's support, and we must

213

repay that support. One way we do that is by playing as hard as we can on the court. Another way is to get involved in the community and try to make it a better place for everyone.

And yet our obligation goes deeper than that. We are obligated as human beings individually, and then as human beings collectively, when grouped together in organizations or corporations, obligated by our morals and values and traditions and beliefs, to use our resources and abilities, and our own good fortune, to help those in need. We are obligated because that is one of the joys of life, to be part of life, to serve life by serving our neighbors and our community.

We, meaning the Suns, the Diamondbacks, and the other teams and departments in the organization, have taken up this responsibility with enthusiasm, and in different ways.

Each team has its own fan base, and so each team has its own charity fund in order to maximize its charitable capabilities and opportunities.

The Phoenix Suns Charities, as befits our oldest franchise, has the most developed and active charitable community relations department and is involved in a multitude of activities. Tom Ambrose, the Suns vice president of public relations, has been with the franchise since 1973 and is in charge of this work for the team.

The team's mission statement says it all:

> The mission of the Phoenix Suns organization
> is to provide the finest in sports and entertainment,
> to be a constant leader in improving the quality of
> life in our community and to maintain a commit-
> ment to integrity, innovation, and a winning tra-
> dition.

I had emphasized the importance of community service from the beginning of our tenure in Phoenix, not only for the organization, but for the players and coaches, too. In short order, we were involved in a multitude of events, large and small, and eventually recognized that we needed to formalize the system that decided what we would do and how we would participate. The Suns formed a board of some fifty leading individuals from the community, to decide how money raised by Suns Charities should be allocated. Our focus has been on helping children in need and families in distress, on issues relating to health, education, and safety.

The board reviews over two hundred requests for monetary donations every year, handing out grants averaging $5,000 to $10,000 to between eighty and ninety groups. Ordinarily, larger grants, such as $150,000 given to the Phoenix Symphony, $100,000 to the Greater Phoenix Economic Council, and $100,000 to the Home Base Youth Center, $500,000 given to the Arizona State University capital campaign, $250,000 to the Phoenix Central Library, and $100,000 to the YMCA are awarded directly by the Suns organization.

On the average, Suns Charities gives out about $500,000 each year, which is augmented by at least an equal amount given by the Phoenix Suns on the corporate side.

In addition to these applications and bequests, we receive another hundred requests each month for player appearances, player-autographed items suitable for charity auction, purchasing tables at fund-raising events, donation of product.

Much of the funding for Suns Charities is raised at our "Courtside Classic," a black-tie affair for which the guests—hundreds of whom paid five hundred dollars each—are handed basketball shoes at the door to wear with their formal duds. The entire team attends, acting as hosts, and approximately $250,000 is raised.

In 1991, the U.S. military and its allies commenced operations in the Persian Gulf, aimed against Iraqi forces, in the campaign known as Desert Storm, on the same night as our gala. To say the least, I was uncomfortable with attending, let alone hosting, a party as our men and women were engaged in combat half a world away. Nonetheless, it was simply impossible to alter plans at the last minute, and canceling was out of the question—too many people and organizations depended upon the proceeds for too many important causes to just walk away from the event.

Seeking some reasonable way to go on with the event without ignoring or slighting our soldiers, I stood at the start of the evening and pledged $50,000 from the gala's take to the Red Cross to support family counseling, youth programs, and other issues related to the war.

Long before we had a board or a formal charity structure, back in 1968, the year we organized the Suns, we commenced with our first major endeavor. In partnership with one of the most esteemed civic groups in the state and the nation, we formed the Phoenix Suns/Boys & Girls Club Basketball League. This statewide youth league has grown to include well over five thousand twelve-to-thirteen-year-old boys and girls, and one thousand volunteer coaches. Every March, the championship game is held at America West Arena, and the team provides the participants with tickets to the Suns' game that immediately follows their contest.

We are working with the Boys & Girls Club on other ongoing projects as well, including the Phoenix Suns Exchange Club and the Phoenix Suns Holiday Party. The former invites six students, selected by their teachers based on academic performance, school attendance and good citizenship, to fly to Oregon each time the team plays the Portland Trailblazers, airline tickets supplied by America West Airlines. The latter program invites nearly one hundred children to America West Arena for a Christmas party, attended by Suns players, and includes gifts and a tour of the place—the Purple Palace, as we like to call it. Subway provides the lunch, and then the kids are escorted to a mall, where Boys & Girls Club board members treat them to a holiday shopping spree.

So many other important initiatives demand attention. The Suns Nite Hoops is an intriguing program, combining basketball with work, educational, and counseling opportunities. Former NBA player Steve Colter directs the effort, in which young men, ages eighteen to twenty-five, who have experienced trouble in their lives (80 percent are referred by the Maricopa County Probation Office), play in an organized league two nights each week from 7 to 11 P.M.—prime hours for crime.

But the league, despite offering the finest in athletic equipment, from gyms to uniforms, as well as coaches and referees, is much, much more than just basketball. One hour preceding each game, the players are required to attend forty-five minute educational workshops, conducted courtside under the auspices of NCTI, a national training and education company under contract by the Suns. The work undertaken during this hour involves group discussions, role playing, and other exercises designed to improve their job interviewing skills, parenting proficiency, educational opportunities, and so on.

Basketball is the medium, but self-improvement is the message. And whether actually getting on the court or through the example of professional athletes, the object is to bring something special and consequential, materially or intellectually, emotionally or spiritually, into the lives of those who can benefit from this involvement or intervention.

Another example of a successful program: Since 1992, the Stay in School program, which involves fifty Maricopa County middle schools, has proven the organization's largest community relations enterprise. The program, conducted in cooperation with the NBA, features visits by former and current Suns to school assemblies to talk about the importance of getting an education, essay contests, and a variety of Suns' gifts in recognition of superior school work and effort. A couple of seasons ago, the year's effort was capped by a "Stay in

School Celebration," where 16,000 students were honored at the arena for their superlative achievement within the program. This extraordinary occasion brought out not only a squad of Suns players, but also Ahmad Rashad and Willow Bay, the hosts of "NBA Inside Stuff," and was broadcast live simultaneously on NBC, TNT, BET, and Nickelodeon.

I could go on for pages detailing the multitude of programs in which the Suns have dedicated a portion of their resources and time: reading programs with the Phoenix Public Library and the Glendale Public Library, involving more than 30,000 children; prizes for outstanding Arizona teachers; sponsorship of a public pool in the summer, which allowed it to remain open longer than the city can afford, keeping the kids cool through the dog days of the season; raising money for Easter Seals through an annual basketball "shoot-out," as kids are invited to gather pledges based on the number of baskets they can sink at the arena; a basketball team entered in the National Wheelchair Basketball Association, sponsored by the Suns, Samaritan Health System, and America West Airlines; "open practices," where fans fill the arena and get to watch the Suns practice in exchange for bringing a can of food, or one dollar, to be donated to the Salvation Army.

But that is just the beginning. We participate with other charities, like the Make-A-Wish Foundation, and dozens of terminally ill children have visited with their favorite Suns players, as well as raise toys, food, and other necessities for groups like Toys for Tots and Shoes for the Homeless. The Foundation for Senior Living, the Community Housing Partnership, the New Day Homeless Shelter, the Downtown Neighborhood Learning Center, the United Food Bank, the Desert Botanical Garden, the Special Olympics, the Glencroft Retirement Home. . . . The list of beneficiaries and partners in the Suns community service literally runs on for pages.

Suns, past and present, and also the team's mascot, the Gorilla, spend countless hours speaking at schools, hospitals, charity events, and any other setting that benefits the community. Seats and suites at America West Arena are donated to good causes and underprivileged kids. The United Way has been a special recipient of our franchise's attentions; I have served as chairman for its county fund-raising campaign, and many others in the franchise have worked long and hard for the organization—not including their personal financial contributions, which have added up to a considerable sum—and we have helped raise millions for the United Way.

The exceedingly prominent media profile that the Suns have gained on the court, and our organization has acquired off the court, through our community efforts, has resulted in a situation where our involvement with a group or cause will spur others to become involved. An example of this is the "Kool Kids" Program, previously mentioned. For twenty-five to fifty cents per child, adding up to a few thousand dollars in total, we were able to keep the Harmon Public Pool in south Phoenix open to occupy some six thousand kids through the entire summer. When we signed up for the program, other companies were prompted to adopt their own pools. In this way, we are able to leverage our name and reputation to greatest benefit.

Not everything we do is through any formal mechanism. Though each Suns player signs a contract that stipulates that he will make six individual personal appearances and another six team appearances on behalf of the franchise's community relations effort, most players end up doing much, much more, and often on their own. Charles Barkley used to visit a homeless shelter each Christmas, then round up all the children in the shelter, take them to a Toys R Us, and let them run free, selecting whatever toys they wanted. Barkley would pay the bill, which would inevitably run into the thousands of dollars.

Charles did this without publicity. In fact, he shunned the media, and refused to promote his generosity in any way, fearing that he would be viewed as just another celebrity seeking press attention and public adulation. He did this because he wanted to, because he thought it was a decent, wonderful thing to do. Through his success on the court, he was in a position to do it, and so he did.

When Barkley left town in the trade that landed him in Houston, we asked Jason Kidd if he wanted to take over and continue Charles's good Christmas deed. Jason enthusiastically embraced the notion and has made this visit, this occasion, his own.

Many of our athletes spend long hours working on their separate charities and causes. Kevin Johnson has met with Native American children each October for over a decade now, encouraging them in their studies, urging them to stay away from alcohol and drugs, counseling them to set life goals. As has been previously noted, KJ has demonstrated his commitment to the community over and over again, through his many good works. On the baseball side, several Diamondbacks have shown similar devotion to helping others. Surely one of the most extraordinary gestures was Matt Williams's pledge, upon signing with the Diamondbacks, to donate $750,000 to the United Way, a contribution that was matched by the team itself. Also prominent among Diamondback activists are Andy Benes and Jay Bell, who, perhaps not coincidentally, are also team leaders.

Our other employees—the ones who work in the office and not on the court or field— also devote long hours to charitable causes. The list of charities that our good men and women have served is too long to spell out here, but let it suffice to say that it includes the American Heart Association, the Arizona Children's Home Foundation, the Arthritis Foundation, Childsplay, Crisis Pregnancy Centers of Greater Phoenix, the Girl Scouts, the Mayor's Committee on Diversity, Phoenix Children's Hospital, the Phoenix Zoo, and Valley Big Brothers/Big Sisters.

Our other franchises are establishing their own community service traditions, gearing their efforts towards either their fans' concerns or something that is of special significance to the team. The Phoenix Mercury is looking to make a difference with regard to some women's issues, raising money for breast cancer research, for instance. The Rattlers have a program, in cooperation with St. Joseph Hospital's Poison Control Center, to alert people about dealing with the dangers of poison, and what to do in the case of a poisoning incident.

The baseball club is seeking to raise a considerable amount of money to fund its Arizona Diamondbacks Charities, introduced to the public as a legally constituted entity on July 10, 1998. Some funds have already been raised, and the foundation will be looking to make an impact in the community in a variety of ways, especially in the areas of youth development and education, assisting health care for the indigent, and providing more housing for the homeless, and low or moderate-income families.

Already, Diamondback players are all over Arizona, getting involved in different activities. A program called "Dr. Diamondbacks" started in August, with first baseman Travis Lee, outfielder David Dellucci, and pitcher Andy Benes representing the team on visits to local hospitals to bring some welcome cheer to young patients. All-star center fielder Devon White hosts the "Future Athletes Youth Baseball Camp" for seventy-five disadvantaged children from south Phoenix. Devon, along with teammates outfielder Bernard Gilkey and pitcher Willie Banks, and coach Marcos Garcia, are encouraging these young people to get involved in both school and the community, with the reward of a baseball clinic awaiting those who excel in these endeavors. Outfielder Karim Garcia represented the franchise as it celebrated the rehabilitation of a Little League baseball field at Joseph I. Flores Academia del Pueblo Elementary School, complete with new field, dugouts, bleachers, and equipment, paid for by the team, the Phoenix Jaycees, APS, and MLB's True Value Field of Dreams program.

In this age of widespread public cynicism and endless media spinning, it is inevitable that many will wonder whether any of this really makes a difference, whether any of this has any influence on people's lives. Indeed, the question continues, are all these fund-raising events and public appearances just one obligatory, public relations sham, perpetuated by a business dependent upon the public's good will?

While I think our work speaks for itself, I'd like to include a letter that we received. Through the year, we receive many letters thanking us for participating or donating or appearing. I have selected this letter to excerpt, not because it represented a sizable monetary contribution, or even a great effort on our part. Nonetheless, it speaks to the impact that even a simple gesture from an athlete can have on a child's life:

> While it is an unspeakable tragedy to lose a child so young, I wanted to let you know what a difference you made in her life. Her family told me how excited she was to have the chance to go to the locker room after the game to meet the players. That visit to the locker room made a huge difference in her short life and I thought you should know.

Could you place a tangible value on such an experience? Expressed another way, can you imagine a more valuable expenditure of time and energy on the part of our franchise, or on the part of any group or organization?

In the end, our community service work—all the money we raise and disperse, all the other companies we entice to join us, all the publicity we attract, all the public appearances we make, all the good we try to do—is dependent upon the fame and reputation of the teams and their players. Those who say that athletes are not role models, that they do not have an impact on how other people, particularly young people, think and feel about themselves and about society, and its norms and values and beliefs, are profoundly mistaken, and simply contradicted by the evidence.

The Diamondbacks held a contest in which children had to write brief essays about their favorite Diamondback player. Stephen Dewson's winning essay spoke well to this question about role models:

> My name is Stephen. I am 7 years old and I love baseball and especially the Diamondbacks. I like to play first base just like Travis Lee. That is one reason why he is my favorite player. He is also a good home run hitter. He seems real nice, too. He sets a good example because he does not throw his bat and he is always calm, even when he gets called out on strikes. I want to be a good player and nice guy like Travis Lee.

Whether Stephen will one day play first base in the majors will only be decided many years from now. However, there is no doubt that Travis's public behavior, and Stephen's positive response to that behavior, has already set Stephen on the path towards becoming a responsible, mature citizen.

This is not to suggest that athletes should be the sole or even foremost role models in any child's life. That position must be reserved for parental example and guidance. But this is not an either/or situation; real life is more complicated than that. Many people influence a child's ideas and ideals, beyond the primary caregiver: grandparents, cousins, teachers, coaches, friends, and those whom the media promotes as celebrities and heroes.

Nonetheless, athletes count. They count because we see

them perform gracefully, skillfully, amazingly. We see them win, and we see them lose. Because we see them at work, because we see them at their highest and lowest moments, we feel we know them. And in some ways, on some level, we do. And that feeling, that belief, based part in fact, part in conjecture, and part in hope, makes them role models.

There's an old saying, that charity begins at home, and it can be true even when that home is a corporation like the Phoenix Suns.

We've already spoken about Connie Hawkins, and how we brought him back into the organization after many years away. But the Hawk wasn't the only former player who came back to the Suns after some time in other places.

As you might recall, center Neal Walk was our pick in the first round of the 1969 draft, after losing the coin flip, and the rights, to Lew Alcindor, a.k.a. Kareem Abdul-Jabbar. Walk performed very well for us, averaging more than twelve points and nine rebounds over five seasons. In 1972–73, he averaged 20.2 points and 12.4 rebounds, still the only Suns center to ever grab more than one thousand rebounds in a single season. In 1974, a trade sent him to New Orleans. He lasted a couple of seasons with the Jazz, then he was dispatched to New York for a year, and then Walk was out of the NBA. At that point, he went over to Europe to play. That was when we lost track of Neal.

Several years passed, until one day, one blisteringly hot summer day, I was standing in front of the Jewish Community Center in downtown Phoenix, when I noticed somebody struggling to get out of a car. The man was paralyzed, and was having an awful time, sweating and pulling, trying to get out of the car and lift himself into a wheelchair.

I suddenly realized, with a shock, that the man was Neal Walk. I learned that he had been confined to a wheelchair since 1987, after undergoing an operation to remove a tumor from his spinal cord.

Shortly after that encounter, Neal joined the Suns' community relations staff and today is the coordinator for the team's speakers bureau. In addition to his job with the Suns, he works with groups across the state to further public awareness of issues facing the handicapped. Within the past few years, he has been recognized for his athletic achievements, including his induction into the Jewish Sports Hall of Fame in 1990, being named the recipient of the 1991 Victory Award for Arizona, and also the 1995 Gene Autry Courage Award.

Neal Walk proved to be quite a remarkable success story, and his rise from tragedy is an inspiration. However, I cannot claim that every tale is one of unqualified triumph.

Gene Williams was a fine athlete out of Kansas State, one of Cotton's former players back in the Sixties. We drafted Williams, but he didn't make the team, and he disappeared from sight. A few years later, I was in my office when I got a call from downstairs. I was told that Gene Williams was here, and he wanted to see me.

I had Gene immediately sent in, and it was readily apparent that he had become a street person and was seriously in need of assistance. Coincidentally, Cotton, who had left the Suns to take the head coaching job with the Atlanta Hawks, was in town with his team. Cotton and I sat down and talked to Williams, attempting to see what we could do to help. Though we offered various options, Gene rejected them all. It was evident that we couldn't do much for Williams, except give him some money to get back to San Francisco, which was his home. We bought him an airline ticket, and urged him to make contact with his family or friends, to try to get his life together, to get some assistance, and to keep in touch.

Neither Cotton nor I have ever heard from Gene Williams again. I hope he is doing well, though I fear that very well might not be the case. The truth is, there is only so much you can do for another. You can provide a helping hand, some money, perhaps an opportunity, but that is all. When I offered Connie Hawkins a job, I expected him to show up in Phoenix within two weeks. Connie chose to show up thirteen months later. Happily, we still had a job for him, and events turned out to everyone's advantage.

There is no denying that it is easy for corporations to dispense funds to worthy causes, nor is there any doubt that some corporations do so just for the favorable PR value, along with the tax deductions. As I've already detailed, all our franchises have made significant contributions to the community.

Nonetheless, I believe that we all have a responsibility as individuals to do what we can for the community. Obviously, those with more to give, either in time or money, should try to give that extra effort. For myself and my family, I hold to the Bible's admonition to tithe a set portion of your income to your church.

In addition, because of my heightened public posture, due to the high profile of our several teams, I am sometimes approached by those in crisis on a one-on-one basis, whom I might meet in our church or other venues, as a sort of relief of last resort. When possible, my family responds, because that is what we should do as individuals, as a family, as citizens.

Then there are those other causes that demand our attention. One reason I have been so proud that we have been able to build our franchises in Arizona has been my conviction that sports, as part of the culture, is essential to the health and well-being of the community. Regardless, sports are far from the sole cultural institution that any community needs, and I have endeavored to be of assistance on occasion. It is the mix of the institutions of the arts—libraries, museums, concerts, plays, films, et cetera—and sports that gives a community verve and vitality.

The Phoenix Symphony was always in financial difficulty,

always struggling from one year to the next to make ends meet. It is tough to concentrate on creating art when artists are worried about making the rent.

The bottom line was that the symphony needed $300,000. That amount wouldn't exactly put the musicians and their management on easy street, but the sum would be sufficient to extract them all from this incessant strife. I was asked to help, and I was glad to try.

The year was 1993. A couple of months passed, and I was still considering the best way to raise the money for the symphony. In the meantime, the Suns made it into the play-offs. The first round was against the Lakers, and the series didn't start well at all. In fact, the Suns not only lost the first two games, but lost them at home.

Another loss and we'd be out of the play-offs, because the first round was the best three of five.

The series shifted to Los Angeles, and the game went down to the very last seconds. The Suns came away with the win, and the team lived to fight another day.

Not long after the game, I received a phone call from Rick Lehman, the chairman and CEO of Bank One. "Jerry," he said, the concern evident in his voice. "Are you okay?"

"Sure," I replied. "Why?"

"Because you looked like you were going to die out there," he said.

It didn't take long to figure out what Rick was talking about. I had traveled with the club to L.A. and had taken a seat near our bench, on the floor. The camera had picked me up as the contest had neared its finish, and I had looked as anguished as I had felt. It's one thing to be in the game; no matter how tight or important the match, there's no time to stop and dwell on the significance of it all, as you battle to gain the victory. It's quite another to be stuck on the sidelines, powerless and removed. Frequently, at least to this old athlete, it's unnerving and tormenting.

Anyway, the symphony dilemma must have been on my

mind because Rick's comment instantly served to crystallize my fund-raising strategy.

"I need to raise a lot of money for the symphony," I said, trying to sound as sincerely in need as possible.

Rick Lehman and Bank One donated $25,000 for the symphony.

Rick's concerned question about my health had given me my lead, and I shamelessly ran with it, over and over.

I called John Teets, Chip Weil of the Arizona Republic, Mark de Michele at APS, and many, many others in the local business community.

"Did you watch the game?" I asked. "You saw how bad I looked? I need $25,000. . . ."

Within a couple of hours, I raised not $300,000, but $350,000.

I'm not normally an advocate of embellishing or playing on people's emotions, but hey, this was for charity.

So allow me to say, once again: whether as an individual or as a corporation, we all must do what we can.

Epilogue

I AM FREQUENTLY asked what I think the future holds for the sports industry. Will professional sports continue to grow? Will greed and arrogance eventually destroy the business by destroying the fans' sense of relationship to the players and teams? Or will the grace and skill and excitement of the athletes and the games continue to capture the imagination of the audience with sufficient power so as to drown out the financial and administrative issues which threaten pro sports?

We have certainly seen some of these questions put to the test in the ongoing turmoil in the NBA. As these words are being written, in the middle of December 1998, the NBA season remains on hold, as the owners and the players cannot reach an agreement to break the contractual impasse, end the lockout, sign free agents, and get the season started. The impact on the basketball industry, and the people who work in the industry—beyond the players and owners—from ushers to parking attendants to concessionaires, and so on—as well as the fans who support the league, has been monstrous and depressing. Whether the season is canceled, a contingency that becomes ever more probable as the weeks pass, or whether a truncated version is cobbled together at the last minute, the league has suffered tremendous damage, not only financially but also emotionally.

This sad state of affairs is a depressing reflection on the status of labor relations between ownership and its players. Where there once was trust and a true sense of partnership, there now appears to be suspicion and antagonism. After thirty-two years in the professional game—and my experience as a member of the labor relations committee—I cannot adequately express my disappointment and frustration that the NBA has grown and succeeded to such an amazing extent only to end up ripped apart by greed and distrust and dissension.

The trouble in the NBA should not be viewed in isolation. Every major sport, including the National Football League, Major League Baseball, and the National Hockey League, has suffered strikes and shutdowns and publicly contentious labor–management disputes, sometimes over and over again. The NBA had somehow escaped the problems facing other sports—until now. I hope and pray that the situation will not happen again. Once is enough in my lifetime.

Of course, sooner or later, the situation will be resolved, the lights will go back on in the arenas, and the players will once again take to the courts. The question is whether the damage done to the NBA is irreparable. Expressed another way, the question is whether the fans will return.

Personally, I have too much faith in the innate glory of the game and the wonderful athletes who perform in the league to believe that pro basketball will not recover from this debacle. I believe the fans, as rightfully angry as they are today, will find their enthusiasm for the sport and their favorite teams rekindled once there is something to cheer about again. Basketball is just too compelling a game, and the players are just too acrobatic and astonishing, to have it any other way.

In contrast, as basketball undergoes its trial by fire, baseball is thriving. Indeed, basketball's problems have afforded me the time and the opportunity to focus on baseball and the Arizona Diamondbacks. The original game plan for the Diamondbacks set a four- to five-year building scheme, starting in the first year by putting together some solid building blocks, and then adding to the base each year, through the free market, trades and the farm system. By year four or five, the idea was to have the club in a very competitive position, ready to vie for the championship.

However, all that changed as I evaluated the state of the organization, and the state of our competition, especially within our division. I took stock in what we had accomplished, where we were headed, and questioned whether or not that original game plan was still the best strategy for the club. I decided that baseball was an area that, with an adjustment in our game plan, we had the chance to really improve our product.

Besides, as a person who relishes not just the challenge of trying to structure a better team, but also enjoys the pure, unvarnished thrill of the action, I could not help but seize on this opportunity.

Additionally, we announced a price increase, across the board, of approximately 12 percent. Some sections—particularly the lower-priced sections—were not affected at all. The one-dollar tickets remained one dollar, the $3.50 tickets remained the same. In fact, the greatest increases were with the most expensive groups of tickets, which are frequently purchased, in all stadiums and arenas, by corporations and business—in other words, those best able to afford it.

Nonetheless, the response from the media and the fans was dramatic. For some reason, media interest was not only local, as might be expected, but national. As far as I was concerned, the media badly overplayed the issue: in 1998, our first season in MLB, ticket prices for the Diamondbacks placed us seventeenth out of the thirty teams, just below the average. Now, in the upcoming 1999 season, our price increase would only move us up to either fourteenth or fifteenth among all clubs—hardly a seismic shift. Furthermore, many teams raised their prices in substantially more dramatic fashion and somehow escaped serious censure. The New York Mets, for example, have increased their ticket prices by fully 20 percent each of the past two years.

In any event, though raising our ticket prices was important and reasonable, it surely did not help our renewal rate with season ticket holders. We had projected somewhere around an 80 percent renewal, but were only running at a 60 percent rate. Season ticket holders comprise the majority of the seats sold in probably every professional stadium, and thus form the foundation of the financial health of the club. Our ability to appeal to them, to keep them excited and interested in the Diamondbacks, was essential.

Hence, I was faced with two issues: trying to raise our on-field performance to another level, which would not come cheaply, while maintaining our fan interest and resulting cash flow.

It quickly became apparent to me that pitching was such an important part of baseball, that if we concentrated on signing position players in piecemeal fashion—a right fielder here, a catcher there—it would take quite a long time to build a contending team. However, if we concentrated on pitching and were able to put together a first-rate pitching staff, we might be able to become competitive immediately.

Though we had found a few fine pitchers during the expansion draft in our first season, the following year—1998—the free-agent market was awash in pitchers, ranging from serviceable to good to outstanding.

We decided to make a run for it early in the free-agent game, and GM Joe Garagiola did a terrific job. The day after we traded for Dante Powell from the Giants, a young and very promising hitter and outfielder, the Diamondbacks signed free agents Greg Swindel, an experienced left-handed reliever, and Greg Colbrunn, one of the game's premier pinch-hitters and fine multiposition player. Armando Reynoso, a right-handed pitcher, who started for the Mets last season before jumping into the free agent market, soon became another excellent addition to the pitching staff.

While Joe concentrated on those deals, I focused on our two biggest targets, two of the best pitchers available in the marketplace.

Todd Stottlemyre was one of those pitchers. He had posted double-digit victorious seasons in eight of his last nine years. Striking out more than two hundred batters in 1998, he helped the Texas Rangers win the American League West championship. At the age of thirty-three, he was at the top of his game, and could prove an extremely valuable asset to our club.

Other teams also recognized Stottlemyre's value, and he had at least half a dozen offers on the table. So what made Todd choose the Diamondbacks? I think Todd explained it best, when he spoke to the media at the press conference announcing his signing. He talked about competing in the past against Buck, and what a great complement of manager and coaches we've assembled. He talked about how we took care of the families of the players, and how we considered our players and their families to be part of our larger organizational family. He talked about how we have ten ex-Phoenix Suns still working for that franchise, which showed our true commitment to this extended family. And then Stottlemyre talked about our one day together and about the impression I had made on him, and what finally decided the issue:

"Ultimately, sitting down, as he looked into my eyes and I looked into his, I saw a fire, a fire of passion, a fire to compete, an intensity. And as a competitor, somebody who takes pride in their intensity and their emotions of being competitive, I saw those same things in his eyes, the passion of being an owner, and I thought, 'Gee, this is it right here.'"

The truth is that every interested party offers these elite athletes lots of money. That being equal, you have to promote other factors, often intangible factors, that will persuade these players to want to play for you. Phoenix is a dynamic, growing city, Arizona is blessed with wonderful weather, and the Diamondbacks have Bank One Ballpark and other terrific sports facilities. Then we have the Diamondbacks organization, which is dedicated, as Todd noted, to building a contender. Todd recognized and appreciated all these factors, including my own determination to winning. And for Todd, those factors made the difference.

With Stottlemyre on board, I concentrated on Randy Johnson, Cy Young winner and one of the most dominating pitchers of the decade. We always felt we had an inside track with Johnson because he lived right here in Paradise Valley with his family. That held open the realistic possibility that if we offered a financial package commensurate with other teams' offers, and were moving towards fielding a really competitive club, on track to compete for the championship, we should be able to sign Johnson.

Johnson was more than just a great pitcher to us. He was also an economic boon, because he was a tremendous draw. Between selling more seats, and then selling more merchandise to those fans in those seats, and an increased television share, we figured that his presence on the Diamondbacks could mean an additional 3 to 4 million dollars per year in revenue.

I met with Randy, his family, and his agent one Sunday night at the Johnson home. We talked about a lot of issues—how competitive we thought the Diamondbacks could be, the other pitchers and position players we recently signed, the family feeling we tried hard to foster, and so on. We also talked about Buck's rather conservative rules and regulations, which included neatly trimmed hair. Given Randy's flowing locks and sizable mustache, which he had no intention of cutting, he recognized that could be a problem, and asked me how I stood on the subject.

I had already discussed this with Buck, who, I must say, had already begun to loosen up a bit on his rules, and so I had my answer ready. I told Randy that if he had tattoos from his head to his toes, plus a big ring in his nose, plus the long hair, I'd have to pass. But considering he only had the hair, I said I'd take him just the way he was, and work on his deficiencies once he was in the fold. He looked at me and gave out a big laugh, and we moved on to other matters.

Randy Johnson signed with us, which immediately led *Baseball Weekly* to pick the Diamondbacks to win the National League Western Division. But we weren't done; shortly thereafter, we signed Steve Finley, the outstanding center fielder from the San Diego Padres.

We had a great meeting with Finley and his wife, and made two offers, both of which were rejected. We let the matter drop, and then a week later, on the day of Johnson's signing, Steve called me and said that he wanted to be a Diamondback. He said, "I felt really comfortable in Arizona and want to be with you."

We were always willing to talk, though we were planning on seriously modifying our offer. I got back on the phone with Steve and his agent, and we worked out the deal.

Again, money is surely the key issue, but it is not the only issue. You have to create an atmosphere that makes the player stand up and notice and think to himself, "I want to play here. I want to be there. I want to be with these guys."

All these multiyear deals together are intended to not only assure the Diamondbacks of, at the least, a successful four-year run on the field, but also dramatically increased revenues. In fact, immediately after signing Randy Johnson, the ticket office received a noteworthy increase in season ticket sales. That is the crux of the sports business, the mingling of athletic and financial concerns. We had to be responsible and creative when structuring the deals for these prominent players, and so, generally speaking, distributed half their money in yearly salaries and half in payments spread over a much longer period, a period ordinarily double the length of their contracts. This structure will allow us to increase our revenues before the bulk of these players' contract comes due, and thus allow us to keep signing players in the future.

The underlying point of this discussion on the Diamondback moves is that while it is essential that our business, same as any business, possesses a well-considered long-range game plan, it is just as essential that the people in charge of that business be intellectually flexible and emotionally open to changing that game plan, no matter how well considered, when the need clearly arises. For the Diamondbacks, I recognized that the need had clearly arisen, and I responded to it. And while the season is still a few months off, and the results have yet to be seen on the field, I am satisfied that we have done the right thing.

Returning to the question that opened this concluding epilogue, a query about the future of the sports industry, I can say with absolute confidence that I do not know what tomorrow will bring. That is not to say that I don't have ideas about possibilities and trends, and I can't take those ideas and extrapolate and arrive at some conclusions. I think and consider and contemplate all the time. But that is far from knowing anything. I don't know what is going to happen and don't pretend to.

I do know that it's neither a cliche nor precisely accurate to say that you can't stop progress. The more exact truth is, you can't simultaneously stop either progress or change. You can't stop the evolution that is taking place. Change is constant and unending, and often unsettling and unpredictable. And when you're a major player in the entertainment industry, as is the case with professional sports, some of your stars become larger than life, become substantial financial forces unto themselves. That goes with the territory, just like in the movie business.

Just as you can't stop change, you can't turn the clock back, and return to a simpler time, an allegedly more innocent era. Competition is the lifeblood of sports, competition for victories and players and fans and media exposure and ticket sales and product sales. Competition for profits and respect and loyalty. Competition for championships. Competition for the sake of competition.

That explains why rival leagues have always popped up in all sports. They either fail or ultimately merge with the already existing leagues. In baseball, the National League, born in 1876, joined forces with the American League in 1903. Many years later, the National Basketball Association faced a challenge from the American Basketball Association. The ABA survived its shaky start and did well enough with basketball fans that the NBA decided that the smartest way to deal with the upstart league was to absorb four of its thriving teams into the senior circuit, causing the rest to die on the vine. So in similar fashion did the National Football League take in the American Football League.

Of course, not every upstart league prospered. Most did not, but instead struggled and suffered and died, forgotten and unlamented. From the National Association, 1871–1876, to the United States Football League one hundred years later, which didn't even last the National Association's five years, the turf is littered with the corpses of leagues that never were much more than ambitious schemes and shiny uniforms. As time passes, the price of admission into professional sports has climbed so high that fewer and fewer adventurers can afford to enter the game—any game. Not much more than ten years ago, when I put together the group to buy the Suns for $44.5 million, it was the highest price ever paid for an NBA franchise. Now, a decade later, our franchise is valued at a nice, round, extraordinary $200 million.

Not a bad investment—especially because neither I nor anyone else could have predicted that back in 1986.

I was very fortunate to have been in the right time and

place—and right frame of mind—to buy the franchise. I didn't have the wherewithal to do it myself, so I found others to join with me. All together, we made it work.

I believed in the franchise, I believed in Phoenix and Arizona, I believed in my ability and the ability of our organization to make it a success. Still, I didn't have a master plan, a long-range goal, a statistical model for future action.

The truth was, we didn't need one. We needed commitment and long hours and a little bit of luck. The commitment and the long hours we supplied. The luck came our way.

I have talked about many of the lessons I've picked up through my years in the sports industry. I know I haven't done so in any orderly fashion, listing my top ten rules for success, that sort of thing, because I don't think business, or life, works that way. I think we try and fail and try and fail—try and make some headway, some progress, maybe eventually effect a breakthrough, and, hopefully, we listen and watch and learn as we go. It's not neat, it's not cut-and-dry, it doesn't fit into a format or a curriculum, but it's reality. And the reality never stops, nor do the lessons, whether you're starting in the mailroom or running the company.

In running the company, the organization, the franchise, I have learned that it's too easy to order things done, too easy to tell others to take care of this and that, too easy to forget what it takes to do a good job. It is imperative to never allow yourself to be isolated from the grind, from the difficulties, from the facts of your business.

You didn't build the business, or get to the top, by standing back while others saw to the company's needs. Thus, it makes no sense to stand back, to stand apart or stand aloof, once that company, all its employees and investors, and all their aspirations and trust, rest in your hands.

While this might seem like the simplest common sense, it runs counter to the impulse of so many who have spent long hours working their ways up the ladder and believe their proper roles now are to supervise, to superintend.

At the same time, though experience is your greatest asset and prime source of knowledge, you can't solely rely on that experience. Everything changes so fast today, that the key is often not what you've learned, but how fast you can learn something new. Challenges arise every day, and few can be overlooked, no matter how solid your rank in your business. Xerox missed out on Canon's challenge to its dominance in the copier field, because Canon only made cameras, just as IBM gave away its overwhelming, controlling role in the computer business because it did not consider the multitude of small hardware companies that cropped up as threats to its position.

Needs and markets will always be met by smart people with inventive ideas. Anyone who believes that he has the answers to every situation probably has precious few answers, and a serious lack of imagination. Jim Crupi, well-known international business consultant and future trends analyst, contends that the future will be not about resources but about will. He has illustrated his point with a story from the Vietnam War. One of our Air Force's major objectives was to destroy the bridges linking the north to the south, stopping the enemy from moving in soldiers and material. Though we bombed incessantly, and hit bridge after bridge, we ultimately failed in our mission goal. Long after the war, a friend of Crupi's was in Vietnam, meeting with a local businessman who had been a young general during the war. At the end of their talk, the American asked the Vietnamese ex-soldier how he kept getting his troops and equipment across the river.

"Well," he replied, "we build the bridges six inches under the water."

Imagine that! The need on the part of the Vietnamese to convince the pilots that there were no bridges left to bomb, and to offer no visual targets, led to a most creative solution. Whether in war or business, the ability to improvise and create, on the spot or in short order, working with whatever is available but relying first and foremost on your intellect, your conviction, and your unshakable determination, will decide success or failure.

As cliched as it might sound, it remains true that in our country, anything is possible. Any goal can be gained, any dream attained. I've heard people talk about not getting opportunities, and that certainly can be the case. Nonetheless, more often than not, the opportunites will come, sooner or later, and maybe in ways not anticipated.

It is important to remember that opportunities are not finished products, but demand that you rise to the challenge and take whatever risks—whatever calculated risks—are necessary. The risk does not have to involve money, as you might immediately assume, because money is not always required to make money. Intelligence, vision, determination: those will take you a very long way. All the way, indeed.

No one—and that includes yours truly—can give anyone else—and that includes you—a blueprint for success, let alone happiness. I can only tell you what worked for me, and what I have learned in the course of my personal journey.

The questions never end, the quest is never complete. I've been striving for a major championship my entire life. I believe that our organization is on track to win one with the Suns in the NBA, and eventually another with the Diamondbacks in MLB. You might be wondering, What then? What would happen if I finally fulfilled my personal quest? It is a question I have been asked many times.

The answer is as obvious as the question: We will try to get another. And another. And as many as we can win. Because the quest, the true quest, is not merely to accumulate championships but to keep striving to learn and improve, to work with purpose and enthusiasm and live with courage and joy.

While there is much to be said for planning your life, planning will usually only take you so far, for the future is always filled with uncertainties and variables. Example: A profession that was recommended for years for its unparalleled job security was banking. Today, the banking profession is in utter tumult as mergers between giant banks consolidate operations and eliminate jobs; and states, corporations, and nations tumble and cost their lenders hundreds of millions or even billions of dollars.

Because of the surprises that life inevitably holds in store, particularly in todays' rapidly changing world, you have to be flexible. You have to be willing to adapt, to change with your industry, or even change industries.

And the changes will never end. A small example, courtesy of our organization: I'm from the old school when it comes to business attire. Throughout my career, I have always worn a suit on most days and for most occasions, and the men and women in our organization have dressed in similar fashion. Times have changed a bit, and so have standards. In accord with many businesses, we established "casual Fridays," permitting our employees to wear casual attire on Fridays during the summer months. I can't say this "innovation" thrilled me, but I understood that it was standard practice today, so I acceded to its adoption by our organization.

But it didn't end there. Bryan has been lobbying for some time to enact casual attire five days a week, twelve months a year, based on what is customary in the sports industry. I have consistently resisted this idea, but just recently acquiesced to his persistent petitioning. While this is not a change I happen to prefer, I grant it is a change that makes sense considering the state of societal standards and business norms.

Time marches on, and you either march with it or get left behind.

Talking about the future makes me think once again about the past, about my beginning in this fascinating business. My good fortune was to get involved in an industry on the verge of tremendous, self-sustaining growth. Of course, I did not know over thirty years ago that I had stumbled upon such a fortuitous situation. I did know, from that very first day, driving through Indiana with Dick Klein, talking about a new basketball franchise for Chicago, that I loved what I was doing. And that passion was more important than stopping to contemplate how many years I would be granted to participate in this wonderful business, or what position and what sort of salary I would eventually achieve.

Passion, and the determination that normally attends it, is the gateway to success, and success has a tendency to breed more success. A certain level of success attracts more opportunities, and that initial success will place you in a stronger position to take full advantage of those new opportunities.

And don't hesitate to try those new opportunities, or whatever other tasks or possibilities or dreams that might present themselves, because time passes quickly and your chance, your moment, can pass you by, if you're not careful, not paying attention.

I have loved every minute of my three decades in sports. The future for my organization and my community—for the Suns and the Diamondbacks, for Phoenix and Arizona, for America West Arena and Bank One Ballpark, for the sports industry and the entertainment industry—is so inviting and so exciting, that my only regret is that I'm not twenty-six years old again, and just starting out, so I can enjoy the extraordinary ride that the future promises.

Our most recent move is a step into the world of new media. Some twenty years ago, the American Cable Company, and then in partnership with Times-Mirror Cable, saw value in acquiring rights to broadcast the Phoenix Suns' games. Though televising sports on cable is now an established, profitable enterprise for all parties, back in those days cable TV was viewed as merely a way to get basic television to rural areas.

Today, cable is a very different business than this original, extremely limited conception. Placing a value of between

$2,500 and $3,500 per subscriber, Cox Cable, the successor to those early systems here in Maricopa County, is now worth at least $1.5 to $2 billion.

Now the cable is changing again, as new technologies provide new capabilities, and new opportunities. Fiber optics, as thin as human hair, carry not only telephone calls, but also television signals, Internet communications, and bank transfers, just for starters. In this spirit, we signed a deal with US West, the telephone giant, to deliver video and other services in cooperation with our organization. In other words, beginning with the 2003–4 season, US West will carry the Suns for the next twenty years. But that is just the beginning. Additionally, America West Arena will be enlarged and extended to include a new US West Pavilion. The pavilion will serve many functions and have ample space for restaurants, offices, video arcades, banquet rooms, and more. It will also be a showplace for US West products. All the amenities and attractions will turn the pavilion into a prime gathering spot for the community, a touch of Times Square brought to Phoenix. (The newly cleaned-up Times Square, that is.)

US West will pay the Phoenix Suns, Inc., some $300 million to complete this deal. Quite a change from the days when the Suns' marketing scheme began with offering free tickets on the side of Carnation milk cartons.

Our corporate partnership with US West has led to my being asked to join the corporation's board of directors. Though my plate is rather full, I accepted US West's offer because I wanted to be on the cutting edge of technology, which translated into being on the cutting edge of virtually every business.

I recently sat through my first board meeting, and listened as the chiefs presented their strategies. I was struck by how much the whole event reminded me, to a certain extent, of sports. Their marketing plans or production plans or design plans found their rough equivalent in game plans. Just as a baseball team (to focus on one sport) needed a good manager, so a business required a strong CEO. The team's top pitching staff had its counterpart in the business's top management group. The analogies continued from there: whether team or business, the players were probably going to hit a bunch of singles, a few home runs, and strike out here and there.

To a certain degree, it all sounded familiar. The one thing I knew for sure: whether on the field or in the boardroom, you can't afford to fail. You have to swing away when the opportunity presents itself, when that ball is just sitting there, round and fat, waiting to be smacked out of the park.

A few years ago, I was inducted into the National Italian American Sports Hall of Fame, which is located in Chicago. Not long ago, I was asked to get involved in the management of the hall and chair the board of trustees. As honored as I was to have been included in such auspicious company, I was now equally dismayed to learn that the hall was in a terrible state of financial disarray. In brief, the place was falling apart. I agreed to join the board only if we determined to take the hall to a new level of success.

On my last visit to Chicago, back in July for Jerry Colangelo Day, as well as the Diamondbacks' series with the Cubs, Mayor Daley gave the hall a generous grant of land, for the purpose of constructing a new Italian American Sports Hall of Fame. The land was situated in Chicago's Italian district.

While this was a wonderful start (the land grant was worth at least half a million dollars), the design for the new hall was going to require raising over one million dollars— and I was going to take the lead in finding the funds.

The new National Italian American Sports Hall of Fame

was to be built on Taylor Street. The area before the hall would be named Piazza DiMaggio and adorned with a glorious statue of the Yankee Clipper at the plate, wearing his old Yankee pinstripes, swinging away. The board decided to announce plans to build the new hall in late September 1998 at the dedication of Piazza DiMaggio, during a weekend of festivities commemorating the hall's twentieth anniversary. It was hoped that the unveiling of Joltin' Joe's statue would launch the fund-raising effort to raise the construction money with a bang.

The weekend began with a black-tie dinner the night before the dedication. The 1998 inductees to the hall were introduced: Gary Beban, the 1969 Heisman Trophy Winner from UCLA, and now president of Coldwell Banker; Tony La Russa, manager of the St. Louis Cardinals; and Chip Ganassi, of the Ganassi Racing Team. Our 1998 Athlete of the Year was Cammie Granato, of the U.S. Women's Gold Medal Olympic Hockey Team.

This was quite an event, important enough for La Russa to change into a tuxedo (without benefit of a shower) after his team finished playing in St. Louis, jump on a private jet, provided by an owner, attend the dinner, and then hurry home for the conclusion of the baseball season, made most memorable by the seventy home runs hit by his first baseman, Mark McGwire.

Tommy Lasorda was the master of ceremonies, I was the honorary chairman, and the special guest—and inevitable center of attention—was Joe DiMaggio.

Joe DiMaggio is not only an icon for the ages, he is a living icon, a man who has managed to maintain both his private standards and public dignity for decades, a remarkable, perhaps unparalleled, feat in our media-saturated society.

Joe DiMaggio is also one of my heroes, and has been since I was a boy. The idea that I would get the opportunity to stand beside him on a podium—any podium—was both daunting and exhilarating. To me, this was more than just a great occasion, it was a great honor, and, in a very real sense, the culmination of my career in the sports industry.

One climatic moment was superseded by the next. When I first met Joe, he surprised me by saying that he had followed my career and was proud of my accomplishments. Coming from Joe DiMaggio himself, this was such an amazing statement that I was struck speechless.

But that was just the start. After the black-tie dinner, I had the chance, along with Tommy Lasorda, to spend some quiet time with Joe DiMaggio. I sat and listened while the two old pros swapped stories about their lifetimes in the game. As I had learned to do so long ago when in the presence of those older and wiser, I sat quietly and listened. These few hours were stimulating and satisfying beyond words.

The next day, at the dedication ceremony, Mayor Daley said that the National Italian American Sports Hall of Fame was important to the city of Chicago for it not only honors Italian-Americans and provides scholarships for student-athletes, but it will be a centerpiece in the ongoing effort to revitalize the old neighborhood.

As I approached the podium to speak, I felt that I had come full circle, that I was returning to my roots. And that's what I told the crowd, that even though Taylor Street was miles north of Chicago Heights, the feeling was one of coming home.

And, I continued, I had no intention of coming home empty-handed. Though we were only here to announce our fund-raising goal, I had gotten on the phone and called around the land. The four major pro leagues contributed $100,000 each, and so did a lot of other people. By this day, I had $1.6 million in the bank—enough to make the building a reality.

Later on, as the weekend came to an end, I said goodbye to Joe DiMaggio. The day before, he had mentioned that he had heard a lot about Bank One Ballpark and would love to visit it. Now, I extended an invitation to him to be our guest at the Diamondbacks' Opening Day the following season. Time will tell if it works out.

I returned to Phoenix for the final game of the Diamondbacks' first season in the majors. It was also Fan Appreciation Night, the last such night in a series of nights, replete with gifts and prizes for the kids and adults, to show how much we value the support of our fans.

The evening quickly turned into something of an emotional event. I went down into the locker room before the game, to talk to the team. Before I spoke, Buck got up. In the course of his talk, he said that the highlight of the year had been an incident in Philadelphia, early in the year. The team was 8–30, and another loss that night had dropped them to 8–31, a most discouraging turn of events and a standard of play that, if it continued through the rest of the season, would put the Diamondbacks in the running to wind up with the worst record in MLB history.

After the game, I joined Buck and his coaches in the visiting manager's office. I attempted to offer some encouragement, trying to keep their spirits up. Whether I succeeded or not, Buck now told the team that my effort meant a lot to him, that, in all his years in baseball, he had never seen an owner make such a gesture.

Eventually, the team did start to come together, and played well enough to end the season at 65–97, finishing better than two other MLB teams, Florida and fellow expansion franchise, Tampa Bay, and tying with Montreal and Detroit. And while that had nothing to do with my postgame pep talk, it was good to stand in the locker room on this final day and be part of this effort.

And that is what I told the men who comprised the Arizona Diamondbacks before that last 1998 game. As a team and as individuals, they meant more to me than just their record, more than just winning and losing. I like to win, there's no denying that—but win or lose, what is more consequential to me is that the work is worthwhile and that everyone involved values the effort.

Out in the stands that night, the mood was also emotional—kind of surprising for a baseball game. People started coming over and asking for my autograph on a program or ball or piece of paper early on in the night. I don't think they were prompted so much because I'm some sort of a celebrity, but because they wanted to have something tangible to help them remember this most memorable first year, and their participation in it.

As the game ended, the crowd around my seat grew larger. I stayed there for over an hour after the last pitch had been thrown, the last ball hit, the final out called. Some embraced me, and thanked me for bringing baseball to Arizona. Many had tears in their eyes. So did I.

On this night, I had no doubt that the work to bring the Diamondbacks and Bank One Ballpark to Arizona had been worthwhile, and everyone in the organization, and hopefully most people outside, ultimately judged it consequential, memorable and valuable.

It is my personal belief that God has a plan for everyone's life. Considering the unexpected course of my own life, what else could I believe? Of course, each plan must be implemented and executed, and that is the responsibility of every individual. It is the mission of every person to strike out and discover what he or she is capable of doing, what he or she is capable of achieving.

Life presents many opportunities, many experiences, many avenues, from which to choose to help you fulfill your destiny. Sports is one such opportunity. Business is one such experience. It has been my good fortune to have had the chance to combine sports and business as primary vehicles to help me find my destiny.

I said at the very start that this book would be about what I believe. In these pages, I suppose I have given some account to many of my beliefs. At the core of my beliefs is this conviction: that every person, in service to their faith and values and dreams, must seize whatever chances arise to make the most of his or her life.

It is a simple thought, no doubt, though not always so simple to live by. Perhaps that makes it the right thought on which to end.

Index

251